Renewal of Catholic Higher Education

Essays on Catholic Studies in Honor of Don J. Briel

Edited by Matthew T. Gerlach

Foreword by George Weigel

Afterword by Fr. Bill Miscamble, C.S.C.

University of Mary Press
Bismarck, North Dakota

Published in the United States of America by
University of Mary Press
7500 University Drive
Bismarck, ND 58504
www.umary.edu

ISBN-10: 0-9988728-1-4
ISBN-13: 978-0-9988728-1-0

Design: Jerry Anderson

Printed in Canada

To Our Lady,
Sedes Sapientiae

In honor of Don Briel
teacher, mentor, and friend

Acknowledgements

Over the years I have been blessed to encounter and collaborate with so many who have dedicated themselves profoundly to the educational mission of the Church and the work of renewing Catholic universities and Catholic intellectual life in America and beyond. Often it was Don Briel who introduced me to such gifted scholars and leaders. I would like to express special thanks to my former colleagues at University of Mary who assisted with the selection and editing of many of the essays contained in this collection: Joseph Stuart, Jared Staudt, Carol Andreini, and Joshua Hren. Heartfelt thanks also go out to two Catholic Studies students, Kateri Krebs and Katerina Schafer, for assisting with this project, and also to Paul G. Monson and Cameron Thompson for their careful scholarly review of the volume in the final stage of editing. I must not fail to mention the tremendous personal and institutional support that was given by University of Mary President, Monsignor James P. Shea, as well as Jerome Richter, Patrick McCloskey and Jerry Anderson, and others, both for the 2014 conference honoring Don Briel and for seeing to it that these essays should be published as a tribute to him. Finally, special acknowledgment is due to my bride, Michelle, not only for her indefatigable assistance with the 2014 conference but more fundamentally for her unwavering support of my intellectual vocation as teacher, administrator and scholar.

— *Matthew T. Gerlach*

Contents

Foreword

In the postwar history of Catholic higher education in the United States, three seminal moments stand out: Msgr. John Tracy Ellis's 1955 article, "American Catholics and the Intellectual Life"; the 1967 Land O'Lakes statement, "The Idea of a Catholic University"; and the day Don J. Briel began the Catholic Studies Program—and the Catholic Studies movement—at the University of St. Thomas.

I've always had the sense that Msgr. Ellis's article has been retrospectively misinterpreted as nothing other than a polemic against Catholic colleges and universities mired in the tar pits of Neo-Scholasticism and intellectually anorexic as a result; I think it's possible to read Ellis as calling for Catholic institutions of higher learning to play to their putative strengths—the liberal arts, including most especially philosophy and theology—rather than aping the emerging American multiversity, of which the University of California at Berkeley was then considered the paradigm. But that's not how Ellis was understood by most, and there is a direct line to be drawn between the Ellis article and the self-consciousness and tacit defensiveness of the Land O'Lakes statement, which seemed to say, yes, we're second-rate, maybe even third-rate, and the way to be first-rate is to be like Harvard, Yale, Stanford and the rest of what would be called, in 21st-century Catholic academic jargon, "aspirational peers."

The problem, of course, is that by 1967, those "aspirational peers" were beginning to lose their minds, literally, en route to the postmodern sandbox of authoritarian solipsism they now occupy today.

So there is another direct line to be drawn: this time, from Ellis and Land O'Lakes to Don Briel's catalyzing the Catholic Studies movement, which is intended to, among many other things, repair the damage that was done to institutions of Catholic higher learning in the aftermath of Land O'Lakes.

But there is far more to Don Briel's vision, and achievement, than damage repair. Nourished intellectually by John Henry Newman and Christopher Dawson, Briel's work has aimed at nothing less than creating, in 21st-century circumstances, the "idea of a university" that animated his two English intellectual and spiritual heroes. And, one might say, just in the nick of time. For the deterioration of higher education throughout the United States in the past several generations has contributed mightily to the cultural crisis of the moment, and the cultural crisis has in turn produced a political crisis in which constitutional democracy itself is now at risk. The answer to that cultural crisis cannot be a retreat into auto-constructed bunkers; the answer must be the conversion of culture by well-educated men and women who know what the West owes to Catholicism as a civilizing force, and who are prepared to bring that Catholic imagination to bear on reconstructing a culture capable of sustaining genuine freedom—freedom for excellence—in social, political and economic life.

Conversion is, ultimately, what "Catholic Studies" and the Don Briel project have been about. The conversion of young minds, hearts and souls to the truth of Christ and the love of Christ as manifest in the Catholic Church, to be sure. But also the conversion of culture through those converted minds, hearts, and souls. According to the common wisdom, Land O'Lakes was "revolutionary." But the true revolutionary in American Catholic higher education over the past decades has been Don J. Briel, who has enlivened an approach to higher education and the New Evangelization as no one else has done.

The breadth of his vision and its implications for the future can be gleaned from the essays that follow, all of which were written in tribute to him. It is a privilege to be able to offer this brief word of introduction to what I hope will be a book that inspires its readers to live out the truths of Catholic higher learning of which another revolutionary, St. John Paul II, wrote in *Ex Corde Ecclesiae*.

— *George Weigel*

Introduction

Catholic Studies and the Renewal of Higher Education

MATTHEW T. GERLACH & R. JARED STAUDT

The collection of essays on Catholic Studies contained in this book was prompted by a conference celebrating the 20th anniversary of Catholic Studies (2013) and honoring Dr. Don J. Briel, the founder of the oldest and currently largest Catholic Studies Program in the United States, at the University of St. Thomas in St. Paul, Minnesota. It was held August 29-31, 2014, at University of Mary in Bismarck, North Dakota, and those in attendance included Catholic educators and scholars, students, seminarians, religious and clergy, along with many other lay friends of the Catholic Studies project.

Honoring Don J. Briel

Dr. Don J. Briel holds the Blessed John Henry Newman Chair of Liberal Arts at the University of Mary. He is the founder, and was for 20 years director, of the Center for Catholic Studies at the University of St. Thomas in St. Paul, Minnesota, where he held the Koch Chair of Catholic Studies. Having grown up in California, Dr. Briel completed his BA at the University of Notre Dame in 1969, where he studied under the legendary Frank O'Malley. He studied literature at Trinity College in Dublin,

Ireland, and earned a Licentiate and Doctorate in Sacred Theology from the University of Strasbourg in France, his main study being the work of Bl. John Henry Newman. After brief teaching stints at the University of San Francisco and St. Mary of the Plains, Briel was hired by St. Thomas in 1981. He was Chair of the Theology Department for many years, the first non-clergyman to hold the position, and served for a time as Assistant Dean of the College of Arts and Sciences.

Briel has exhibited a set of talents not often combined in one person. He is a keen scholar and a beloved teacher. He is also an excellent administrator, a notable entrepreneur and an educational visionary, all of which goes some way to account for the success of his endeavors. Seeing the need for a renewal of Catholic higher education and a reengagement of the whole of the Catholic intellectual tradition, Briel and a few of his colleagues founded the Center for Catholic Studies. It was the first such program in the country. Under Briel's 20 years of leadership, a small interdisciplinary program grew into a Center with its own interdisciplinary department and a graduate program. Briel founded *Logos*, a highly respected journal of Catholic thought and culture, and engineered the establishment of three institutes connected to the Center: the John A. Ryan Institute for Catholic Social Thought, the Murphy Institute for Law and Public Policy and the Habiger Institute for Catholic Leadership. In all of his work, his aim is to go to the heart of the key educational and spiritual and societal challenges of the day, finding ways to encounter the broader culture with the strength of the Catholic faith and tradition.

He founded and developed the Bernardi Campus of the University of St. Thomas in Rome. It is the "gold standard" of study-abroad programs in the Eternal City, at which the intellectual, spiritual and social lives of the students achieve an impressive and transformative integration. Briel's work has not gone unnoticed, nationally or internationally. There are currently close to a hundred Catholic Studies programs around the country and abroad, many of which see their model in the St. Thomas program Briel founded. The Center at St. Thomas, through the Ryan Institute, regularly collaborates with the Holy See, especially with the Office of Justice and Peace, their most recent work being an internationally published Vatican document entitled "The Vocation of the Business Leader." The Murphy

Institute, housed both in the St. Thomas Law School and the Center for Catholic Studies, has worked with the Holy See's mission to the United Nations on developing its position papers. The Center regularly hosts seminars and lecture series, bringing together some of the best and most energetic Christian minds to collaborate on questions of business, law and government, biomedical ethics, marriage and family, and theological and philosophical matters of current interest.

SITUATING THE PROJECT OF CATHOLIC STUDIES

Four dates define the unique educational approach of Catholic Studies. First, in May and June of 1852, Bl. John Henry Newman delivered a series of lectures to the newly organized faculty of the Catholic University of Ireland. Newman's lectures, later published as *The Idea of a University*, provide the most compelling account of the essence of the university, whose mission it is to seek universal knowledge. True education should not impart disparate facts, because the mind has the "power of viewing many things at once as one whole" in an integrated fashion.[1] Theology plays a key role in this integration as "religious Truth is not only a portion, but a condition of general knowledge."[2] Newman also laid out the goal of liberal education in the formation of a philosophical habit of mind, "of which the attributes are, freedom, equitableness, calmness, moderation, and wisdom."[3]

In 1909, as a young man of 19, the great historian Christopher Dawson sat on the steps of the church, Ara Coeli, next to the Forum in Rome, where Gibbon had decided to write his *Decline and Fall of the Roman Empire*. Dawson, facing Rome's many churches, decided to write a history of culture, in which, unlike Gibbon's account, he would argue that religion plays the leading role in forming culture. Many years later, as the culmination of this project, his book, *The Crisis of Western Education*, argued that university education must focus on Christian culture as a unifying principle to overcome the crisis of identity faced in modern culture. Dawson argues that "the essential function of education is 'enculturation,' or the transmission of the tradition of culture, and therefore it seems clear that the Christian college must be the cornerstone of any attempt to rebuild the order of Western civilization."[4]

Later in the same century, in 1990, Pope St. John Paul II, recognizing the crisis and secularization of Catholic higher education, issued a constitution on Catholic universities, *Ex Corde Ecclesiae*. He called not only for fidelity in theological teaching, but also laid out a broader vision of interdisciplinary study and holistic formation:

> While each discipline is taught systematically and according to its own methods, *interdisciplinary studies*, assisted by a careful and thorough study of philosophy and theology, enable students to acquire an organic vision of reality and to develop a continuing desire for intellectual progress. In the communication of knowledge, emphasis is then placed on how *human reason in its reflection* opens to increasingly broader questions, and how the complete answer to them can only come from above through faith. Furthermore, the *moral implications* that are present in each discipline are examined as an integral part of the teaching of that discipline so that the entire educative process be directed towards the whole development of the person.[5]

Only a few years later, drawing these three seminal points together, Dr. Don Briel founded the nation's first Catholic Studies program in 1993 at the University of St. Thomas in St. Paul, Minnesota, the growth of which was outlined above. The University of Mary seeks to continue Briel's legacy with its own Catholic Studies program, which has also grown quickly in its six years to become the second-largest Catholic Studies program in the country. Though drawing inspiration from Briel's work at St. Thomas, the University of Mary's program brings its own distinct approach, embracing the motto *ora et labora* to provide further incentive for the integration of the liberal arts and the professions.

There is one conspicuous absence from the four foundational dates mentioned above: the Catholic imagination. We could add a supplemental date of 1964, which marks the death of a great Catholic artist, Flannery O'Connor. O'Connor, though not a central figure in the Western canon, nonetheless marks an important moment in American Catholicism, in which a Catholic could communicate a sacramental vision to a non-Catholic audience in the United States. O'Connor describes the vision she brought to an increasingly secularized and wounded culture:

When fiction is made according to its nature, it should reinforce our sense of the supernatural by grounding it in concrete observable reality. If the writer uses his eyes in the real security of his Faith, he will be obliged to use them honestly and his sense of mystery and acceptance of it will be increased. To look at the worst will be for him no more than an act of trust in God.[6]

In the midst of a secular culture, which sees only "concrete observable reality," O'Connor speaks of infusing our vision, even of its grotesque elements, with the supernatural.

Literature, along with the arts more broadly, assists, in particular, with the formation of a Catholic imagination or, speaking more broadly, a Catholic vision of the world. Unlike theology, which more narrowly focuses on the understanding of God's revelation, Catholic Studies explores the broad, living tradition of Catholicism, tracing its impact across all of the disciplines and its instantiation within culture. While it draws upon theology, which provides its access to the supernatural life of faith, it extends to philosophy, history, literature, the arts and even the professions. Catholic Studies is an integrative project, with three general tasks: reuniting faith and reason, faith and culture, and faith and life within the Catholic university.

THREE INTEGRATIVE TASKS OF CATHOLIC STUDIES

Blessed John Henry Newman wrote that the "object of the Holy See and the Catholic Church in setting up universities" is "to reunite things which were in the beginning joined together by God, and have been put asunder by man."[7] The essential purpose of universities, Newman suggests, is unitive, integrative; universities are to overcome artificial disjunctions, dichotomies and divisions found in culture. Christopher Dawson pointed out how increasingly opposed things are to Newman's "unitive" vision of the university.[8] Underlying many of the ills plaguing the modern university is the tragedy of the "schism between religion and culture" that has been undermining higher education for centuries.[9] In response to this schism, Catholic Studies seeks to bring integration to collegiate studies, in particular by undertaking three integrative tasks.

First Integrative Task: Synthesis of Faith and Reason in the Arts, Sciences, and Professional Training

The first task for Catholic Studies involves the integration of knowledge through the ongoing dialogue between faith and reason. Catholic Studies seeks to facilitate this dialogue through its interdisciplinary approach within its classes and by providing a forum for interdisciplinary collaboration and discussion outside of the classroom. The unity of knowledge is one of the essential aims of the university. The explosion of specialties and rigid compartmentalization of the different disciplines makes the integration of knowledge challenging. Newman had already pointed out in The Idea of a University that it is the primary task of the university in and through its professors and students to seek diligently the unity and integration of knowledge, "to assign to each study, which it receives, its proper place and its just boundaries; to define the rights, to establish the mutual relations, and to effect the intercommunion of one and all."[10] The explicitly interdisciplinary activities of Catholic Studies, which affirm not only a plurality but a hierarchy of disciplines, invite faculty and students to yearn and labor toward a holistic vision of knowledge. By promoting the dialogue between faith and reason both inside and outside the classroom, Catholic Studies aids the university in its mission to seek and bear witness to this one truth and the complementarity of these two distinct, but legitimate, orders of knowledge.

Second Integrative Task: Evangelization of Culture, Inculturation of the Gospel

Pope St. John Paul II states in *Ex Corde Ecclesiae*: "A Catholic University, aware that human culture is open to Revelation and transcendence, is also a primary and privileged place for a fruitful dialogue between the Gospel and culture."[11] The Church is missionary in nature, which means that Catholic universities must instantiate in a manner proper to them the Church's vocation to evangelize culture, in both the sociological and the humanistic senses of "culture."[12] Thus the second integrative task of Catholic Studies extends the first, bringing the Gospel into the social dimensions of human existence in every time and place. This second integrative focus of Catholic Studies can be understood as one mode of the universal Church's task of "inculturation," a process aimed at "the intimate transformation of authentic cultural values through their integration in Christianity and the insertion of Christianity in the various human cultures."[13] In and through the particular challenges and tensions that arise, the process of inculturation implies a mutual enrichment or "cross-fertilization." On the one hand, the Church communicates the absolute newness of the Gospel to cultures, and on the other hand, positive elements of human cultures are taken up and incorporated or assimilated by the Church, thereby creating new "Christian culture." Catholic Studies seeks models of inculturation in the legacy of Christian culture we have inherited. This present task thereby draws upon the history of the encounter between the Gospel and culture throughout all the ages of the Church.[14] This "cross-fertilization" should have roots in the kind of educational culture fostered by Catholic Studies, which should itself be a microcosm of what the Church undertakes especially through the lay apostolate of missionary disciples in the world. Catholic Studies thus seeks to assist students and the Church more broadly in the task of evaluating contemporary cultures and "discern their positive and negative aspects, to receive their authentically human contributions, and to develop means by which it can make the faith better understood by the men and women of a particular culture."[15]

THIRD INTEGRATIVE TASK: UNITY OF FAITH AND LIFE

The third task for Catholic Studies entails unifying faith and every aspect of one's own life. The Fathers of the Second Vatican Council had already underscored the "split between the faith which many profess and their daily lives" as one of "the more serious errors of our age."[16] At the modern university this error is exacerbated by several fragmentations. Being surrounded by the "jungle of competing specialisms" makes it difficult not only for faculty and students to discover the unity of knowledge at the theoretical level but also for them to see how the practical skills and theoretical knowledge might all be integrated within an individual's life.[17] Alisdair MacIntyre describes the tendency to live a fragmented life in different roles and settings, including within the university:

> So the classroom may be treated as a place for rigorous testing of ideas, while conversation outside the classroom remains mindless and philistine. So the chapel may be treated as the place where the significance of one's life is disclosed, while this disclo-

sure is for the most part ignored in the other areas of the university's life. So the modes of athletic activity may proceed without regard to anything that happens in classroom or chapel. And to the extent that student social life is thus compartmentalized, no reform of the curriculum that aims to provide an integrative education is likely to be successful.[18]

Catholic Studies, in response to this such compartmentalization, has the special focus of helping students see how the different areas of their lives, both on- and off-campus and both inside and outside the classroom, can be conceived and lived as parts of an integrated whole.

SUMMARY OF ESSAYS

The essays within this volume largely relate to one or more of these three integrative tasks, offering a vision that can guide not only Catholic Studies programs, but the renewal of Catholic university education more broadly. The essays in Part I offer a constellation of principles and examples by which Catholic universities may navigate the turbulent strong currents of cultural decay and disintegration, whereas Part II's essays propose reflections on the potential and actual transformative pedagogy undertaken by the "Briel approach" to Catholic Studies.

The first essay of the volume is based on Don Briel's keynote address from the 2014 conference. In "A Reflection on Catholic Studies," Briel offers his recollection of the origins and character of Catholic Studies that he and his collaborators established at the University of St. Thomas, St. Paul, Minnesota. What distinguishes Catholic Studies under Briel is that it is conceived and undertaken as a work of the Church, more of an intentional community of conviction, a communion of persons comprised of students and faculty functioning as a "creative minority" within the larger university. The program exists more in the people than in the curriculum, more in the faculty than in the texts. Moreover, the classroom experience of students overflows, through friendship, into various forms of residential experiences, which Catholic Studies facilitates: the Rome campus, Catholic Studies houses, special floors in dormitories. In such extracurricular activities, not to mention retreats, leadership programs, and collaborative endeavors with the Church local and universal, students undergo a fuller intellectual, spiritual and human integration and formation than they would be able to experience merely by taking classes—as essential as these are. In this range of expression and activity, Catholic Studies is able to serve the wider university as a catalyst for reflection on, and a particular realization of its commitment to, the distinctive ends of Catholic university education.

In his essay "Naming the New Lions: The Challenge of Contemporary Culture to Christian Faith," Paul Murray, O.P. exposes the "new lions" of the culture that threaten Catholic colleges and universities. Our culture is riddled with three deadly ideologies and attitudes, each of which spring from and lead to deadly spiritual decisions: relativism, fundamentalism, and pessimism. Like Daniel in the Old Testament, Catholics who seek to live their faith today as in the past face "lions" that threaten to devour them. Murray answers the threat of the new lions with faith, charity and hope—the three theological virtues—springing from a life of prayer. The lion of cynical relativism can be met by engaging and leavening contemporary culture with confidence in the strength and beauty of faith, setting the Gospel handed on by the Church on a "lampstand" for all to see. Grim fundamentalism is best overcome by the exercise of charity, a charity that combines strong conviction concerning the "fundamentals" that often contradict modern culture on the one hand with an openness of spirit in joy and mercy that fosters a culture of encounter and discerning dialogue. Finally, the fatigue and disenchantment in the lion of pessimism leading to despair or resigned mediocrity can be successfully fought off with hope—the extravagant hope and ardor for holiness, for sanctity. Hope and ardor for holiness will supply a remedy against the temptations to fatigue and disenchantment as students seek to live their faith and leaven the culture around them with the Gospel. Just as every culture depends on spiritual roots, so Christian culture is ultimately rooted in the theological virtues of faith, hope, and charity.

In the essay "What St. Benedict Taught the Dark Ages—His and Ours," F. Russell Hittinger illustrates the wisdom and well-lit path given by Benedict and his *Rule* to those who dwell in the "vespers" or evening of human culture and civilization. In the midst of the "disorganized disaster" of the fifth century, order began to rise again in the monastic community. Living in such an enclosed community led the monks to reproduce, or reinvent, the "whole of the civilization." What the self-sustaining and divinely focused monks of St. Benedict discovered and shared with those who dwelt around the monastery was how to "divide a day unto wisdom." In the ordering of a life they discovered how to reproduce the whole of the civilization by seeking to live a life worth living together. The monks rediscovered how to live life as an organic whole. Benedict gave the Dark Ages a "curriculum," a course of study that requires one to become and remain childlike. "Benedict taught an integrated and integrating knowledge," knowledge that is taught "materially, politically and poetically." Finally, Benedict teaches us to "hearken," to heed, to obey, to return to the Father again and again. Hittinger's essay highlights the unique promise that Benedictine monasticism holds out to the integrative tasks of the Catholic university; it provides direction to those who would draw from the Christian culture of the past for addressing the challenges of education in our own day.

Jonathan J. Reyes' essay, "Catholic Studies and Formation of Life: On the Integration of Intellectual and Moral Education in the Catholic University," takes up the challenge of providing holistic formation opportunities for students of Catholic Studies. One of the major divisions students experience is between the intellectual knowledge they acquire and the choices they make outside the classroom. The cordoning off of intellectual education from moral formation, Reyes argues, is grounded in two errors: first, the severance of intellect and will (flawed philosophical anthropology and moral psychology), and second, the desire not to coerce students or impose a particular morality on them (ethical relativism). Reyes recounts the stages of the modern university's "abandonment" of any moral authority and then suggests ways the university might retrieve and reclaim this moral authority as an essential part of its educational mission, helping students to achieve intellectual-moral integration. The approach of Catholic Studies, as a catalyst of this intellectual-moral integration within the university, should include initiatives and programming, curricular, extracurricular and co-curricular, that will assist students and faculty who live in a divided world in the reunifying of their intellectual and moral lives. This reintegration of the intellectual and the religious, intellectual knowledge and moral discipline, requires something as intentional as Catholic Studies if students are to have a chance on our Catholic campuses in the post-Christian world in which they live.

In his essay "Revitalizing and Institutionalizing Mission: Business Education at Catholic Universities," Michael J. Naughton provides a way forward for business programs and business schools. The response to "mission drift," Naughton proposes, is to "institutionalize mission." He explains how institutions and organizations undergo "mission drift" and gives a three-step process for overcoming this and "institutionalizing mission": 1) to know the end or distinctive purpose of the Catholic university; 2) to evaluate the current state of the business program or school in light of this purpose; and 3) to find ways to close the gap between the purpose and current operation/state. Thus, to "institutionalize" the Catholic university's mission in a professional program like business requires knowing the distinctive end or purpose of the Catholic university in offering professional training in business, evaluating the business program's current state in light of this purpose and finding ways of closing the gap between purpose and current state (i.e., how to bring the Catholic liberal arts tradition into the professional training in business). Naughton's own work in the Opus School of Business at St. Thomas, Minnesota demonstrates how mission can be "institutionalized" in a significant way.

The essays in the second part of this volume highlight the transformative pedagogy spring from the Catholic Studies approach to university education. First, R. Jared Staudt argues in his essay "Poetic Knowledge, Catholic Studies and the Formation of Culture" that Catholic Studies depends upon "an examination of Catholicism from an incarnational and sacramental perspective." Staudt claims that Catholic Studies rests on a particular way of encountering Catholicism poetically, through direct sensory and experiential knowledge. Catholicism cannot be understood simply as an idea, but must be approached in faith as a divine reality and holistically in its historical and cultural embodiment. The Incarnation itself provides the foundational point of reference as God enters the world and founds a Church rooted in the sacramental communication of grace. If Catholic Studies approaches Catholicism in this fashion, it must also facilitate an encounter with the reality of Catholicism outside of the classroom, an experience of the living, sacramental reality of Christian culture. The university is poised to become a center not only for such an encounter, but also for the creation of Christian culture in the life of its students and in society more broadly.

Elizabeth Lev's essay, "In Defense of Christian Art," argues that, despite the dominant bias, considerations of form and style are not sufficient to account for the significance of art. Lev challenges the prevailing disjunction in the discipline of Art History between the formal qualities of a given work of art and the subject matter and motivations behind that work. From this perspective, "Christian art" does not really exist because it always shares formal qualities characteristic of its time and place. Lev, attempting to reunite the formal and the material elements of art, holds that "Christian art" does exist as something for art historians to study and that these works of Christian art are worthy of study as *art for Christians*. Teaching works of art to Catholic Studies students, who bring a "Christian lens," has led her to reach the conclusion that two qualities define art as distinctively Christian: first, the unique doctrine of the Incarnation permeating a work, and second, the purpose and function of art in the life of the Christian viewer. The city of Rome offers unique opportunities to encounter, study and contemplate works of art as a Christian and let that art transcend its particular historical period into the present and be participated in by the viewer. Lev suggests that encountering great works of art in a sacred setting such as Rome, by students who are there as pilgrims as well as scholars, allows the Christian subject matter as well as the intended sacred purpose for which the art was created or commissioned to figure more prominently. When the fuller "poetic" power of the work of art is experienced, the subject and purpose may be more easily integrated with the formal elements of the work as well as the life of the student.

In his essay on the place of literature in Catholic Studies, "Between the Beatific Vision and a Record of Man in Rebellion: Catholic Literature Revisited," Joshua Hren suggests a contrasting, though complementary, perspective to Lev's: namely, that the "Catholic literary tradition" did not exist so much in actual literature written by Catholics or for or about Catholics as it has developed; rather, it existed as a traditional way Catholics taught and learned literary texts. Hren argues that Catholic Studies must include multiple ways of teaching and studying literature if it is to live up to its claim to study Christian culture. Applying the analogy of literature and reading, multiple "texts" and various ways of "reading" culture (as a complex whole and in its various parts) will be essential to account for the complex reality of "Catholic culture," especially as a tradition. Hren's essay contributes something absolutely indispensable to this volume by underscoring something that often is left out of discussions of Catholic Studies. He draws attention to the fact that those who reflect on, write about and dialogue with "non-Catholic culture" with a Catholic mind become participants in the tradition of Catholic thought and culture.

Joseph T. Stuart's essay, "Catholic Studies and the Science of Culture," attempts to defend the academic foundations of Catholic Studies as a field of study by examining its object of knowledge: Christian culture. The nature of culture, revealed in the etymology of the word, is so complex that two very different traditions of thinking about it have developed in the West. The socio-historic view of culture examines it objectively and empirically as the common way of life of a people understood and judged on its own terms (cultural relativism). The humanistic view of culture studies it contemplatively as those learned intellectual and spiritual qualities that a people should have, that they ought to strive for to better their humanity, often revealed in their significant texts and artifacts. This is a prescriptive view of culture as essential to the formation of the human person and as such is worth defending because truth matters. The argument here is that Catholic Studies must combine these two views of culture in its conception of itself. Students and teachers should ask empirical and prescriptive questions about culture together, not divorced from each other in separate classes. They should study culture sociologically and historically but also as the place in which Christian faith and reason are lived out today in families, parishes, professions, regions and nations. In this way, Catholic Studies is not a special kind of theology, a catechetical program, a cultural studies program or a Great Books program. It is a liberal arts-based education integrated by the study of Christian culture, even as it can serve as more than simply an academic program within the university.

In "A Roman View of American Catholicism: Thinking Hemispherically," which concludes Part II of this volume, Paul G. Monson explains why an on-site study-abroad semester in Rome as part of the Catholic Studies experience impacts students so profoundly and formatively. Paradoxically, Rome forces students to encounter in greater profundity both the Church in America and the Universal Church. The Rome experience calls into question U.S. students' "myopic sense" of their faith and the Church and challenges the dominant "American exceptionalism" they bring with them. Encounters with the concrete history and culture of Rome and those who have left their mark on it help to liberate American students from their myopia. A term abroad in pilgrim-trodden Rome, Monson argues, helps Catholic Studies accomplish its educational task by conducting students down a threefold path of conversion, communion and solidarity. Experiencing firsthand these three elements opens students up to a more "hemispheric" and truly global perspective of their faith and the unity-in-diversity of Catholic culture.

Borrowing the root metaphor of James Burtchaell's book *The Dying of the Light*, Wilson D. Miscamble's essay, "Maintaining the Light: Don Briel, Catholic Studies and the Future of Catholic Intellectual Life in America," rounds off the book. Miscamble observes that despite the decline in Catholic identity and mission within Catholic institutions of higher learning, there is a host of creative, diverse and growing initiatives in the U.S. that are reviving, cultivating and extending serious Catholic intellectual life and culture, both within and outside the academy. Catholic Studies have emerged precisely within this context, as part of this overarching narrative of decline and renewal. Miscamble's essay thus provides an intellectual "landscape" for appreciating the rise and activity of Catholic Studies in the U.S. These programs are "incubators" that generate Catholic intellectuals, professionals and leaders of the future, tranformatively engaging culture both within and outside Catholic institutions of higher education.

CONCLUSION

This book is by no means intended to be exhaustive. There are many important scholarly treatments of Catholic Studies and disputed questions concerning it which are not directly engaged in this present collection. But the volume was occasioned by a widespread desire to honor someone who has contributed immensely to Catholic Studies and who possesses a distinct and robust vision of the project that may continue to serve as a guiding light for addressing the present and future challenges in Catholic higher education. Moreover, the very nature of Catholic Studies requires that it remain open-ended; the three integrative tasks are undertakings that can never be fully and definitively achieved, once and for all. History and culture require our perseverance, hard work and imagination. We also ask the reader to consider this collection an invitation to scholars, artists, and professionals not represented by these essays who are nonetheless doing fine work in Catholic Studies. Perhaps other collections already in existence or ones to come might compensate for their absence in this volume. At least two rather fundamental topics are particularly conspicuous by their absence: a special essay on the central significance of the Sacred Liturgy and Sacred Scripture, and an essay on the indispensable function of the study of philosophy for Catholic Studies. We have long been of the conviction that in addition to history, theology, and literature, a fourth core discipline of Catholic Studies is philosophy, which we believe must be anchored in—or at least compatible with—Thomistic realism. No single volume, especially a collection of essays such as this, could ever do justice to the nature and promise of Catholic Studies for higher education in America. But it is our firm hope that these essays will provide some signposts for positive developments in the decades to come.

Celebrating the first 20 years of Catholic Studies and the leadership of Don J. Briel provides an excellent opportunity to reflect on the fruits of Catholic Studies programs throughout the country, such as those at the University of St. Thomas and the University of Mary. Catholic Studies has emerged at a pivotal moment in the history of Catholic education, as Catholic universities increasingly drift from their religious identity and mission and accept the overspecialized and compartmentalized approaches of secular universities. Catholic Studies programs have made a significant step toward reuniting the various strands of university life, which have been unraveling for some time, or, as Newman wrote, toward reuniting "things which were in the beginning joined together by God, and have been put asunder by man." If Catholic Studies can fulfill its three integrative tasks—wedding faith and reason, faith and culture, and faith and daily life—it is poised to contribute significantly to the Church's mission to bring the Gospel into higher education and to evangelize afresh every dimension of human life and thought.

NOTES

[1] John Henry Newman, *The Idea of a University* (London: Longmans, Green and Co., 1931), 137.

[2] Ibid., 70.

[3] Ibid., 101-02.

[4] Christopher Dawson, *The Crisis of Western Education* (Washington, DC: The Catholic University of America Press, 2010), 115.

[5] §20, http://w2.vatican.va/content/john-paul-ii/en/apost_constitutions/documents/hf_jp-ii_apc_15081990_ex-corde-ecclesiae.html.

[6] Flannery O'Connor, "The Church and the Fiction Writer," in *Collected Works*, ed. Sally Fitzgerald (New York: Library of America, 1988), 810.

[7] John Henry Newman, "Intellect the Instrument of Religious Training," in *Sermons Preached on Various Occasions* (New York: Longmans, Green and Co., 1908), 13.

[8] In particular, see Christopher Dawson, "The Historic Reality of Christian Culture," in *Christianity and European Culture*, ed. Gerald Russello (Washington, DC: Catholic University of America Press), 89-91.

[9] Ibid., 90.

[10] Newman, *The Idea of a University*, 457-58. This passage is cited in footnote 19 of *Ex Corde Ecclesiae*.

[11] Pope John Paul II, *Ex Corde Ecclesiae*, §43.

[12] See note 16. This, in our view, mandates that Catholic universities and institutions of higher learning should take a leading role in carrying out the intellectual tasks of the Church's mission to evangelize; Catholic Studies as we conceive it should facilitate and catalyze this. "Evangelize" here is not merely a one-on-one "sharing of the faith with others" but a demonstration of how the faith transformationally relates to the historical and social realities of human life in light of, and in intellectual service to, the Church's mission to evangelize.

[13] Pope John Paul II, *Redemptoris Missio*, 1990, §52.

[14] Cf. Christopher Dawson's "Six Ages of the Church," in *Christianity and European Culture*.

[15] Pope John Paul II, *Ex Corde*, §44.

[16] *Gaudium et Spes* (Pastoral Constitution on the Church in the Modern World), §43.

[17] Dawson, "The Historic Reality of Christian Culture," 90.

[18] Alisdair MacIntyre, "Catholic Universities: Dangers, Hopes, Choices," in *Higher Learning and Catholic Traditions*, ed. Robert E. Sullivan (Notre Dame, IN: University of Notre Dame, 2001), 18.

Part I

Catholic Studies and Contemporary Challenges of the Catholic University

I

A Reflection on Catholic Studies

Don J. Briel

On this celebration of the anniversary of Catholic Studies I hope that you will permit me to indulge in my own recollection of its origins and character. In order to do so, I need to say something about my own experiences of Catholic education. I take as justification Newman's claim that in attempting to give an account of the deepest truths of life, egotism is true modesty.[1] I can speak for myself and do not have a right to speak for others, although it is important to underline the fact that Catholic Studies has been the work of a community of scholars who reflect a variety of influences and emphases.

The Radical Changes in Catholic Higher Education Beginning in the 1960s

I arrived at the University of Notre Dame nearly 50 years ago during the last session of the Second Vatican Council. As the product of Catholic elementary and secondary education, I had not encountered a lay teacher in seven elementary schools, and in the diocesan high school I attended, priests and religious predominated. In the concluding months of the Council's deliberations and in the initial phases of the transition to the vernacular liturgy, it was clear that the Church was moving away from a relatively settled institutional self-understanding, one which had been fortified by a long cultural and deep intellectual tradition to a more open and less adversarial engagement with the modern world.

At Notre Dame I encountered a rich remnant of Catholic culture: priests and brothers of the Congregation of the Holy Cross in habit present throughout the university, not merely as faculty and administrators but also as rectors in residence halls; daily Mass not only in Sacred Heart Church but also in each hall chapel; the symbols of faith everywhere, the grotto, the statue of Edward the Confessor outside my bedroom window, the log chapel, statues of the Sacred Heart and Edward Sorin, shrines, the mosaic of Christ on the face of the new library; eight required courses in both theology and philosophy including courses in Scripture, morality, metaphysics, logic and ethics; Moreau Seminary; and an attentiveness to issues of Catholic thought and culture which pervaded nearly every course, including those taught by non-Catholic faculty. This was true in courses in literature, in which I first encountered serious figures such as John Donne, Paul Claudel, Georges Bernanos, Richard Crashaw, Evelyn Waugh, Francois Mauriac and Romano Guardini; in history, in which I first grasped the importance of the Catholic foundations of Western culture; and even in a course on Jewish thought taught by a local Reform rabbi. There were key figures who guided this encounter with the larger Catholic tradition, including Frank O'Malley in literature, Joseph Evans in philosophy and James Tunstead Burtchaell in theology.

But one began to sense a growing unease arising from this new openness to the assertions of modernity and an accompanying loss of confidence in what had appeared to be the settled claims of baroque Catholic culture. By the time I left Notre Dame four years later, much had changed, not only the cultural shift from the requirement that students wear a coat and tie to dinner but also the removal of the religious habit, a growing resistance to the general requirements in theology and philosophy, a deepening sense of the central importance of social activism and the importance of political change, and an increasing diversity of backgrounds and commitments among the faculty and—to a lesser extent—among the students.

Daniel Patrick Moynihan, then a staff member at the Nixon White House, delivered the commencement speech at my graduation exercises

in 1969, and having begun with an apt citation from Bernanos, he continued with a warning about the growing danger of the heresies of liberalism,
heresies which would be "procedural in nature, for it is in process that a
liberal society defines itself...."[2] He pointed to a pervasive suspicion about
traditional authorities within the academy, government and the Church
and was particularly attentive to the dangers of an increasingly radical
dependence on political solutions to complex social and moral problems,
citing Michael Polanyi's sharp recognition that in the absence of God, a
bad society is inexcusable and "to achieve a comprehensive improvement
of society, you need comprehensive powers, so you must regard all resistance to yourself as high treason and must put it down mercilessly."[3]

This led Moynihan to the important conclusion, one that had a particular resonance with me following the disastrous presidential campaign
of 1968 in which I had traveled with Robert Kennedy's presidential team
both in Indiana and in Nebraska, that the essential crisis of the time was
not political but, in essence, religious. For "it is a religious crisis of a large
number of intensely moral, even Godly people who no longer hope for
God."[4] They had begun to hope instead for procedural political solutions.
He insisted that government could not give values to those who had lost
them, supply meaning to life for those who had none, or provide the basis
for the moral energy needed to live life fully. He concluded with a call
for the recognition of the limits of politics and the need to expand the
province of moral philosophy. I was drawn increasingly to an educational
vision conscious of this problem and the urgency of its solution.

It had not been long before I arrived on campus that Notre Dame,
in line with Catholic higher education as a whole, had replaced required
courses in religion with new requirements in theology. The earlier
assumption had been that the study of religion would promote the possibility of an integration of life in which the claims of the intellect would
find a complementary formation in virtue and devotion. Now the Catholic university moved to focus its distinctive intellectual claims in the
emerging field of academic theology. In doing so, it implicitly distanced
itself from the task of the moral and religious formation of its students.

This marked a twofold departure from the older tradition of Catholic education, for it had classically been philosophy that had served as the
integrating discipline of Catholic general education, and theology was

understood to be an ecclesial discipline whose primary setting was the seminary and not the university. But, as Philip Gleason has noted, the loss of the organizing principles of Neo-Scholasticism in the 1940s had left the specific intellectual claims of the general curriculum in some disarray.[5] But it was the changed understanding of theology itself that provided the greatest novelty. Newman, too, had argued for a central role of theology, insisting that it was the "fundamental and regulating principle of the whole Church system," and he argued as well that it had a critical role in achieving that philosophical habit of mind that is the primary object of university teaching.[6] But Newman wrote at a time in which he could still assume the active role of what he called the *schola theologorum*, that body of theologians who exercised a fundamental critical role in the life of the faith precisely because of their conscious ecclesial vocation and formation. But by the late 1960s this formation, which presupposed a certain intellectual and spiritual integration, had begun to be replaced by an understanding of theology as an academic discipline among disciplines. No longer must it be assumed, as the Fathers had, that in order to be a theologian, one had to be a saint. Nor was it even more modestly required—as Balthasar had insisted—that theology must be done on its knees. The focus now became the urgent need to gain intellectual credibility within the dominant claims of the natural and social sciences, to gain a place at the table. That long, slow, theological preparation made possible in seminaries and religious houses of formation was replaced by the need for young, largely lay scholars to complete their work expeditiously in order to meet the new specialized expectations of the academy. Several years ago, Matthew Lamb had addressed this emerging reality, wondering aloud whether one could sustain a distinctive Catholic theology within this new cultural context.[7] He also raised the issue of the loss of that training in languages and in philosophy made possible by the older system of formation.

In a 1967 essay, "Theology and the Layman," Daniel Callahan, who had served as Christopher Dawson's assistant in his years at Harvard as the first Chauncey Stillman Chair in Roman Catholic Studies, argued that the study of theology was necessary for the laity in order for them to overcome a tendency to superficial piety. Newman had also argued for theology's role in the university on similar grounds, insisting that without it—as young men became more educated in secular thought and culture and comparatively uneducated in the claims of faith—they would collapse into either naive piety or superficial skepticism. But here again it is important to stress that from Newman's perspective, theology must always depend upon the authority of the Church, for Revelation itself has been given to the Church's authority to proclaim and to defend, and as a result theology must be exercised within this tension of relations with the Church.

In contrast, Callahan suggested that academic theology would be the means of empowering the laity and of enhancing opportunities for autonomous choices. He noted that this heightened consciousness would be necessary in order to overcome the world's proffering of "innumerable tranquilizers to ward off anxiety, to keep the larger questions of life and existence from pressing too hard."[8] And he warned of the danger of a pious fideism that closes off the necessary dangers of a conscious life. He conceded that the Catholic layman himself would be tempted by that tranquilized peace of mind made possible by avoiding the questions of meaning and truth, but that "he can choose to be different. He can risk the trouble of taking on problems and difficulties, obscurities and mysteries.... And theology is a risk: the risk of having the old certainties destroyed, of new and perplexing problems raised, of great challenges placed."[9]

But these assumptions now require a new appraisal. They require as well perhaps a reminder of Chesterton's recognition that the great advantage of living within a coherent, venerable, authoritative tradition is that it frees us from the arbitrary tyranny of the unexamined assumptions of our own time.[10]

In July of that same year, a group of prominent Catholic educators met at Land O'Lakes, Wisconsin, to draft a statement on the nature of Catholic universities that Philip Gleason has called a declaration of independence from the hierarchy.[11] The statement famously insisted on the Catholic university's "true autonomy and academic freedom in the face of authority of any kind, lay or clerical, external to the academic community itself."[12] At the same time the signers of the document insisted that Catholicism must be "perceptibly present and effectively operative" within the Catholic university. However, if it was not its ecclesial character that provided that providential agency by which Catholicism would shape the life of the university, what might replace it? Here again we find an emphasis on the role of theology. The Catholic university must commit to the creation of a faculty of theology that would oversee the work of scholars in all branches of theology, a work that is "essential to the integrity of a university." The creation of a theology faculty will make possible a broader interdisciplinary dialogue with all areas of knowledge. But the signers acknowledged that for this to be possible it would be necessary that there be "present in many or most of the non-theological areas Christian scholars who are not only interested in and competent in their own fields, but also have personal interest in cross-disciplinary confrontation."[13] It is perhaps debatable whether Catholic universities of the time possessed a faculty with this disposition and intellectual formation, but to have fulfilled this commitment Catholic universities would not only have had to assemble a certain kind of faculty of theology but also to have developed a robust hiring for mission practice and a concerted set of faculty development programs to draw new faculty whose own training was increasingly specialized into cross-disciplinary conversations/confrontations and to a sustained attentiveness to the role of faith in the academy. One has to say that the uncritical confidence in the ability of theology to exercise this integrative role now strikes one as remarkably naive.

But the signers did not stop there, for they defined the Catholic university as constituting the critical intelligence of the Church, the guardian of its intellectual heritage. As such the Church was now to be understood to depend formally on the critical evaluation of the university and not the reverse:

> Every university, Catholic or not, serves as the critical reflective intelligence of its society. In keeping with this general function, the Catholic university should carry on a continual examination of all aspects and all activities of the Church and should objectively evaluate them. The Church would thus have the benefit of continual counsel from Catholic universities. Catholic universities have hardly played this role at all. It may well be one of the most important functions of the Catholic university of the future.[14]

The romantic and idealized vision of the university as the "critical reflective intelligence" of society may have been a matter of wishful thinking, but in the growing suspicions about the authority of both the Church and civil society, the academy saw an opening for its own enhanced pretensions to provide the organizing principles of social order.

The new autonomy proposed for theology arose from a complex history. In one sense, the need for a certain freedom for the theologian is self-evident. Newman had argued that it is impossible for a theologian to work well under the lash of a superincumbent authority, but he was equally conscious of the fact that the mind is most creative not when it is undisturbed by authority of any kind but rather within an active engagement with it, in a tension of relations with authority even when that authority possesses infallible powers. It is the necessary cycle of the life of the Church, like the ebb and flow of the tide, that emerging theological insights will over time provoke the response of the authorities of the Church in order to situate the new knowledge within the larger tradition of the faith. And such judgments, even of the highest kind, do not arrest the movement of the cycle, for immediately there is the need to determine where that authoritative declaration does and does not apply. And so we turn back to theology. Newman does not hesitate to use the language of warfare to describe the various collisions and reconciliations inherent in such a process. For him, the Church is simply necessary for the life of the mind and as such is necessary for the university to be a university at all, not simply by adding a religious principle to a secular project but by assisting the university in securing that fragile circle of knowledge in which each discipline finds its own distinctive role and characteristic limit.[15]

Newman wrote at a time when the fragmentation of the circle of knowledge was quickly advancing, and he recognized that the elimination of theology from the university curriculum, already underway in London and proposed for the Queen's College system in Ireland, would result not merely in a vacuum, an absence, but in the disordering of the relations of all of the disciplines. Theology was essential, Newman thought, but insufficient to secure the tensions of the circle of knowledge. The authority of the Church was necessary to sustain the tensions of the circle and to secure the two vital principles of the university: the unity of knowledge and the ultimate complementarity of faith and reason. Newman noted that when liberal education was pursued without the assistance of the Church, it would inevitably lead in one of two directions, the pursuit of truth as beauty or sentiment (perhaps now the prevailing temptation of the humanities) or truth as power (the consistent temptation of the applied sciences and professions). Both tendencies now converge in the life of the modern university.

John Cavadini recently warned of the consequences of the modern Catholic university's attempts to define its Catholic claims not in its relationship to the Church—that living incarnational, historical mystery overseen by the apostolic claims of often very human and sometimes poorly educated bishops—but rather in a relationship to the Catholic intellectual tradition, an idealized, gnostic alternative of our own invention.[16] In this he reminds us of Dietrich Bonhoeffer's sharp insight, one with considerable Scriptural warrant: "Only he who believes is obedient and only he who is obedient believes."[17] And if obedience is required for faith, to whom shall we go?

CATHOLIC STUDIES AS RESPONSE TO THE GROWING PROBLEMS OF MODERN UNIVERSITY CULTURE

All of this is a background and context for the creation of Catholic Studies over 20 years ago. It seemed to me that we had to confront a number of interrelated problems.

- The loss of a sense of the fundamental purpose of the university, which is, as Newman insisted, to form a habit of mind in its students enabling them to see things in relation and to form a right judgment about complex realities. This had largely been replaced by an emphasis on narrowly specialized expertise for faculty and narrowly defined career preparation for students.

- The fragmentation of the circle of knowledge resulting in an incoherent and unintegrated educational experience.

- The loss of a sense of the Church's role in securing the university's intellectual claims.

- The abandonment of the language of formation, increasingly perceived as imposing coercive restrictions on adult consumers of education and the substitution of the language of therapy for that of religion. As Harry Lewis, the former dean of Harvard College, noted, Harvard no longer claims to form the good person, merely the well person. "The university has lost, indeed it has willingly surrendered," he wrote, "its moral authority to shape the souls of its students."[18] We are content now with safety and health as measures of well-being. Of course, this is not to suggest that the souls of students are not being formed within the university, for surely they are, but it is not a formation for which the university itself claims responsibility.

- The substitution of a critical sense for a creative or even commonsensical one. I think of T.S. Eliot's observation: "When a poet's mind is perfectly equipped for his work, it is constantly amalgamating disparate experiences; the ordinary man's experience is chaotic, irregular, fragmentary. The latter falls in love or reads Spinoza, and these two experiences have nothing to do with each other, or with the noise of the typewriter or the smell of cooking; in the mind of the poet these experiences are always forming new wholes."[19] This substitution has greatly increased the compartmentalization that now marks so much of contemporary life and certainly the life of the university.

Many of us were influenced not only by the thought of Newman but also by his fellow English convert Christopher Dawson, who shared Newman's sense of the dangers inherent in a culture increasingly marked by the absence of faith. In a sermon titled "The Infidelity of the Future," Newman had warned that for the first time in history, we would live in a culture without religious foundations, a culture that would inevitably have dehumanizing effects.[20] Two generations later, Dawson saw the artificiality of the experiment and also noted that its deepest tendency would be toward violence since without an integrating spiritual principle it would have to impose coercively a superficial organizing principle, a historical insight later reiterated by Moynihan. And so we confront in the 20th century a culture that is at once the bloodiest and, as John Paul II noted, the most fearful in human history.

The response to this historical situation, as in the earlier five ages of the Church identified by Dawson, would require not merely the necessary addition of a spiritual principle to what he called the Great Leviathan of bourgeois culture, but the need "to view the cultural situation as a whole and to see the Christian way of life not as a number of isolated precepts imposed by ecclesiastical authority, but as a cosmos of spiritual relations embracing heaven and earth and uniting the order of social and moral life with the order of divine grace."[21] This same view was expressed more recently by Pope Benedict XVI to a group of American bishops on their *ad limina* visit to Rome:

> Faith's recognition of the essential unity of all knowledge provides a bulwark against the alienation and fragmentation which occurs when the use of reason is detached from the pursuit of truth and virtue. In this sense, Catholic institutions have a specific role to play in helping to overcome the crisis of universities today. Firmly grounded in the vision of the intrinsic interplay of faith, reason and the pursuit of human excellence, every Christian intellectual and all the Church's educational institutions must be convinced, and desirous of convincing others, that no aspect of reality remains alien to or untouched by, the mystery of the Redemption and the Risen Lord's dominion over all creation.[22]

Let me respond then to each of these problematic aspects of modern university life and attempt to indicate how they shaped our understanding of the task of Catholic Studies.

We began with the assumption that Catholic Studies would be a work of the Church, not necessarily in its formal juridical structure (although from the beginning we sought to secure this in a clear canonical form). We had first explored with the Congregation for Catholic Education the possibility of a pontifical charter for the Center for Catholic Studies. We were persuaded that this would be difficult to achieve and so began to explore the possibility of canonical archdiocesan recognition. Because the University of St. Thomas was in the process of reconsidering its own relation to the local Church, it was decided to postpone these discussions. Nonetheless, from the beginning, the work of Catholic Studies was not merely intellectual but also apostolic, for we sought to form not merely a habit of mind among students but also to integrate their intellectual and spiritual formation in an organic form. But its chief intellectual feature was its interdisciplinary focus, for with Dawson and Newman, we realized that we needed to form our students in such a way that they could experience life as Eliot noted: in the context of forming new wholes.

It is important here, I think, to distinguish the work of interdisciplinary and multidisciplinary studies. As we understood interdisciplinary studies, the task was to integrate the methods and insights of a variety of disciplines within a complex but coherent vision of reality. In contrast, multidisciplinary studies seek to take into account the methods and insights of a variety of disciplinary perspectives while leaving them autonomous, their mutual relations undefined. The first lends itself to the pursuit of the unity of knowledge and the study of the relations of faith and reason. The latter does not. Moreover, it seemed to us that academic theology, although indispensable in this work, would be insufficient in itself to achieve such unity. We needed to recover the imaginative tradition of the faith, its approach to beauty, the great-souled world of literature, the deep artistic traditions of Catholicism, its understanding of the human person and of the range and the limits of politics. For we shared the view of Dawson that "the Christian culture of the past was an organic whole. It was not confined to theology, it expressed itself also in philosophy and in literature, in art and music, society and institutions, and none of these forms of expression can be understood completely unless they are seen in relation to the rest. But under existing conditions this is impossible."[23] Impossible but essential, and it struck us that new forms of study would be necessary to achieve it.

John Paul II stressed the central importance of the disciplines of theology and philosophy in *Ex Corde Ecclesiae*, but he equally stressed the importance of interdisciplinary studies that not only complement these disciplines but in some measure correct them.[24] And perhaps particularly in our own time we need the insights of poets, and not only the great Catholic poets of the past—Prudentius, Dante, Hopkins, Rimbaud, Eliot and Stevens—but also contemporary poets. I think of Christian Wiman's recent description of Christ as a shard of glass in the gut, for "to walk through the fog of God toward the clarity of Christ is difficult because of how 'unlovely,' how 'ungodly,' that clarity often turns out to be."[25] He notes that human love catalyzes the love of Christ, but at the same time he cites Augustine's recognition that although we search for this love, and continually yearn for it, "we barely touch it in a quick shudder of the heart."[26]

We placed the incarnational principle at the heart of our attempt to overcome the fragmentation of knowledge that haunts the modern university. We hired faculty with broad interdisciplinary formation and commitments and invited students not only into courses but also into conversation and extracurricular formation programs that offered them an opportunity to explore the implications of that unity of knowledge at the heart of the claims of a Catholic university. We sought to embody that incarnational principle not primarily in the comprehensive claims of a curriculum but rather in a communion of persons disclosed in the program's faculty, in their mutual relations and disputations, in their friendship. At the heart of Catholic Studies has been the encounter not merely with a set of texts but with living Catholic minds who share in that *gaudium de veritate*, that "joy in the truth" that Augustine had described in the *Confessions* and that John Paul II described as lying at the heart of the life of a university, properly understood.[27] Here I am reminded of Pope Benedict XVI's lecture to Catholic educators in Washington in April of 2008 in which he spoke of Catholic education as a work of intellectual charity. He stressed the dignity and distinctiveness of the Catholic teacher, for "this aspect of charity calls the educator to recognize that the profound responsibility to lead the young to truth is nothing less than an act of love.... In practice intellectual charity upholds the essential unity of knowledge against the fragmentation which ensues when reason is detached from the pursuit of truth."[28]

The end of this intellectual charity is not merely that of faith but also of hope, for as the pope noted, "Once their passion for the fullness and unity of truth has been awakened, young people will surely relish the discovery that the question of what they can know opens up the vast adventure of what they ought to do. Here they will experience 'in what' and 'in whom' it is possible to hope, and be inspired to contribute to society in a way that engenders hope in others."[29]

We sought to disclose this ecclesial character of the work in its relation to the university with its emphasis on the role of the lecturer in promoting the unity of knowledge and the relations of faith and reason but also in relation to the college, that residential formation overseen by Newman's tutor, which provided that combination of personal formation and elementary studies that so shapes the lives and hopes of young students.

The Church, Newman insisted, had to be present in both, and we sought to incorporate that principle not only in our academic programs but also in our programs in Rome in which we had the opportunity to integrate in an intentional residential community intellectual, spiritual and human formation. That experience has been for most of our students the defining moment of Catholic Studies. It was important to us that we create not merely another American study-abroad program in Rome but that we instead create a truly Catholic community of conviction. Our affiliation with the pontifical Dominican university, the Angelicum, our chapel, the community of faith which unites students, seminarians, faculty and staff in a common purpose, expressed most directly in liturgical life, has had a lasting impact on the lives and vocations of our alumni. It was here that we sought to embody most fully the collegiate principle and the influence of the tutor. In addition to Rome, we offered other community living opportunities for men and women on our St. Paul campus. This took the form not only of floors in residence halls but also Catholic Studies men's and women's houses in which students formed an intentional community of friendship and conviction in which they lived a life of friendship in community. The students themselves form the rule of life in each house. We also created leadership formation programs that invited students to reflect on the ways in which their formation might assist them to serve as leaders in the Church and in civil society. In addition to our Leadership Intern Program for juniors and seniors, we launched a Latino Leadership Program that has drawn students from around the country.

The Center also developed a series of summer faculty development seminars; a quarterly journal, *Logos: A Journal of Catholic Thought and Culture*; three endowed institutes focusing on Catholic social thought, the relations of Catholic thought, law and public policy, and the formation of a new generation of young Catholics for service to the Church and civil society; lecture series and faculty book discussions; retreats; and collaborative efforts with the Pontifical Council for Justice and Peace, the Holy See's Mission to the United Nations in Geneva and the Archdiocese of St. Paul and Minneapolis.

In a recent conversation I had with a philosopher teaching in a major seminary in the United States, she argued that the Catholic university as a whole should embody the integrative commitments and ecclesial character of Catholic Studies. This strikes me as fundamentally unrealistic unless she was describing a relatively small Catholic liberal arts college. Catholic Studies is, in effect, a creative minority, a college within the larger university, an intentional community of students and faculty seeking to realize an organic intellectual, spiritual and human formation within the broader work of the university that focuses on the abstract and theoretical claims of the various disciplines. This necessarily requires an economy of scale. It is simply not possible for a large comprehensive university, perhaps even a medium-sized institution, to constitute a community of this kind, and it is precisely these intentional residential communities that the modern university requires.

The conversation continued with other colleagues, several of whom complained about the loss of a genuine engagement in learning among students who appear neither to seek conversation with their peers nor to seek advice from their faculty. I was struck by the difference in my experience in Catholic Studies. When I leave a Catholic Studies course, I have to thread my way through groups of students who are in crowded conversation with others about the course they just left and who are often waiting to continue the conversation with their teachers. Again I am reminded of the importance of intellectual charity and its relation to friendship. Christopher Blum recently noted that "teachers who find it difficult to cultivate friendship and practice it as a high ideal are unlikely to be able to understand, much less shape the lives of their students, whose whole collegiate lives are engulfed in friendship's concerns."[30] But the compartmentalized character of the modern university's life does not provide a rich soil for the flourishing of intellectual charity. Here, I think, we have an important reminder of the importance of the distinction Newman makes between education and mere instruction.

Alasdair MacIntyre has identified the need to overcome the compartmentalization of the modern university, and he has also noted the disastrous results of narrow specialization in recent economic, political and military crises. A student should have, he argues, an organic experience of the interdependence of a set of apparently isolated encounters in the classroom, the residence hall, the chapel and the sports field.[31] But as I mentioned earlier, the contemporary university has largely abandoned this integral vision of intellectual and personal formation. Catholic Studies seemed to us an essential response to that shift, not only inviting students to a more radical encounter with truth but also to a new formation of life which discloses a deep sense of personal vocation.

Newman warned that the deformations within the modern university posed such a fundamental danger to the intellectual lives of students that they might well be advised to forgo a university education entirely. "How much better," he wrote, "is it for the active and thoughtful intellect, where such is to be found, to eschew the college and the university altogether, than to submit to a drudgery so ignoble, a mockery so contumelious! How much more profitable for the independent mind, after the mere rudiments of education, to range through a library at random, taking down books as they meet him, and pursuing the trains of thought which his mother wit suggests."[32]

This loss of an integrating educational vision was viewed by Dawson as fundamental to the modern cultural crisis. He noted, "A common educational tradition creates a common world of thought with common moral and intellectual values and a common inheritance of knowledge, and these are the conditions which make a culture conscious of its identity and give it a common memory and a common past. Consequently, any break in the continuity of the educational tradition involves a corresponding break in the continuity of the culture."[33] Newman had argued that the modern university posed a fundamental danger to the intellectual lives of students if it failed to realize this integral vision. That is to say that the modern university offers not merely a partial education but a deformed education.

I am persuaded that Catholic Studies is an essential element in the renewal of the contemporary university, partly because I think it provides one critical way in which we might respond to the diminishing presence of the religious women and men who founded so many of our institutions, who not only disclosed the distinctive claims of their identity in their work and in their vision but who, in large measure, carried those wider claims in their personal and communal witness within the universities they founded. Nothing has replaced that witness, and in a real sense nothing fully can. But a group of faculty whose primary intellectual and indeed spiritual work is to take up this distinctive interdisciplinary task, a faculty largely lay in character, of necessity, but also incorporating priests and religious, will have a considerable role to play in securing this legacy. That integrated witness cannot be compartmentalized. In the absence of that organic vision of the relations of prayer, intelligence, obedience and formation of life, we find the modern academy with its separation of pastoral formation, intellectual instruction and human development. In "Intellect the Instrument of Religious Training," preached at the University church in Dublin in 1856, Newman argued that the "object of the Holy See and the Catholic Church in setting up universities" is "to reunite things which were in the beginning joined together by God, and have been put asunder by man." He insisted that he wanted "to destroy that diversity of centers, which puts everything into confusion by creating a contrariety of influences." He continued:

> It will not satisfy me, what satisfies so many, to have two independent systems, intellectual and religious, going at once side by side, by a sort of division of labour, and only accidentally brought together. It will not satisfy me, if religion is here, and science there, and young men converse with science all day, and lodge with religion in the evening. It is not touching the evil to which these remarks have been directed, if young men eat and drink and sleep in one place and think in another; I want the same roof to contain both the intellectual and the moral discipline.... I want the intellectual layman to be religious and the devout ecclesiastic to be intellectual.[34]

Newman reminded us of the task of the university, in calling the attention of the young men before him to the image of St. Monica forming the mind and heart of her son Augustine. Such is the image of the university as an *alma mater* knowing her students one by one and not in anonymous abstraction. This has been the work of Catholic Studies. As such, it has been a great experiment. As I mentioned to graduating seniors, when I think of Catholic Studies, I am reminded of the English titles of the two volumes of memoirs of Raissa Maritain, *Adventures in Grace* and *We Have Been Friends Together*. For this has been the work of genuine community.

I note that Catholic Studies is indispensable in this work of renewal, but it is also clear that it is, in itself, insufficient to realize it. It can serve as a catalyst for reflection and renewal in forming a generation of students and can provide forums for sustained reflection on the history and contemporary relevance of Catholic thought and culture for faculty. It cannot, however, replace the larger university-wide task of creating robust hiring for mission plans and faculty development programs for the university as a whole. This is the responsibility of university trustees, of the president and senior administration. If Catholicism is to be "perceptibly present and effectively operative" within the Catholic university, it will require a more comprehensive effort than Catholic Studies can provide. Nonetheless, Catholic Studies constitutes one of those creative minorities on which larger cultures, in this case academic culture, depend. As such it reminds us of the great tradition of Catholic thought and culture and invites students and faculty to an encounter with those great things that Dante described as the source of awe and wonder on which the soul finally depends.[35]

NOTES

[1] John Henry Newman, *An Essay in Aid of a Grammar of Assent* (Oxford: The Clarendon Press, 1985), 248.

[2] Daniel Patrick Moynihan, "Politics as the Art of the Impossible," in *Go Forth and Do Good: Memorable Notre Dame Commencement Addresses,* ed. Wilson D. Miscamble, C.S.C. (Notre Dame: University of Notre Dame Press, 2003), 187.

[3] Cited in Moynihan, 191.

[4] Moynihan, 190.

[5] Philip Gleason, *Contending with Modernity: Catholic Higher Education in the Twentieth Century* (New York: Oxford University Press, 1995), 297-304.

[6] John Henry Newman, preface to the Third Edition, *The Via Media of the Anglican Church* (London: Longmans, Green and Co., 1897), xlvii.

[7] Matthew Lamb, "Will There Be Catholic Theology in the United States?" *America* 162 (May 26, 1990): 523-34.

[8] Daniel Callahan, "Theology and the Layman," in *The Role of Theology in the University* (Milwaukee: The Bruce Publishing Company, 1967), 11.

[9] Ibid.

[10] G.K. Chesterton, *Orthodoxy* (South Orange, N.J.: Chesterton Institute Press, 2008), 135.

[11] Philip Gleason, *Contending with Modernity: Catholic Higher Education in the Twentieth Century* (New York: Oxford University Press, 1995), 317. For the actual statement North American region of the International Federation of Catholic Universities, see " 'Land O' Lakes' Statement on Catholic Universities (1967)," in

American Catholic History: A Document Reader, ed. Mark Massa with Catherine Osborne (New York: New York University, 2008): 110-18.

[12] Land O'Lakes Statement, §1.

[13] Ibid., §4.

[14] Ibid., §5.

[15] John Henry Newman, *Apologia Pro Vita Sua,* ed. Ian Ker (London: Penguin Books, 1994), 225-27.

[16] John Cavadini, "An Open Letter to the Notre Dame Community Regarding Catholic Identity," *The Observer,* April 19, 2006.

[17] Dietrich Bonhoeffer, *The Cost of Discipleship,* trans., R.H. Fuller, rev. ed. (New York: Macmillan Publishers, 1960), 54.

[18] Harry R. Lewis, *Excellence without a Soul: How a Great University Forgot Education* (New York: Public Affairs, 2006), 159-60.

[19] T.S. Eliot, "Metaphysical Poets," in *Selected Essays* (London: Faber and Faber Limited, 1932), 247.

[20] John Henry Newman, "The Infidelity of the Future," in *Faith and Prejudice and Other Unpublished Sermons of Cardinal Newman* (New York: Sheed and Ward, 1956), 113-28.

[21] Christopher Dawson, *The Crisis of Western Education* (Washington, DC: The Catholic University of America Press, 2010), 115.

[22] Pope Benedict XVI, "Address to the Bishops of the United States of America (Regions X-XIII) on Their 'Ad Limina' Visit," May 5, 2012.

[23] Christopher Dawson, "Civilization in Crisis," in *Christianity and European Culture,* ed. Gerald J. Russello (Washington, DC: The Catholic University of America Press, 1998), 79.

[24] Pope John Paul II, *On Catholic Universities: Ex Corde Ecclesiae* (Washington, DC: United States Catholic Conference, 2000), 15-18.

[25] Christian Wiman, *My Bright Abyss: Meditations of a Modern Believer* (New York: Farrar, Straus and Giroux, 2013), 121.

[26] Ibid., 21.

[27] Saint Augustine, *S. Aureli Augustini Confessionum Libri Tredecim,* ed. Martinus Skutella,(Leipzig: Teubner, 1934), X, xxiii, 33, 234, line 24; Pope John Paul II, *Ex Corde Ecclesiae,* §3.

[28] Pope Benedict XVI, "Address to the Participants in the Meeting with Catholic Educators," April 17, 2008.

[29] Ibid.

[30] Christopher O. Blum, *Rejoicing in the Truth: Wisdom and the Educator's Craft* (Front Royal, VA: Christendom Press, 2015), 166.

[31] Alasdair MacIntyre, "Catholic Universities: Dangers, Hopes, Choices," in *Higher Learning and Catholic Traditions,* ed. Robert E. Sullivan (Notre Dame: University of Notre Dame Press, 2001), 1-21.

[32] John Henry Newman, *The Idea of a University*, ed. Ian Ker, (Oxford: The Clarendon Press, 1976), 132.

[33] Christopher Dawson, *The Crisis of Western Education* (Washington, DC: The Catholic University of America Press, 2010), 5.

[34] John Henry Newman, "Intellect the Instrument of Religious Training," in *Sermons Preached on Various Occasions* (London: Longmans, Green and Co., 1921), 13.

[35] Dante Alighieri, *Convivio*, trans. William Walrond Jackson (Oxford: Oxford University Press, 1909), 281.

2

Naming the New Lions:
The Challenges of Contemporary
Culture to Christian Faith

PAUL MURRAY, O.P.

I cannot say how delighted I am and honored to contribute to this book in honor of Don Briel. Few people in my life have inspired me so much as Don Briel. I revere Dr. Briel not only as the founder of the Catholic Studies Program, and for the impressive courage and wisdom he has shown, over many years, in that particular role, I revere him also as a wonderful friend—indeed, among the gifts of providence I have received so far, one of the most unexpected and most delightful.

I would like to begin by drawing attention for a few moments to the celebrated account of Daniel in the Old Testament—the story, that is, of the enormous courage possessed by this young man when faced, all of a sudden, with the threat of the lions' den. My aim in recalling this story is to raise one question in particular, namely: What are the forces, the oppo-sitions—"the new lions" —that most threaten us today as believers? What are their names? At a time of enormous challenge, when we find ourselves confronted more and more by the culture of death, how can living faith survive and thrive? As you know well, in the Daniel story, of central impor-tance is the remarkable dedication of Daniel to the practice of prayer. But if we consider our own situation today, what possible impact can prayer be expected to make? How can such a humble and simple practice as prayer help us confront the challenge of "the new lions"?

King Darius, according to the biblical account, signed an interdict that no one was to address any petition "to any God or man for thirty days," otherwise he would be "cast into the den of lions" (Dan 6:7). Even after Daniel heard that this law had been signed, he continued his custom of going home to kneel in prayer and give thanks to his God in the upper chamber three times a day. However, some of Daniel's enemies spied on Daniel and reported his disobedience to the king, insisting that Daniel be punished. The king wanted to spare Daniel, but he was bound by the law that he himself had promulgated. And so, with deep regret, he "ordered Daniel to be brought and cast into the den of lions" (Dan 6:16).

To Daniel the king said: "May your God whom you serve so constantly, save you"...Very early the next morning, the king rose and hastened to the lions' den. As he drew near he cried out to Daniel sorrowfully: "O Daniel, servant of the living God, has the God whom you serve so constantly been able to save you from the lions?" Daniel answered the king: "O king, live forever! My God has sent his angel and closed the lions' mouths so that they have not hurt me" (Dan 6:16; 19-22).

One detail among others that strikes the modern ear as strange in this story is the fact that Daniel was thrown to the lions simply because he said his prayers. But we who are living now—in what we imagine to be a more enlightened age—do we have the right, I wonder, to be so shocked? Not many years ago, in Europe, as it happens, a similar kind of persecution took place, and in an unusually shocking way in Communist Albania. I had the opportunity to visit Albania not long after the final collapse of Communism. (I was giving a retreat, at the time, to some of the sisters of Mother Teresa.) A man I met when I was there, an Albanian, told me a story about his uncle. The Communists were still in power when his uncle became ill and had to go into a hospital, where he underwent a serious operation. After the operation, when he returned to the ward and started to come back to consciousness, he began to groan quietly: "O God, O God!" One of the male nurses in the ward immediately contacted the Communist authorities and told them that, in open violation of state law, a man, a patient, was praying publicly in the ward. The police came at once, and the man was forcibly removed from the hospital. Then, together with all his family who were rounded up by the police, the man was thrown into prison and, in spite of his sickness, held there for many months without trial.

The king ordered Daniel to be brought and cast into the lions' den. In our own day, how are we to understand the significance of this powerful, biblical image? What are the lions of today that threaten us and would devour the body of our faith? Communism is no longer the lion that it once was, so it's worth asking ourselves the question: Who or what are the new lions now confronting us? I would like to name three. There are other challenges or other threats I could name, which you yourselves would no doubt be able to propose. But the particular trio I have in mind are these: first, the lion of relativism; second, the lion of fundamentalism; and third, the lion of pessimism.

THE LION OF RELATIVISM

Perhaps the best way to understand relativism is to understand its aim, which, at least in its philosophical form, is to convince us that no human being, no human intelligence or spirit, can ever know or grasp ultimate truth in itself. It says to us: "What you think you know, or believe in, are merely appearances. Your conviction about God, for example, is a reflection, or a projection of your own, on a limited, human scale. In the end, all the words of faith you possess, all your convictions, represent, at best, only one way among others—and a very subjective way—of looking at reality."

This voice of relativism, so apparently sane and humane, is heard today in many of the corridors of learning, in university forums and classrooms, for example, and in philosophical seminars and discussion groups. But its voice, its message, echoes in other places as well, many of them closer to home. It has found its way, for example, into the everyday world of books and films, kitchen-table talk and coffee-bar conversation, and also, and on more than a few occasions, I am sad to say, into Sunday homilies!

But why should we consider relativism a great or significant problem? The question arises because, at first glance, it doesn't seem to be a threat comparable in any way to that of atheistic Communism at its height. Communism was not only a theory—it was also a social and political reality. It assumed a worldwide, visible form. In contrast, relativism is neither a political party nor a movement. It does have its public disciples, of course, but they tend to be academics. And so, one may well be tempted to dismiss the whole thing as a mere fad of certain intellectuals, and not therefore as a real threat.[1] But, in fact, relativism has already made an enormous impact, not only on society in general but also on the life of the Church herself. In the United States a huge number of the faithful have abandoned the Church in recent years, choosing to live, whether with full consciousness or not, under the tenets of moral and spiritual relativism.

Relativism, I suspect, will emerge in the long run as a much more deadly threat to Catholic faith, and to human culture, than any past or present threat of Communism. Like almost nothing else I can think of, it draws away the lifeblood of strong religious conviction. Attempting, however, to confront it as a community of believers is by no means an easy task. For in spite of its challenge to the faith, it possesses a disarmingly benign appearance. It approaches us *not* "like a lion seeking someone to devour," but rather like a domesticated tabby, a house cat, so common and so tame it seems almost a part of our everyday, mental furniture. Identified in the popular mind with such fine and necessary things as tolerance and affirmation, openness and freedom, relativism never seems to behave—at least not on the surface—like a prowling lion. Its opinions, unlike those of Communism, never roar. Its convictions never snarl, never bite. In fact, it never seems to frighten us at all. More like an atmosphere than an ideology, with a strangely quiet, almost imperceptible movement, it slides up close to wherever we are, settles down on our intellectual lap and begins to purr! But are we not finding ourselves disarmed, just at the moment when we should be *armed* and standing up to this disguised but grave threat "strong in faith"? Surely now is the time for us to hold fast to our Catholic faith and joyfully proclaim it?

As an encouragement to this end, it is well worth remembering here the moment, in spring or early summer 1979, that marked the beginning of the end of modern Communism. St. John Paul, the first Polish priest or bishop ever elected pope, returned home to his native Poland for his first pastoral visit since his election. The plan was that he would celebrate Mass before a million people in Warsaw's Victory Square. Before he arrived, all the people were wondering: "What will he say in his homily?" Poland, after all, was still dominated by the Communist regime: The priests and the people were forced to practice their faith under very difficult circumstances. So, no doubt, that day, the Communist authorities themselves were also wondering: "What will he say? What *can* he say?" After the Gospel had been read out, there was a great silence in the Square. John Paul II, Karl Wojtyla, was about to deliver what some people have called the most important homily of his life.

Up to this moment in the country, the Communist Party had tried its best to relegate Christ and the Catholic faith to positions of minor importance or of no importance. But now, with enormous confidence, John Paul declared: "Christ cannot be kept out of human history in any part of the globe ... the exclusion of Christ from human history is an act against the human being."[2] At one point, toward the end of his sermon, the form of the homily changed into that of a prayer—an unforgettable prayer: "I cry from all the depths of this millennium, I cry on the vigil of Pentecost: 'Let your Spirit descend. Let your Spirit descend, and renew the face of the earth, the face of this land.' "[3]

The reason, John Paul said, why he had come to Poland was to reaffirm the fact that Christ was "an open book of life," a book that teaches all of us in the world about human dignity and human rights. What he was asking for, then, together with his fellow countrymen and women—what he was praying for, in the great Sacrifice of the Mass—was that in Poland, as elsewhere in the world, "Christ will not cease to be for us an open book of life for the future."[4]

The message was clear. Christ was no longer to be kept out of the universities or the schools or the factories. It was at this point in the Pope's homily that the people, crowded into Warsaw's great square, began to clap loudly, and to cheer, and to chant in unison, over and over again: "We want God, we want God!" The clapping, the chanting, never seemed to end. It lasted all of 14 minutes. A Dominican confrere of mine, a Polish priest, Wojciech Giertych, the present papal theologian, who happened to be present at the Mass in Warsaw, told me afterwards that those 14 minutes changed the history of Poland, and indeed the history of Europe. The seed of a new confidence had been sown.

Recalling this event, and more especially the background to it—the enormous suffering endured by Catholic believers under State Communism—we may be inclined to consider our own situation as believers today a happy one, living, as it appears we do today, in an apparently free and open society, whether we happen to be living in the States or in Europe. Up until fairly recently our governments, and indeed the general culture of our age, seemed content to leave us, for the most part, to our own religious devices. We had been accommodated. But that situation is, of course, changing and changing fast.

In the face of this new and growing opposition, we might be tempted to retreat into the comfort of our own tribe, as it were. But it would, of course, be a betrayal of the Gospel if, deciding to focus only on our own peace and security, we gave up all serious attempts at transforming the world around us. The manifest desire of Christ is that we strive to leaven the whole dough of society: the culture, the mores, the social practices, the laws. In this matter, inspired by the writings of George Bernanos, Hans Urs von Balthasar declares: "The Christian thrives only in the open air, hardened by the dangerous world in which Christ has placed him and into which he has expressly sent him."[5]

Owing to the impact of relativism in modern America, many years ago Cardinal Avery Dulles remarked: "The general climate of ideas, especially among intellectual elites, is unfavorable to the Gospel."[6] In the meantime, matters have by no means improved. In fact, the situation in many respects has worsened. Avery Dulles noted that part of the task of the Church in our time is "to dispel the thick clouds of relativism."[7] I wholeheartedly agree with that. But how to dispel these "clouds"? It will, obviously, never be enough simply to issue condemnations. If that is all we do, we risk becoming as dark and angry as the "clouds" themselves! No—our primary task in this situation is, if I may extend the metaphor, somehow to shine through the clouds: to allow, that is, the strength and beauty of what we believe in to become apparent in our every word and gesture, to demonstrate to the world that the culture of life we are seeking to create is a culture that upholds the rights of the poor, for example, and respects the dignity of women. Our task, as followers of Jesus, is to set our light— that is, the light of the Gospel and the light of the Catholic spiritual tradition—on a lampstand, where it can be seen and can give light to all.

St. John Paul, during one of his visits to the United States, spoke of two kinds of responses to contemporary culture, one affirmative, one critical: "Sometimes," he said, "witnessing to Christ will mean drawing out of a culture the full meaning of its noblest intentions ... At other times witnessing to Christ means challenging that culture, especially when *the truth about the human person* is under assault."[8] The cultural situation in which we find ourselves today is very different, in one or two respects, from that of 60 or 70 years ago. Then the main issue was the challenge of secularization, whether in the parish or outside it. That challenge remains, but there is another challenge today, and it comes, paradoxically, from the field or realm of spirituality.

The change is, in itself, welcome, of course. It is a cause of no small encouragement, for believers today, to witness, among our contemporaries, a newly felt craving for some deep, living contact with the divine mystery. But spirituality, it should be noted, is not necessarily faith in the living God. In fact, on occasion, it can be little more than a well-disguised form of secularism and can assume some very strange forms indeed. There comes to mind here that sharp comment often attributed to G.K. Chesterton: "When people stop believing in God, they don't believe in nothing—they believe in anything!"

The present enthusiasm among our contemporaries for spirituality can mark the beginning of something truly impressive. But it can also indicate merely the pursuit of new experiences. Fashion, not faith; the taste of transcendence but not the bite. Cardinal George, in an interview on one occasion, made a few very wise comments on this subject. He remarked:

> Spirituality is in. You can have a search for the transcendent, and everybody will think that's wonderful. But faith is out. If you put a word like "Jesus" on that God you're searching for—well, that's limiting. Who has ever died for a spirituality? But a lot of people have died for the faith. The relationship between spirituality and faith has to be drawn or else spirituality can become narcissist. The search for spirituality is good, it's an opening. But it also can paradoxically turn people away from genuine faith, from really meeting Jesus Christ.[9]

Given the plurality of spiritualities that surround us nowadays, our situation as Catholics begins more and more to resemble the situation that confronted the first Christians. For, today we find ourselves stripped of much of the grandeur and glamour and triumphalism of what was once called Christendom. The message we preach is no longer taken for granted. Our words about Christ, about his death and his resurrection, begin to sound strange. And we, who are the bearers of this message to the world, can begin to look like fools. Pope Emeritus Benedict, when he was Cardinal, remarked in a paper entitled "Relativism: The Central Problem for Faith Today": "Those who want to stay with the faith of the Bible and the church see themselves pushed from the start to a no man's land on the cultural level and must as a first measure rediscover the 'madness of God' (1Cor.1:18) in order to recognize the true wisdom in it."[10]

Culture, human culture of any lasting significance, remains always dependent on living faith tradition, and particularly dependent, I would say, on what is one of the undoubted fruits of living faith, namely confidence—the golden seed of confidence—that deep inner hope, that element of spirit without which there can be no real flourishing of life, no survival, no harvest. As William Blake once put it, in a brief, stunning aphorism: "If the sun and moon should doubt, / They'd immediately go out"![11]

THE LION OF FUNDAMENTALISM

Years ago my old spiritual director alerted me to the fact that when, with my index finger, I am pointing at something or someone—when I am naming them—I am with that same gesture, with three of my other fingers, pointing back at myself! It was, I'm sure, a needed, salutary lesson at the time, and one that is also worth remembering here as I continue attempting in this talk to name, one after the other, the new lions. For the inescapable fact is that there are lions prowling within ourselves as well as lions outside. "Within the heart," we read in the homilies of St. Macarius, "there are unfathomable depths ... It is but a small vessel, and yet there are ... lions there."[12]

The phenomenon on which I now want to focus attention I call the lion of fundamentalism. It may strike you, at first, as a surprising choice. We don't normally consider fundamentalism a particular problem for Catholics. We associate it more with extreme forms of Islam or, in this country, with certain hard-line branches of the Reform tradition. And we point the finger in those directions. But if we examine our conscience and our history on the matter, we begin to realize that, at least as a tendency, fundamentalism has been with us in the Church almost from the beginning. The first fundamentalists, in fact, it could be argued, included some of the earliest followers of Jesus—all of them Jews—who rejected outright the idea of accepting non-Jews, the Gentiles, into the communion of Christ's Church. These Jewish converts were genuinely sincere men and women, people of principle, holding fast to what they understood and accepted as God's will. But on one crucial issue, their minds and hearts were closed all the same.

Something of St. Paul's exasperation in trying to come to terms with this phenomenon in the early Church is echoed three centuries later in a completely different context by St. Augustine. The group Augustine sets out to address is clearly resolute in its adherence to a number of the teachings of the Gospel. But in classic fundamentalist spirit, they somehow manage to ignore all the rest of God's truth. Augustine writes: "The clouds of heaven thunder forth throughout the world that God's house is being built. But these frogs sit in their pond and croak: 'We're the only Christians'!"[13]

Unfortunately, something of that "croaking" noise has survived the centuries and can still be heard today in a number of voices and ideologies within the Church. Hans Urs von Balthasar, although delighted at the emergence within Europe of a number of small groups determined to return to the fundamentals of the Catholic faith, found it necessary, at the same time, to warn them about the risk of a Catholic fundamentalism—a phenomenon he described as "the temptation of an enclosed autonomy."[14]

The witness to Gospel truth and to Catholic life such groups could give was, he said, "the Church's greatest need," but it was also "a great danger."[15] In spite of their enormous potential, there existed, in these groups, a tendency toward a sort of sectarian pride, a group arrogance or group narcissism. He wrote: "After the humbling of hierarchical triumphalism, there still remains a more subtle, spiritual triumphalism, the triumphalism found in the ideology of communities or groups ... On the one hand, there is the temptation to be too involved in the world; on the other hand, there is the temptation of an enclosed autonomy. The only solution is openness to God's revelation in its unabbreviated Catholicity."[16]

The emergence of Catholic Studies Programs is, I am persuaded, a phenomenon that would have delighted Hans Urs von Balthasar. I say this because it represents, first and last, a return to the fundamentals of the Catholic faith. But what of the threat to which he drew attention, namely the lion of fundamentalism? What of the temptation to group arrogance and group narcissism, the temptation, that is, to fall back into the safety of an enclosed autonomy? In my own experience of Catholic Studies—an experience that stretches back several years—I never witnessed, not even once, the unhappy phenomenon Balthasar describes, the descent into an elitist spiritual triumphalism. On the contrary, what has impressed me, again and again, in both the students and professors in the Catholic Studies Program is the way strong conviction concerning the fundamentals of the faith combines with an impressive openness of spirit and with a joy—both natural and supernatural—clearly manifesting the very opposite of a grim fundamentalism. What's more, the phenomenon I've been describing can, I have no doubt in my mind, be directly attributed to the "unabbreviated Catholicity" of Dr. Briel's original vision.

One of the temptations to which Balthasar refers is "the temptation to be too involved in the world." With regard to the priesthood, that particular temptation is linked, perhaps forever in our minds, with the period immediately following Vatican II. At that time, the secular dimension of the priestly vocation was emphasized. The calling of the priest, his very identity, seemed at times almost to coalesce with the aims of people like social workers and politicians, who were trying to transform human culture by promoting peace and justice in the world, the alleviation of poverty, health care and other works of mercy. The problem for the priest, however, the risk, was in allowing these great and necessary tasks to obscure something fundamental to the vocation of the ministerial priest, namely the sacred and cultic character of his role. Naturally, I don't think we should ever separate priesthood from an active concern for the poor or for the downtrodden, a Gospel imperative articulated brilliantly in our own day by Pope Francis. However, I have been greatly impressed and encouraged, over recent years, by the manifest recovery among young Catholics and young Catholic seminarians of the understanding of the sacred role of the priest.

Von Balthasar spoke of two temptations. The first temptation, he said, is "to be too involved in the world." The second is the temptation to draw back from our social and political responsibilities and inhabit what

Balthasar calls "an enclosed autonomy." Those who follow this route, whether they are priests, seminarians or laypeople, are very often sincere men and women, deeply passionate about their faith and their convictions. But being so intent on holding fast to these convictions, they can become somehow rigid and hard-nosed and begin to treat the faith as if it were their own personal and tribal possession.

"Sometimes," Pope John Paul II remarked, addressing a group of young seminarians, "priests of excellent virtue and zeal drastically reduce the efficacy of their ministry because of their impatient, unfriendly temperament and lack of balance. It is necessary, therefore, to form for oneself a good, open, understanding, patient character."[17] If nowadays, as priests or laypeople, we should find ourselves guilty of what John Paul calls "lack of balance," if we allow ourselves, that is, to be taken over by some kind of spiritual fundamentalism, it will mean that the door has finally been closed on any serious attempt at evangelization.

We are called, as Catholics, to be "carriers of the Word of life." But if, in practice, all we carry around in our minds or express with our words is a harsh fundamentalist creed or a hard-line ideology—a so-called left-wing or right-wing ideology—then we will never begin to transform the culture of the world we live in. And why? Because what we will be preaching will be our own word, and not the Word of God. The Dominican preacher Vincent McNabb remarked once to his brethren in the English province: "The world is waiting for those who love it ... If you don't love men don't preach to them—preach to yourself"![18]

When I spoke earlier about the lion of relativism, I suggested that we stand up to it "strong in faith." But what answer can we give to this second lion, which threatens us both from outside and from within, the lion of fundamentalism? We have to confront it, obviously, and head-on; we have to give an answer to those who question our faith. "Put in my mouth," we read in the Book of Esther, "persuasive words in the presence of the lion" (Esther 4:24). That said, however, the best response to fundamentalism, the most compelling and effective answer, but an answer that might, at first, look weak and ineffective is, of course, love.

Hans Urs von Balthasar, in a late interview on the subject of faith and modern culture, suggested that far from withdrawing from the complications and confusions of modern society and modern culture, the Christian should be active "on all levels on which a Christian commitment can humanize whatever is threatening to slide into the inhuman."[19] Earlier in the interview, Balthasar put this question to himself: "What can be done amid this want of culture wrought by the machine?" And he replied: "I suppose one can try to build islands of humanity, and in this project Christians could and should be leading ... From islands like this, true culture, Christian culture, may spread across the earth."[20]

We are not, of course, to forget our own spiritual needs, but we are asked by the Gospel to lift our gaze away from ourselves and consider the needs of the world. Apologetics has been recovered recently by many young Catholics as a means of confronting the present crisis. That recovery has been long overdue. But as Catholics, our best apologetics, I would suggest, is the love we show to the poor, and of course the love we show to our Risen Brother and Lord in the Eucharist, and in the other sacraments as well. Love, then—God's love for us in Christ and our love for one another—is the best way to overcome the present crisis.

THE LION OF PESSIMISM

A few years ago, I came by chance upon one of the most disturbing statements about priesthood I ever read. It appeared in a short article entitled "The Pastor with the Empty Soul." The author, a priest himself, claimed that a number of his fellow-priests stand up "week after week ... in front of their congregations, and proclaim the Gospel message, not with passion and conviction but from the hollowness of their empty soul." Then he said, and the phrase is terrible: "They are burned out without ever having been on fire." The author, a middle-aged American priest, was, I hope, exaggerating. But his statement compels us, here and now, I would suggest, to put to ourselves the question: How, in our own lives as priests, or as seminarians, or as lay-believers, are we to confront the threat of losing heart, of losing hope? How are we to come to terms with the specter of manifest fatigue and disenchantment? How are we to overcome the lion of pessimism?

The answer, I think, is contained in the small word "hope." Paul VI defines Christian hope as "hope for something that is not seen, and that *one would not dare imagine*."[21] That last phrase holds the key, the secret.

For what we are talking about is not some sort of educated or half-educated optimism. Christian hope does not consult the polls. It does not read the editorials. Grounded in a living experience—a prayerful experience—of God's power to save, it is a thing extravagant in its range and scope, a heart of flame, a virtue striking in its imaginative daring. Wise, therefore, and worth remembering, are the words from this passage in *The True Believer,* by Eric Hoffer. He writes: "Those who would transform a nation or the world cannot do so by breeding and captaining discontent or by demonstrating the reasonableness and desirability of the intended changes or by coercing people into a new way of life. They must know how to kindle and fan an extravagant hope."[22]

One form of that "extravagant hope" —given the tendency we have to weakness and mediocrity—is that we are each one of us called to holiness. Each one of us, as members of Christ's Church, has a vocation to sanctity. John Paul II, in *Redemptoris Missio,* declared: "It is not enough to update pastoral techniques, organize and co-ordinate ecclesial resources ... What is needed is the encouragement of a new 'ardor for holiness.' "[23] With regard to that challenging statement, one commentator noted: "Only holiness, spiritual beauty, and the truest human integrity will heal the soul of man and plant the seeds of a new culture. Whatever is true, whatever is just, whatever is lovely, 'we must think on these things' (Phil.4:8)."[24]

We must think on these things. That Pauline injunction sums up in one bright phrase the intellectual venture undertaken by both students and professors in the Catholic Studies Program. Nowadays, in books of spirituality, we are quite often invited to move from the head to the heart, to concentrate not on thinking but feeling. And there can, of course, be a point to that. For goodness *is* the holiness of the heart. But thinking, serious thinking about the Gospel and about the world we are living in, can itself be a form of holiness, and a necessary form. For what we discover, at the end if not at the beginning of our studies, is that truth is nothing other than the holiness of the mind.

Given the enormity of the challenge facing us all, whether as lay-believers or priests or future priests or deacons, the contribution we ourselves might make will seem, perhaps, very small indeed. But we can take heart from the humble yet passionate words of Good Pope John, St. John XXIII. "An old world," he said, "is disappearing. Another one is being formed, and with this I am trying to conceal some good seed or other that will have its springtime, even if it is somewhat delayed, and comes after I am dead."[25] Yes, seeds, small seeds it may be that we are planting in a difficult soil at a difficult hour, but seeds containing an extravagant hope.

CONCLUSION: THE PRIMACY OF PRAYER

In this essay I have suggested so far three things: that we confront the lion of relativism with faith, the lion of pessimism with hope and the lion of fundamentalism with love. Faith, hope and love—these are the three gifts we need today if we are to confront the challenges of contemporary society and begin to plant the seeds of a new culture. Without this triune grace we will, inevitably, start to rely too much on other aids—useful in themselves—but offering little or no protection against "the lions."

With regard to the question of protection from "the lions," I want in a moment to turn our attention to the question of prayer. But first, permit me to repeat a joke about lions that may well be familiar to you. A man— not a very prayerful man, an atheist, in fact—is being pursued by lions. He runs and runs, but they are fast on his heels. He falls to the ground, covers his face with his hands and in desperation starts to pray: "O God," he cries, "if there is a God, help me and change the lions into Christians." There is a deadly silence. The man thinks: Is it possible my prayer has been answered? He takes his hands away from his eyes just in time to hear one of the lions say: "For what we are about to receive may the Lord make us truly grateful"!

A number of years ago, when I was on retreat on the island of Malta, I came upon an article in a local newspaper written by a young man who had just left the priesthood. His name was Peter. "It never crossed my mind," Peter wrote, "that I might one day decide to go back on my calling … When I entered into training it was with some very high ideals … The years of training were long and dry and it was my ideals that kept me going … I threw myself into the priesthood … Finally I could start to do what I had studied for all these years …I wanted to do something rather than just talk."[26] By his own account, Peter, as a young priest, almost immediately began to experience opposition and disappointment. "I started to feel I was not being allowed to use my full potential … I decided to opt out.

I was suffocating. I felt I no longer had a sense of belonging and I could no longer fulfill my own spirituality."[27]

The focus of Peter's spirituality was all on *doing*. He never once mentions prayer, and instead of the three gifts that would no doubt have transformed his life, and perhaps saved his vocation—faith, hope and love—he lists three other things instead, all of them once again focused on *doing*. "I tried to live my priesthood," he writes, "with a lot of energy, creativity and productivity."[28] Three good and useful things in themselves, it has to be said—but these, together with his ideals, were never enough to help Peter make the impact on society that, for so many years in the seminary, he had dreamed of making. His plans to "make a difference," his ideals for priesthood, his dreams, were all of them, within a few short years, very quickly devoured by the lion of pessimism. What was admirable in young Father Peter was the desire to make some kind of impact on the contemporary world, to Christianize in some way modern culture. But the methods he employed and the spirit in which he approached his task reflected in large part the very world that he wanted to change.

Few people among our contemporaries have made more impact on the modern world than Mother Teresa of Calcutta. I remember a conversation I had with her once at San Gregorio in Rome that relates to our present topic. On that particular day, the convent of San Gregorio, the sisters' main house in Rome, seemed completely taken over by the media. There were journalists everywhere, and with them all kinds of special lights and cameras and electrical cords and microphones. They wanted Mother Teresa to do an interview, which would form part of a video they hoped to produce and which, they promised her, would go all over the world. These men certainly had "energy" and "creativity" and "productivity." Mother calmly said, "No, not today, thank you." As it turned out later, there was very good reason why Mother Teresa should not have participated in this particular project.

The journalists stayed on late into the afternoon, refusing to believe that Mother Teresa would not accede to their request. Finally, after they had gone, I sat down together with Mother on the long gray stone step in the middle of the convent. After a few words of greeting, Mother said: "You know, they don't understand. Jesus came on earth to bring the most important message of all time to the world. He had only 33 short years in which to do it, and he spent 30 years doing nothing!"

Whatever the full meaning of her words, one thing is clear: When it comes to the question of making an impact on the world or of transforming human culture, God's ways are not our ways. Sometimes, faced with the enormity of the challenge of evangelization today, it happens that those of us who are entrusted with the task in a particular way begin to take ourselves and our own efforts far too seriously. Losing the Gospel sense of our role, we also lose our sense of humor and sense of proportion. We start to think of all that must be achieved in business terms only, in the language, that is, of human productivity and human success.

Mother Teresa said something on another occasion that relates directly to our topic. It was at Casalina, the sisters' main house of formation in Rome. I was having breakfast in a small room with another priest, an American, some minutes after having celebrated Mass for the sisters. Mother Teresa joined us, and the conversation turned to the subject of China. I can remember, as if it were yesterday, her reply to one of the priest's questions—a question innocently couched in the language of big business. He asked: "Mother Teresa, is there any particular group in China that you're hoping to target?" She replied at once to his question, her words utterly genuine and utterly simple. "My great desire," she said, "is to meet anybody who has nobody."

As contemporary believers, whether young or old, we need many things. But first and last, we need faith and hope and love. In prayer—and in prayer more than anywhere else—we receive these gifts. In private prayer, and in the prayer of the Eucharist, we find faith to overcome relativism, love to overcome fundamentalism, and hope to overcome pessimism. In prayer, in the humble earth of our desire for God, seeds are sown for a new culture of life, a new birth, a grace of energy and form, to take root first in our own lives and then to spring up and flourish on the earth. In prayer, faithful prayer, watchful prayer, we meet the God described for us at the close of Chapter Six in the Book of Daniel. Let me read it now to finish: "He is the living God enduring forever; his kingdom shall not be destroyed and his dominion shall be without end. He is a deliverer and saviour, working signs and wonders in heaven and on earth, and he delivered Daniel from the lions' power."

NOTES

1   Of course, the leaders of totalitarian regimes of the 20th century, such as Communist states, proudly based their philosophies on relativism.

2   Pope John Paul II, "Homily of His Holiness John Paul II, Victory Square, Warsaw," June 2, 1979, par. 3a.

3   Ibid., par. 4.

4   Ibid., par. 3b.

5   Hans Urs von Balthasar, *Bernanos: An Ecclesial Existence*, trans. E. Leiva-Merikakis (San Francisco: Ignatius Press, 1996), 585.

6   Avery Dulles, S.J., "Seven Essentials of Evangelization," *Origins* 25, no. 23 (1995): 400.

7   Ibid.

8   Pope John Paul II, "Homily of His Holiness John Paul II, Oriole Park at Camden Yards, Baltimore," October 8, 1995, par. 6.

9   "Cardinal George on the Synod of America," *Our Sunday Visitor*, October 26, 1997, 10.

10   Cardinal Ratzinger, "Relativism: The Central Problem for Faith Today," *Origins* 26, no. 20 (1996): 312.

11   William Blake, "Auguries of Innocence," in *Poetry and Prose of William Blake*, ed. G. Keynes (London: Nonesuch Press, 1946), 121.

12   Pseudo-Macarius, *The Fifty Spiritual Homilies*, 15:32; 43:7, ed. G.A. Maloney (Mahwah, NJ: Paulist Press, 1992), xvi.

13   St. Augustine of Hippo, *Expositions on the Psalms*, in *Nicene and Post-Nicene Fathers, First Series*, vol. 8, ed. Philip Schaff, trans. J.E. Tweed (Buffalo, NY: Christian Literature Publishing, 1988), Psalm 96: 11.

14   Hans Urs von Balthasar, cited in Peter Henrici S.J., "Hans Urs von Balthasar: A Sketch of His Life," in *Hans Urs von Balthasar: His Life and Work*, ed. D.L. Schindler (San Francisco: Ignatius Press, 1991), 41.

15   Ibid., 40.

16   Ibid., 40-41.

17   Pope John Paul II, "Mass for Students of the Pontifical Major Seminary of Rome: Homily of John Paul II," October 13, 1979, § 3.

18   Spoken by McNabb during a retreat in 1927. See Father Vincent McNabb O.P., *An Old Apostle Speaks*, ed. G. Vann (Oxford: Blackfriars Publications, 1946), 3.

19   *Test Everything: Hold Fast to What Is Good: An Interview with Hans Urs von Balthasar by Angelo Scola*, trans. M. Shrady (San Francisco: Ignatius Press, 1989), 52.

20   Ibid., 50-51.

21   Pope Paul VI, *Evangelii Nuntiandi*, §21.

22   Eric Hoffer, *The True Believer: Thoughts on the Nature of Mass Movements* (New York: Harper & Row, 1951), 9.

23   John Paul II, *Redemptoris Missio*, §90.

[24] Stratford Caldecott, *"Kairos:* Towards a Culture of Life," *Communio: International Catholic Review* 21 (Spring 1994): 116.

[25] Giancarlo Zizola, *The Utopia of Pope John XXIII* (Maryknoll, NY: Orbis Books, 1978), 17.

[26] Cited in Mark Wood, "Poverty, Chastity and Disillusion," *The Malta Independent* (March 30, 1997), 18.

[27] Ibid.

[28] Ibid.

3

What St. Benedict Teaches
the Dark Ages—His and Ours

F. Russell Hittinger

The Renaissance humanist Petrarch first introduced the term *tempus tenebrae* in the 14th century in order to mark and to scorn the time in which the barbaric tribes had defiled Latin language and literature.[1] Later, Enlightenment thinkers would see the dark ages not so much in terms of literary snobbery, but as Immanuel Kant put it, a "self-imposed immaturity." "Immaturity," he explained, "is the inability to use one's understanding without guidance from another."[2] But the Gospel of John speaks of a deeper darkness and a different light:

> The true light that gives light to everyone was coming into the world. He was in the world, and though the world was made through him, *the world did not recognize him*. He came to that which was his own, but his own did not receive him. Yet to all who did receive him, to those who believed in his name, he gave the right to become children of God—children born not of natural descent, nor of human decision or a husband's will, but born of God. The Word became flesh and made his dwelling among us. We have seen his glory, the glory of the one and only Son, who came from the Father, full of grace and truth. John [as a voice "calling in

the desert"] testified concerning him. He cried out, saying, 'This is the one I spoke about when I said, 'He who comes after me has surpassed me because he was before me.' "

In the wilderness, the Gospel sounds the most profound theme of Christian experience: A Light appears in the darkness of the fallen world. For the Christian imagination formed in Scripture and monastic culture, the Evangelist's "dark age" did not represent a period of cultural history, as it did for the Renaissance.

Rather, for the monastic culture, the notion of a "dark age" was drawn from theological anthropology and Christology. The story was summed up in the first chapter of John and the fourth chapter of Luke. Adam and his progeny were cast from paradise into a desert—into what St. Augustine called "a region of dissimilitude"—where the race of men were caught in the brambles of sin, knowing not the Light, and therefore not truly understanding themselves. And so the New Adam went into the desert in search of the old Adam. Praying, fasting and being tempted by the devil for 40 days, the Incarnate Word showed the way back to the house of the Father.

St. Benedict was not the first Christian who went into the desert to discover this Light. But he is justly renowned for molding a simple but sturdy institution for those who are in search of it. At least in this sense—and also in a secondary, historical and cultural sense—Benedict is the patron saint of Lent, the season of the desert and for overcoming darkness.

I would like in this essay to suggest the significance of St. Benedict for his "dark age" as well as our own by means of four little compositions along the lines of nocturnes. Nocturnes, of course, were the night offices said in a monastery, a spiritual analogue to the nocturnal plant; in biology, a nocturne can mean a plant that flowers in the dark. But in modern times, a nocturne is a musical composition evoking a nighttime theme or being performed at night. And so I offer the following four vignettes: Owl of Minerva, Dark Ages, Curriculum and Harkening.

THE OWL OF MINERVA: WISDOM IN TWILIGHT

Hegel once wrote:

One more word about giving instruction as to *what the world ought to be*. Philosophy in any case always comes on the scene too late to give it.... When philosophy paints its gloomy picture, then a form of life has grown old. It cannot be rejuvenated by the [philosopher's] gloomy picture, but only understood. Only when the dusk starts to fall does the owl of Minerva spread its wings and fly.[3]

Hegel's aphorism can be interpreted in different ways. He probably means to say that life rather than philosophy is prescriptive. The Philosopher can grasp the whole of a thing only when it is complete, in the face of which there is no point legislating what *ought* to be. Perhaps Hegel also means that only when a civilization approaches its demise can the Owl of Wisdom take stock of its essential genius, which Hegel calls its life form (*Gestalt*). *Only at the end of a civilization do its geniuses appear*, like a swan who sings one beautiful song before it dies. Hence, the Owl of Minerva takes flight not at the morning star or in the noonday sun, but in the dusk.

From a monastic perspective, the Minervian moment is marked at the seventh liturgical office of the day, which Benedict calls Vespers. The word Vesper is taken from Greek mythology: *Hesperus* is the personification of the evening star, the planet Venus in its evening appearance; the *Vespera*, then, are prayers at the time of shadows. Measured from the first light of morning-tide, the vespera fall sometime between the 10th and the 12th hours, between 4 and 6 p.m., depending on the season. In Cap-41 of the Rule, Benedict prescribes that these prayers are to be chanted before the need of artificial light.

This time is distinguished from the *very* end of the day, which is marked by the office of Compline [from the verb *complere*, to complete]. Compline is chanted at about 8:30 p.m. With it, the hours of the day are finished, and the monks, in hope of the resurrection, submit themselves to the Great Silence: to a darkness that swallows all human knowledge, like the tomb that awaits every son of man. *Wisdom therefore must come in the shadows, just as Hegel suggested—in the dusk, rather than the night;* just when things are complete enough for us to take their measure and to consider "what the world ought to be," but not so complete that wisdom itself slips into the oblivion of darkness.

For the monastic tradition, the *vespera* represent a time of judgment—of the hours of the day, of the individual soul, of the people, of the race of man. No less an authority than St. Augustine himself speculated that after Adam and Eve sinned, and hid from God, He came to find and to judge them at the hour of vespers.[4] Why at this time? God can judge the defendant while there is still light—not just physical light, but more importantly the *lumen synderesis*, the light of conscience, which was already partially in eclipse by the shadows of sin.

In monasteries under the Rule of Benedict, four consecutive psalms are usually chanted at Vespers: Psalm 109 (He judgeth among the nations, making their ruin complete); Psalm 110 (He hath shown His people the power of his works); Psalm 111 (Blessed is the man that feareth the Lord ... He shineth to the righteous as a light in darkness); and Psalm 112 ("From the rising of the sun to its going down let the Name of the Lord be praised"). Then the monks proceed to chant an ancient hymn entitled *Lucis Creator* with its verse: "Creator of Light, who joins morning and the shadows, and for our instruction calls it a day." *Wisdom depends on our ability to know a day and how to take its measure.* Thus were monks enjoined, at Compline, to say with the Psalmist: "So teach us to number our days, that we may apply our hearts unto wisdom" (Ps. 90:12; cf. RB 18).[5]

Let us return, for a moment, to Hegel's image of wisdom arising, phoenix-like, just as a civilization reaches its demise. The *clear* and the *obscure* are mixed together, such that what is clear is all the more intelligible because of the shadows. Applied to history, we see the beginning only at the end—but the *chiaroscuro* consists chiefly in this: that the beginning is the very thing that is ending, and ending is the beginning of something else. The greatest historical figures occupy this time of vespers. They represent with a proper and profound ambiguity the best of what has declined and the seeds of what will come. The Catholic Church of Late Antiquity provides us with two such Minervian figures: Augustine and Benedict.

Augustine was born in 354, the son of a minor official in a provincial town in Roman North Africa. He was formed in the trivium: grammar, rhetoric and logic. Although he complained about the intellectual shallowness and the moral turpitude of his own education, anyone who would pick up his work is bedazzled by what he learned. For elegance of style and for the power of speculative intellect, Augustine was, I dare say, the greatest thinker produced by Roman culture. When he died in 430, his city was surrounded by the Vandals. In retrospect, we are entitled to think that this was the vespers of the ancient world. Augustine himself didn't think so; he believed that he lived in the very cultural-political world of Graeco-Roman civilization. All of Augustine's fathers—which is to say, his teachers—were ancient grammarians, rhetoricians, philosophers and theologians. And one is always laid to rest with one's fathers, not with one's great-grandchildren.

For his part, Benedict was born in 480, 50 years after Augustine's death. He, too, came from a provincial Roman town, Nursia (today, Norcia), in the mountains of Umbria; going back some 1,200 years, this was the borderland of the Etruscans and the Samnite tribes. He too was the son of a Roman civil official. As an adolescent, Benedict was sent, along with his nanny, to Rome to learn the very same trivium studied by Augustine. First, he needed to become a *grammaticus*. What was grammar? The knowledge of words. According to the ancient wisdom: "Everything which does not deserve to pass into oblivion and has been entrusted to writing, belongs necessarily to the province of grammar." Like Augustine, Benedict absorbed himself in grammar but worried that rhetoric was morally corruptive. Augustine did not pray for an emancipation from rhetoric until his was in his mid-30s (indeed, in Bk. 9 of the *Confessions* he describes his baptism as a liberation from rhetoric); in stark contrast, Benedict renounced rhetoric at the age of 16 or 17. So far as we know, he studied only the first segment of the trivium.[6] He never renounced grammar—indeed his Rule requires that the brothers learn to read, in order to appropriate the external word of scripture 1) as it is on the page and 2) as it is expressed as a liturgical word in choir. And thus Benedict represents the via media between the loquacious Augustine and the hermit monk St. Antony, the greatest of monks, who remained illiterate in order to attend only to the *internal word* that manifests itself in the desert and brambles of the soul.

Abandoning his formal education, Benedict tried to live the monastic life as a hermit in caves in the vicinity of Subiaco, not far from Rome. Like the desert father, St. Antony, Benedict learned experimentally. He became so proficient in knowledge of the divine word that other monks asked him to be their master. In the Rule, Benedict says that he intends to found a school—in Latin, a *schola*—for the service of God.

Yet his first attempts to educate and govern other monks were troubled, to say the least. On at least two occasions, his monastic sons tried to murder him—indeed, in the old-fashioned Italian way, which was by poisoning. Benedict was discreet and prudent, eventually learning how to govern monks—he even went so far to allow a bit of wine every day to combat "sadness" and to relieve the temptation of "murmuring."[7] Control over murmuring is a greater achievement than eloquence in letters.

Learning by trial and error, he went on to found 13 monasteries. Moving to Cassinum, some 70 miles southwest of Rome, Benedict ascended the 1,800-foot-high Monte Cassino in 529, and there, at the summit, over the top of a demolished temple of Apollo, he laid the altar for his greatest monastery. A year later, he began to write his Rule. Written in vulgar or ordinary Latin, and amounting to fewer than 9,000 words, it is quite different than Augustine's work. It has neither eloquence nor speculative power. Untold thousands of souls have been converted by reading Augustine, but it is hard to imagine anyone being converted merely by reading Benedict's Rule.

If Augustine was the greatest stylist and speculative thinker of the Roman world, Benedict exemplified, in the vespers of that civilization, the genius unique to Rome. Romans always knew that their language and speculative tradition were inferior to the Greeks; that their religion was inferior to the Eastern religions, especially the Egyptians; that their aesthetics were inferior to the Greeks and the Carthaginians. Rome's destiny was different. As Virgil boasted in the *Aeneid*:

Roman, remember by your strength to rule Earth's peoples
—for your arts are to be these:
To pacify, to impose the rule of law,
To spare the conquered [and] battle down the proud.

The shadows had lengthened since the time of Augustine. Benedict was born 70 years after Alaric and his Vandals sacked Rome, less than 30 years after Attila's Huns had swept through Italy, and only two years after the demise of the last Emperor in the West, Romulus Augustulus. *In this sense—and only in this sense—can Benedict be regarded as a Minervian owl. As Roman civilization collapsed around him, he established a Christian institution that nevertheless carried the stamp of Roman genius.* Albeit in ways unimagined and unanticipated, Benedict's Rule proved to be the greatest pacification program in Western history. Otherwise, there is no evidence that Benedict thought of himself or his monastic Rule as either the end or the beginning of any epoch. As a man of the ancient world, he had no intention to transmit any wisdom other than the ancient one.

After all, Christianity and monasticism first arose and were practiced as an ancient wisdom. Benedict perhaps first learned of monasticism from Syrian hermits who lived in caves around Norcia. These and other monks simply believed that they were imitating Christ and his apostles. The monks had read the scriptures and sought to imitate Luke 4: Led by the Spirit into the wilderness for 40 days, Christ prayed, fasted and was tempted by the Devil. We return again to the story recapitulated by the monastic search. The first Adam sinned and was expelled from the garden of delights—thrown into a wilderness—like the Prodigal Son in the plantation of sorrows, eating food not fit for the swine and not knowing the way back to the house of the Father. As Augustine explained, "For on whatever place one has fallen, on that place he must find support that he may rise again."[8] The new Adam begins where the old Adam fell. Christ went into the desert to confront Adam's nemesis.

Many things and institutions have their origin in the medieval centuries: parliament, romance vernaculars, the heavy plow, tidal mills, cannons, the spinning wheel, universities, glass mirrors and percussion drilling, invented by Cistercians. But monasticism is not an invention of the Middle Ages. It comes instead from a more ancient light discovered in the desert, from an ancient wisdom molded by Benedict's Roman genius. In the last chapter of the Rule, chapter 73, entitled, "The Whole of Just Observance Is Not Contained in This Rule," Benedict insists that whatever is taught in this Rule is only a part of what is transmitted from the Holy Fathers. And by the "Fathers" he meant 1) the Apostles, 2) the authors of Holy Writ, 3) the example of the Desert Fathers and 4) those who have written Institutes for the governance of monks. He concludes: "Whoever you are [quisquis] hastening toward your heavenly homeland; fulfill with the help of Christ this little Rule for beginners ... " And this is perhaps the key sentence in the Rule. *Benedict founds a school for beginners.*

To be sure, it includes rules for reading and writing, for chanting, for using and cleaning farm implements, for greeting strangers, for determining prices for goods sent to market, for the organization of crafts and many other simple, practical details. The school is free—no tuition by way of social class or money. We learn in Ch. 58 that the only thing necessary is a willing heart to seek God (*quaerere deum*) and adherence to the Rule under the Abbot. Benedict's Rule governs a monastery in which the rich and the poor alike begin as beginners. And these beginners begin where the Light first appeared—in the desert.

But Benedict's wisdom, genius and "legacy," for which history rightly esteems him, certainly extend beyond the modest walls of the monastery or the humble souls of the monks. If one goes to Benedict's hometown of Norcia, a little town of about 4,600 souls nested in the mountains of Umbria, one quickly happens on the Piazza di San Benedetto. On the far end of the piazza stand a church and a monastery built over the top of the Roman-era apartment building in which Benedict was raised. In the center of the piazza is a statue of Benedict, made by Giuseppe Pinzi in the late 19th century. The inscription reads:

> Founder and Father of Monasticism in the Western regions, he was driven by the Spirit to a life hidden from society. From whence there arose a renaissance of letters, the useful arts, agriculture, and sciences.

The inscription is quite astute. Benedict, it suggests, is the patron saint of Europe not so much because of the civilizing of culture accomplished by his monasticism but *because he went into the desert*. This reveals the spiritual root of European culture. Europe's claim to fame, in other words, is not so much that it relearned and perfected the arts and sciences preserved by monks during the Dark Ages, but rather that *Europe is a civilization grown from a cultivated desert*. This is a quite radical claim, made in our own day more than once by Pope Benedict XVI, who suggested that the current crisis of European identity should be understood in terms of what the Benedictines did in the wasteland: Were they merely technicians who invented tools to till the soil, or were they about the business of clearing the weeds growing in the human soul?[9]

If Benedict's Rule established nothing but a trade school for learning the useful arts—slightly eccentric monks who figured out how to build windmills—it quickly would have made itself obsolete. For it is in the very nature of such an enterprise to graduate its students into more advanced skills. This is how humanists in modern times interpreted the story of Benedict's "school." *But* if the monastic school teaches its students to awake from the mortal slumber of the Old Adam, and like the Prodigal to run to the Father, no one (in this life, anyway) can claim to be a graduate, and the capacity of monastic culture to renew culture from within is truly boundless.[10]

How to be "a beginner": This is the first thing Benedict teaches the Dark Ages, his and ours. To be a beginner in this way is not a primitive condition to be outgrown but rather a sign of advancement and the mark of a return to the most essential. It is what everyone needs to relearn each Lent and learn again amid the vespers of our present age.

DARK AGES

In 1911, the 11th edition of the *Encyclopedia Britannica* stated that the period from the fifth to the 10th centuries is called "the dark Age."[11] Yet by the time of the Second World War, the 14th edition had a change of heart, now insisting that "the contrast, once so fashionable, between the ages of darkness and the ages of light has no more truth in it than have the idealistic fancies which underlie attempts at medieval revivalism."[12] No self-respecting scholar today, it suggests, would use the term "dark ages" to periodize, categorize or otherwise to mark historical time and events, much less culture.

In my view, however, it is a mistake to drop "dark ages" altogether. The collapse of Roman order in the West *was* devastating.[13] That Roman order was urban and urbane; in the early fifth century it included something like a thousand municipalities, bound together by a civilian, demilitarized aristocracy that spoke Latin and Greek. At its zenith, the city of Rome had more than a million inhabitants; it was served by 11 aqueducts bringing water from as far as 59 miles, over arches 100 feet tall.

These cities, including those of much smaller caliber, were the center of civilization: of business, politics, fine art, patronage, libraries, buildings on a large scale, artisans, diplomacy. The patriarchs and metropolitans of the Christian Church led Christians from the major cities: Rome, Constantinople, Antioch, Alexandria, Milan, Ravenna.

Stationed along the Empire's borders was an army of roughly a half million men, along with a couple hundred thousand auxiliary and part-time units. All told, it was about the same size as the U.S. Army and Marines Corps today. To equip and provision this enormous and highly mobile force required more than 50 state factories, which made swords and arrows, processed leather for various gear and made woolen products such as socks and shirts. About half of the imperial budget went to feeding, equipping and paying the army; another third went to the maintenance of key cities, including the grain and oil handouts to the urban masses; and the rest to the bureaucracy. It is estimated that taxes on agricultural yield from land was constant at about 25 percent. This was the cash cow that maintained the army and the urban projects.

But when the barbarians penetrated and then overwhelmed the imperial armies beginning in the fifth century, the tax revenue evaporated. The agriculturally rich North Africa, where Augustine lived, was lost to the Vandals in 439, causing an 80 percent reduction in taxes from that region alone by the sixth century. In the aftermath of all this, what emerged in the West was a Libertarian heaven—monies for large public projects would disappear for hundreds of years. But so would cities of more than 50,000 people. By the 13th century, only a handful of cities in the West could support 100,000 people: London, Paris, Milan and perhaps Genoa. Here are just a few things that indicate the "darkness" that fell upon this period:

- Fourth-century levels of maritime trade across the Mediterranean would not be restored until the 19th century.

- Drilling through the ice pack in Greenland, scientists have discovered that as the factories closed, the pollution caused by the smelting of lead, copper and silver fell to prehistoric levels, not to be regained until the 17th century.

- The art of making pottery on a wheel disappeared from Britain for more than three centuries.

- Abundant coinage disappeared; household utensils, such as cups with glossy surfaces, easy to wash and easy to stack due to standardized shapes, became unknown to men.

- With the demise of cities came the demise of literacy. Consider that Charlemagne, the emperor, circa 800, never could quite get the hang of writing.

It is possible to continue for some time in this vein, simply enumerating all of the things that vanished first from the earth, and then from common human memory.

But what is most important to understand for our present purpose is why the falling dominoes were so hard to put back into place. The answer is that the Empire depended on an extraordinarily far-flung division of labor and knowledge. A northern Italian peasant of the third or fourth century might eat off tableware from Naples, store liquids in amphorae from North Africa, sleep under a roof consisting of tiles from the south of Gaul and be governed by a civil administrator from Tuscany. Along the Tiber as it snakes through Rome is a place called Monte Testaccio. Here, archaeologists discovered the remains of some 53 million amphorae, all imported from Iberia, in which approximately 6 trillion liters of oil were imported from overseas.

It is important to draw the right moral lesson from this story. The Dark Ages were dark not merely because the lights of technology were extinguished, but because *no one knew how to reproduce the whole of the civilization.* The "light" that was lost was not the tool or *techne* but knowledge and wisdom. And we too are capable of losing that light even in the midst of our highly advanced tools and technology. A "dark" age does not consist merely of technological ignorance; worse yet is having forgotten how to live a good life rather than a life of mere subsistence. Consider all of the things we might not know how to do without sharing in a tradition of wisdom.

- Prepare a corpse for burial.

- Decide whether grandma is dead.

- Adjudicate conflicting legal claims between business enterprises.

- Recite from memory Jewish and Christian scriptures. Throw in the U.S. and state constitutions.

- Remember all of the countries.

- Judge what is an authentic and an inauthentic copy of a book.

- Recall one's paternal ancestors by name five generations back.

- Distinguish carefully between what is established fact and what is mere speculation in any given physical science.

- Distinguish between law and mere force.

- Distinguish what is pleasant to the senses from what is good.

- Distinguish what is good from what is morally good.

- Distinguish between transitory relationships keyed to survival and enduring memberships, such as one's status in a family or in a polity.

Every day would be a disorganized disaster. It is worth reflecting on the possibility that technology alone is not the only factor that marks civilization from a dark age. The European Dark Ages teach us that the more diversified the functions of a civilization, the more necessary it is that at least some people know what is a life worth living versus a life worth merely enduring. The Dark Ages were dark because people simply forgot what the Owl of Minerva understands—namely, the way the world ought to be or, at least, the way it once was.

As one will discover when reading the Rule, in addition to their commitment to poverty, chastity and obedience, like other consecrated religious, the Benedictine monks also promise stability (*stabilitas*) and reform of manners (*conversatio morum*). Stability was perhaps the most important vow for the Dark Ages. For when the Benedictines established a community, they were there to stay. Unlike the warrior class, which was mobile and just short of nomadic, the monks would arrive, clear the forests, and irrigate and cultivate the land. Within earshot of the bells, laypeople could begin again to measure time. From the monks they learned how to properly bury the dead, how to read and write—how to do things that transcend a life of mere subsistence. *In summary fashion, this is what Benedict taught the Dark Ages: how to live life as a whole when forces of disintegration and confusion abound.* Not a life of worldly success so much as one of human success. Not only how to divide a day, but how to divide it unto wisdom.

CURRICULUM

If monastic life according to the Rule, as a "school for beginners," can be said to follow any "curriculum," this is because Benedict taught an integrated and integrating knowledge. This he did along three fronts: He taught *materially, politically* and *poetically*. But it is the poetic that suffuses the Benedictine school. All three return us to the fundamentals of knowledge, to the "beginning" of that wisdom and integrity of life still possible in the desert and evening of an age.

First, as regards the *material of life*, nothing is more important than light and dark: namely, an answer to the question, "What suffices for a day?" Infants and very young children are ignorant of what constitutes a day. I am told that even college students have problems in this regard—that a collegiate "day" is a 24/7 flow of flickering images resembling a casino in Nevada. Like the practical wisdom displayed in Genesis, Benedict begins with a Day. A day equally measured: eight hours of prayer, eight hours of labor, eight hours of rest, adjusted for the seasons.

A day having been properly established, the Rule prescribes a unity of things that the ancient world had usually kept apart: on the one hand, the free or liberal arts and sciences, cultivated and practiced by the nobility. This was called a *universitas personarum*, things tending toward one *in and for* the dignity of human persons. On the other hand stood the work of artisans and manual laborers. This was called a *universitas rerum*, a unity for the sake of the things being organized: the bricks, the streets, the monies. Benedict taught the proper order of these things. Tools for the sake of monks, monks for the sake of God—hierarchy of action without distinction by class.

In the ancient world, personal dignity was measured by its remotion or distance from tools and labor. Indeed, the rural warrior class in these centuries of the Middle Ages did not work the land. They killed with their hands, but they did not work with them. Benedict's motto was *Ora et Labora et Lectio*: prayer, work and reading.[14] The monks therefore are at once contemplatives and laborers.[15]

Reading is essential in Benedict's school, for it joins together prayer and work. Consider the acts associated with reading, and the materiality involved: speaking; meditating, cogitating; imagining; remembering, understanding, desiring.[16] By summoning so many different mental and physical actions or postures, reading can be profoundly integrative. It forms a clearing in the forest of the sensations of the soul and creates a place for study and prayer. Lent, whether liturgically speaking or cultur-

ally speaking, should be a time for reading, at least in the sense understood by the monastic culture.

As regards the *social organization* of human persons in the monastery (political knowledge), three things are extremely important from a
sociological perspective: First, it is characterized by easy entrance and difficult exit. The monastery is a voluntary society that is not especially picky
about who joins. Within a month or so, the applicant is inside the walls;
a few years later he is professed, and solemnly professed a couple of years
after that. Yet the learning curve is long—the rest of one's life. Second,
each abbey is quasi-autonomous and self-sufficient under the rule of its
own abbot. The key to self-sufficiency is the vow of stability. This is the
Benedictine understanding of 1 Peter 2:5: "You also, like living stones, are
being built into a spiritual house." Third, the Benedictine Rule emphasizes
equality among the brothers. For most public purposes, monks are distinguished only by their date of entrance—that is, according to a principle of
seniority. Even the youngest monks can vote in an abbatial election.

All of these add up to a sturdy social structure in the wilderness: liter-
ate men or women, under a common rule and superior, knowing how to
divide a day and how to live a stable life in a certain place, not only within
a day but over years; competent to contemplate and to work with their
hands; having as their only standard of admission that the novice have a
willing heart; and all of them counting themselves as beginners from the
day they enter the monastery until they die. From inside the monastic
perspective, it does not really matter too much whether the whole thing
is destroyed so long as it starts again—since it can always begin again. It
was never meant to be anything but a school for beginners. And there is
always another child of the Old Adam who awakes from slumber and will
become a brother.

The third of Benedict's ways of teaching, and to my mind the most
important, is one fit for a child—or someone seeking to be childlike. One
teaches a child through the senses and the imagination—that is, *poetically*. In one of his greatest essays, "The Mission of St. Benedict," John
Henry Newman reckoned that the three great paradigms of teaching in
Latin Christianity were Benedict, who taught *poetically*, Dominic, who
taught *scientifically*, and Ignatius of Loyola, who taught *practically*.[17]

By poetry Newman did not necessarily mean the craft of poetry, which is the craft of constructing metered verse. Rather, he meant a way of learning that arises from sense, experience and imagination. Its special feature is wonder, or what the Latin speaking peoples called *ad-miratio*. Admiration is taken from the adjective *mirus*, wonderful. We could call it *knowledge touched by the thing being known*. For his part, Aristotle used the word "thaûma" (θαῦμα), meaning "miracle" and "thaumazein" (θαυμάζειν), which means "to admire." Wonder lies at the root of knowledge, which begins in the senses: "ALL men by nature desire to know. An indication of this is the delight we take in our senses; for even apart from their usefulness they are loved for themselves; and above all others the sense of sight."[18]

Thus, the genius of the Benedictine method of teaching and learning involves knowledge touched by the thing being known through the senses. Newman contrasts this "poetic" pedagogy to the "scientific" approach:

> Reason investigates, analyzes, numbers, weighs, measures, ascertains, locates, the objects of its contemplation, and thus gains a scientific knowledge of them. Science results in system, which is complex unity; poetry delights in the indefinite and various as contrasted with unity, and in the simple as contrasted with system. The aim of science is to get a hold of things, to grasp them, to handle them, to comprehend them; that is (to use the familiar term), to *master* them, or to be superior to them... But as to the poetical, very different is the frame of mind which is necessary for its perception. It demands, as its primary condition, that we *should not* put ourselves above the objects in which it resides, but at their feet; that we should feel them to be above and beyond us, that we should look up to them, and that, instead of fancying that we can comprehend them, we should take for granted that we are surrounded and comprehended by them ourselves. Hence it is that a child's mind is so full of poetry, because he knows so little; and an old man of the world so devoid of poetry, because his experience of facts is so wide.[19]

As Newman sees it, the scientific mentality requires one to stand above the things being studied. Here the dignity of the mind tends to replace the worth of the object.

Poetic learning is for the youth, scientific proof for the mature and perhaps wisdom for the old. But wisdom itself is more like poetry than proof. In Latin, the word *sapiens* denotes a person who can savor or taste. Wisdom is knowing something that one can savor. In chapter 19 of the Rule, Benedict prescribes that psalms are to be chanted *sapienter*, wisely. In his life of St. Benedict, Gregory the Great comments that he was *scienter nescius et sapienter indoctus*, "learnedly ignorant and wisely uninstructed." Benedict did not have a scientific theology of the Psalms, but rather a Rule for savoring them: "My heart and flesh sing for joy to the living God" (Psalm 84:2).

The Rule was written for youth in a world grown old. Not the world as it ought to be but, alas, cannot be; rather the world as seen by a youth—which is to say, a world that is admired just the way it appears and is first known through a contact suffused with emotion.

Benedict's "poetic method," moreover, extends to the entire range of material and symbolic culture of the monastery. Newman refers to a "Poetry of life, the poetry of ceremonies,—of the cowl, the cloister, and the choir.... " (Today the power of this "poetry of life" helps explain the enduring fascination children have with the world of *Harry Potter*.) First, the black hood, the cowl, or what was called the *cucullus*—a poncho worn by children in ancient Rome. Then, the cloister—the internal space of the monastery, like a child's house or bedroom. Finally, the choir, which is the place of beauty. Newman notes that in this kind of world, a person can take "each new day as a whole in itself ... and doing works which cannot be cut short, for they are complete in every portion of them."[20] Imagine, now, chanting all 150 psalms once a week—the variety of images, moods and emotions. Each psalm is chanted and is complete itself; the one psalm repeatedly is complemented by the next, and by the next office, and the next day without any effort to tie disparate parts together into a scientific system of theology—any synthesis is left to the poetic imagination under the regime of the Holy Spirit.[21]

In view of such poetic, childlike instruction, one becomes aware of the slowness of the Good. We may remember what it was like to learn that way, when we were younger: when a summer seemed like a lifetime. Almost effortlessly, a youth can learn more in three months than an adult in three years. The life envisaged by Benedict is not like a five-year plan, or a senior thesis, or a job report. The monk's life is rolled out like the verses of a psalm—little parts that cumulatively become something more.[22] Benedict's poetic teaching calls him to become again like a little child, to begin again.

Again, this is what Benedict taught the Dark Ages, his and ours. The slowness of the good, which is experienced as incredibly rich if one becomes as a child. Tertullian said of the incarnate Christ, that He "suffered Himself to be conceived in a mother's womb .... [and] wished to be sated with the pleasure of patience."[23] In the Middle Ages, Lent was taken from a Germanic word for *long*; in Benedict's school, however, the Latin adverb *lente* (slowly) is the better term. Life in the Benedictine monastery was to be a perpetual Lent, a linking of patience with poetry.

HARKENING

Finally, and briefly, let me take you to the beginning of the Rule, where, presumably, all of us who read Benedict's Rule begin. The first words: "Harken, my son, and with the ear of your heart hear the precepts of your Master." The poetical approach jumps right off of the page. *Harken!* Not read, study or merely listen. To harken is to attend to something that is immediate. The notion of a knowledge touched by the thing being known is highlighted (*auscutator*, a hearer who heeds) by means of the scriptural image of the *ear of one's heart* (from Ps. 44). One is bidden to incline, to turn toward something as from an inner principle. Benedict continues:

> Readily [*libenter*] accept and faithfully follow the advice of your pious Father [*admonitionem pii patris*], so that through the labor of obedience you may return to Him from whom you have withdrawn because of the laziness of disobedience. My words are meant for you, whoever you are [*quisquis*], who laying aside your own will, take up the all-powerful and righteous arms of obedience.

Here, Benedict embeds the story of the Prodigal Son. The *filius* or *filia* (the son or the daughter) turns to the voice of the Father: "Therefore, let us arise ..., and arising he went unto his Father."[24]

The text shifts from the verb *obsculta* (*auscultare*, harken, heed) to its linguistic sister, *ob-dire*, to listen toward a word. Obedience. Benedict's student would have been familiar not only with the story of the Prodigal Son but also with the ideal of the Roman father: the *paterfamilias* who is by right a domestic magistrate, invested with public charge inside his household, including the capital powers of life and death over his wife, sons, slaves and domestic animals. In the Roman world, what does the son owe to the father, and the father to city, and the city to the protecting gods? *Pietas*. It is a kind of reverence of an inferior to a superior; more precisely, *pietas* is the proper response on the part of someone who can never fully pay back what is received.

Yet it's clear that the Prologue of Benedict's Rule is *not* referring to that kind of daddy. In fact, the word *paterfamilias* is used but once in the Rule (Ch. 2), and it pertains to Christ as the Good Shepherd. Here's what's important. Benedict is referring to a Father who is Himself Pius—that is, tender. *Pater piissime*. A tender and merciful Father, who has the virtue of piety toward what is lower than himself. To the *humanum* created in his Image. And now we are back to the parable: the Father, who sees from afar the son trying to return, and who takes the initiative. This is not the stern Roman *pater*. The monastery is a school of the Pater Noster, the Our Father. Again, a school for beginners ... to become childlike again.

Let me take you to one more paragraph into the Prologue to the Rule. We read: "Let us then at last arise, since the Scripture arouses us saying: *It is now time for us to rise from sleep*" (Rom. 13:11). Interestingly, Benedict has embedded Lazarus (from John 11, *Lazare veni foras* ... Come Out!) into the story of the Prodigal (Come Back), and Easter into the story of the Passion (Arise!). The paragraph continues: "And let us open our eyes to the deifying light; let us attune our ears to what the divine voice admonishes us, daily crying out: *Today if you hear his voice, harden not your hearts*." Benedict is evoking, along with Scripture, a favorite communion chant of the ancient church: "Come, O sons, listen...O taste and see... and be radiant" (Psalm 34). In the Prologue he writes, *"Currite dum lumen vitae habetis* ... hasten while you have the light of life."[25]

Father Benedict teaches through these verbs: "harken," "hasten," "awaken," "arise," "turn," "obey," "leave aside," "listen," "incline." The whole Prologue bristles in this mood, but in a way that is strangely soothing— one reason, perhaps, is that this is precisely what the ear of the heart desires. The most famous monk of the Middle Ages, Bernard of Clairvaux, said that as sin entered the world through sight (beholding the fruit of the tree), so salvation comes first through the ear. Recall Deuteronomy 6.4, "Hear, O Israel, the Lord our god is One." Benedict requires that when the bells summon to prayer, eight times a day, the monk must drop everything, turn toward the sound (incline, awake, arise, harken) and go to prayer. Eight times a day, 56 times a week, 2,912 times a year, one leaves everything behind and turns toward the voice. Here we have a splendidly simple reenactment or recapitulation of the Gospel—*come back, come out, arise*. The Psalms' interior meaning, as well as the Eucharistic liturgy, is the *voice* of Christ. And if you say *Ego* (Prol.) —"I'm the one" —then Benedict says, here is a school for the doing of it. "In instituting it we hope to establish nothing harsh or oppressive." Whatever rules are laid down for correcting vices, maintaining equity and conserving the order of love will be hard at the beginning but not overwhelming.

CONCLUSION: WHAT BENEDICT TEACHES THE DARK AGES

And so now I can conclude by summing up what Benedict teaches the Dark Ages—not from a standpoint external to the Rule (the judgment of history, economics, aesthetics, agricultural sciences and arts), but from a point of view internal to the Rule.

The monastic school does not exist for the purpose of surviving the Dark Ages or for helping barbarians to learn to count on something other than their fingers, even if it did have these results. Benedict taught the monks to have a certain contempt for all of that, although not a naïve or callous disregard of the fact of the world's ignorance or misery (read for yourselves the chapters on feeding the poor and welcoming strangers). Rather, *he taught the monks that there is something better to do, something higher and more worthy of their daily labor.* The monastery is nothing other than a school that turns *prodigals* into *pilgrims*. Beginners. That is what we become, once again, each Ash Wednesday, as we commence Lent. In the last stanza of his poem "Ash Wednesday," T.S. Eliot writes:

> I renounce the blessèd face
> And renounce the voice
> Because I cannot hope to turn again
> Consequently I rejoice, having to construct something
> Upon which to rejoice

Eliot's meditation reminds us that the simplest, most natural and super-naturally the most urgent thing always proves to be the most difficult: to begin, to turn once again. This is the "one thing necessary." This is what Benedict taught then and teaches now: how to begin, how to receive life as Lent and Lent as a new springtime of life, to become young and like a child again, to seek first the Kingdom. Here we discover the fine line, perhaps only a hair's breadth, between the prodigal and the pilgrim. In the end the one infallible "solution" to the new Dark Age upon us would be to address the darkness in ourselves and turn again and again back to Him who is the "true Light" coming into the world, the One who brings us the light, joy and peace of Easter through patient suffering in the desert, of the Cross.

Notes

[1] Theodore E. Mommsen, "Petrarch's Conception of the 'Dark Ages,' " *Speculum* 17, no. 2 (1942): 226-42.

[2] Kant, "An Answer to the Question: What is Enlightenment?" (1784), in *Perpetual Peace and Other Essays*, trans. Ted Humphrey (Indianapolis: Hackett Publishing, 1983), 41.

[3] George W.F. Hegel, *The Philosophy of Right*, trans. T.M. Knox (Oxford: Oxford University Press, 1967), 12-13.

[4] See St. Augustine, *On Genesis: Two Books on Genesis Against the Manichees; And, On the Literal Interpretation of Genesis, an Unfinished Book,* Fathers of the Church, Vol. 84 (Washington, D.C.: Catholic University of America Press, 2001), 119:

> Toward evening God was walking in paradise [Gn. 3:8], that is, he was coming to judge them. He was still walking in paradise before their punishment, that is, the presence of God still moved among them, when they no longer stood firm in his command. It is fitting [that he comes] toward evening, that is, when the sun was already setting for them, that is, when the interior light of the truth was being taken from them. They heard his voice and hid from his sight. Who hides from the sight of God but he who has abandoned him and is now beginning to love what is his own? . . . For the human soul can be a partaker in the truth, but the truth is the immutable God above it. Hence, whoever turns away from that truth and turns toward himself and does not rejoice in God who rules and enlightens him, but rather in his own seemingly free movements, becomes dark by reason of the lie.

[5] Ps. 90 is the only psalm explicitly used by Satan to tempt Christ. See Matt. 4:6. Hence, the monastic theme of the night and the ruler of darkness, the dragon.

[6] The hermit Antony, who was a spiritual model and inspiration for both Augustine and Benedict, was illiterate, despite being reared in an affluent family. St. Athanasius says of the young Antony: "he could not endure to learn letters" (*Life of St. Antony*, §1). The father of Christian monasticism, he was given entirely to the "inner Word." "His memory," Athanasius remarks, "served him for books" (§3). *Select Works and Letters*, vol. IV, Nicene

and Post-Nicene Fathers, Series II, eds. Philip Schaff and Henry Wace (Grand Rapids, MI: Eerdmans, 1980), 195-96.

7 *Rule*, Cap. 40.

8 Augustine, *De Vera Religione*, XXIV, 45.

9 Benedict XVI, *Spe Salvi* (2007), §15. See also Benedict's "General Audience," April 9, 2008, and also his "Address to the World of Culture," September 12, 2008.

10 How else can we explain the fact that, over the subsequent centuries, Benedict's sons and daughters created thousands of these schools under the "little rule for beginners"? By the 11th century, the great Benedictine monastery of Cluny in France had nearly 1000 daughter houses and affiliated monasteries, constituting a vast, trans-national corporation. Within the Cluniac system alone, there were more Benedictine monasteries than there are McDonalds in France today. A 19th-century scholar claimed to have found evidence for the existence of some 37,000 Benedictine houses. (By way of comparison, today there are about 4,100 universities, colleges and two-year colleges in the U.S.). A mid-19th century enumeration put it down as follows: 37,000 houses, 30 popes, four emperors, 46 kings, 51 queens, 1,406 princes, 1,600 archbishops, 600 bishops and 15,000 abbots and learned men. And who knows how many souls who lived in those cloisters whose names and numbers are long forgotten! For Newman's counting in the 19th century, see Newman, "The Mission of St. Benedict," in *Historical Sketches*, vol. 2 (New York: Longmans, Greens, and Co., 1906), 372.

11 The so-called monastic centuries (or "Benedictine Centuries") coincide with the Dark Ages. In the West, we are speaking roughly of 500 years, from the sixth century to the end of the 11th century.

12 *The Encyclopedia Britannica*, 14th Edition, eds. James Louis Garvin, Franklin Hooper, and Warren E. Cox, vol. 15 (The Encyclopedia Britannica Company, Ltd, 1929), 449.

13 In the next few paragraphs I collate data drawn mostly from two recent books: Bryan Ward-Perkins, *The Fall of Rome and the End of Civilization* (Oxford: Oxford University Press, 2005) and Chris Wickham, *Inheritance of Rome: Illuminating the Dark Ages* (New York: Viking Penguin, 2009).

14 The common, shorter version of the motto, *ora et labora,* seems to have been invented rather recently. Paul G. Monson argues that the motto actually originates in America, not Germany, with Martin Marty: "*Ora et Labora*: A Benedictine Motto Born in America?" in *God Has Begun a Great Work in Us: Embodied Love in Consecrated Life and Ecclesial Movements*, eds. Jason King and Shannon Schrein, College Theology Society Annual, vol. 60 (Maryknoll, NY: Orbis, 2015), 66-86.

15 Jedis who do the work of artisans and serfs: a very powerful and useful combination. See Jude P. Dougherty, "'Intellectuals with dirt under their fingernails': Attitudes toward Sciences and Technology and the Difference They Make," *Communio* 9 (1982): 224-237 and earlier essay by Lynn White, Jr., "Dynamo and Virgin Reconsidered," in *Dynamo and Virgin Reconsidered: Essays in the Dynamism of Western Culture* (Cambridge, MA: MIT Press, 1968), 57-73. Not surprisingly, it would yield great fortunes for some monasteries. Look especially at chapter 57 of Benedict's Rule on how to price monastic products sent to market (in a spirit of charity and poverty, the monks ought to sell them under the market rate).

16 For the monk, each word is like a hook, catching hold of other words; the monk was like a living concordance. As Dom Jean Leclercq puts it, reminiscences are not quotations,

but the words of the person using them. Monastic readers become like a living concordance. *The Love of Learning and the Desire for God: A Study of Monastic Culture* (New York: Fordham University Press, 1982), 77.

[17] Newman, "The Mission of St. Benedict," 366.

[18] Aristotle, *Metaphysics*, Book I.

[19] Newman, "The Mission of St. Benedict," 387.

[20] Ibid., 409.

[21] *Lectio divina*—a snippet of scripture that suffices unto itself.

[22] The longest span of time worth considering is a liturgical season: four weeks of Advent, 40 days of Lent, 50 days between Easter and Pentecost. Again, Ps. 90: "So teach us to number our days, that we may apply our hearts unto wisdom." From a point of view within the monastery, it doesn't matter whether one's allotment of time is an hour, a day, a week, a season or many seasons.

[23] Tertullian, *On Patience*, ch. 3.

[24] Lk 15:20.

[25] Cf. Jn 12:35. Then Jesus told them, "You are going to have the light just a little while longer. Walk while you have the light, before darkness overtakes you. The man who walks in the dark does not know where he is going."

4

The Integration of Intellectual and Moral Education in the University

Jonathan J. Reyes

The modern university has abandoned any moral authority to shape the souls of its students. This is true first on the grounds of the separation of intellect and will: After all, what has scientific study or academic excellence to do with what you do in your home or your dorm room? Second, on the grounds of freedom from coercion: What right does a university have to tell its students what to believe or to shape their moral convictions? On most college campuses, educators and administrators demonstrate a genuine anxiety that they not be perceived as imposing a morality. This reluctance has made "formation," at one time a respectable word for an important dimension of education, a negative term. The contemporary situation is summarized well by Harry Lewis, professor and onetime dean of Harvard: "Harvard teaches students but does not make them wise."[1]

While at many Catholic institutions of higher education the idea of moral education has not been abandoned, it has nevertheless been severely marginalized. This should give us pause given the Catholic commitment to an integrated view of the human person that understands education to be at the same time moral and intellectual. John Henry Newman put this well in his 1856 sermon, "Intellect, the Instrument of Religious Training," insisting at once on both the intellectual and "religious" formation of university students:

> Here, then, I conceive, is the object of the Holy See and the Catholic Church in setting up Universities; it {13} is to reunite things which were in the beginning joined together by God, and have been put asunder by man... I wish the intellect to range with the utmost freedom, and religion to enjoy an equal freedom; but what I am stipulating for is, that they should be found in one and the same place, and exemplified in the same persons... It will not satisfy me, what satisfies so many, to have two independent systems, intellectual and religious, going at once side by side, by a sort of division of labour, and only accidentally brought together. It will not satisfy me, if religion is here, and science there, and young men converse with science all day, and lodge with religion in the evening. It is not touching the evil, to which these remarks have been directed, if young men eat and drink and sleep in one place, and think in another: I want the same roof to contain both the intellectual and moral discipline.[2]

Catholic Studies, as a subsidiary "institution" within the context of the modern university, serves for many a "single roof" that brings together the intellectual and moral development of students. Often Catholic Studies is suspect because it is perceived as transgressing that which is strictly academic and intellectual, for example, by sponsoring a regular "community night," encouraging liturgies, organizing service activities and socializing around some form of recreation—not obvious activities for an academic program. Indeed, it is true that Catholic Studies embraces a broader approach to education that is inclusive of moral formation. In its "extracurricular" programming and events as well as its emphasis on the intrinsic link to some form of collegiate, residential or intentional community element, Catholic Studies can offer the university a partial means of recovering some of its moral authority and its intentional role in the holistic formation of students.

The purpose of this essay is twofold: first, to offer a brief historical account of the gradual separation of moral and intellectual education in

Catholic higher education and draw a few lessons from this history; and second, to offer some practical recommendations for the way forward, based both on the history of higher education and my own experience with Catholic Studies and other endeavors sharing a family likeness. Throughout, I hope at least to suggest something of a rationale for Catholic Studies as a "more-than-academic" program and to set forth some initiatives that might be fruitfully supported or sponsored by Catholic Studies programs. The integrative approach of Catholic Studies to education includes by necessity initiatives and programming that seek to assist students and faculty to reunify their intellectual and moral lives. Because of this, Catholic Studies should be understood as one promising way that Catholic higher education can "reunite what man has divided" in respect to the intellectual and moral aspects of education. This integration requires something like Catholic Studies on our Catholic campuses in the post-Christian world in which we live.

A Brief Historical Account of the Separation of Moral and Intellectual Formation in Higher Education

When Newman criticized the separation of religion and science in higher education, he was combating what he believed was already a widely held view. In fact, Newman was speaking into a larger, and, by 1856, decades-old debate over the reform of higher education in England. There was disagreement at the most fundamental level as to the nature and purpose of higher education. Was the purpose of higher education to form professional researchers whose mission was to advance the seas of knowledge? Or was the purpose to educate, both intellectually and morally, future leaders of England? Is a university education for the accumulation of knowledge or for instilling a habit of mind?

One attempt to unite these two ends is particularly relevant in this context. Some argued that research in itself was a moral education. Research, after all, requires a great deal of discipline and a dedication to scientific truth, and therefore it trains students in perseverance and increases their love for truth. Newman's response to Robert Peel's version of this argument produced—in the judgment of his biographer Ian Ker—perhaps his best piece of polemical writing. Newman concludes his pamphlet on *The Tamworth Reading Room* in this way:

I consider, then, that intrinsically excellent and noble as are scientific pursuits, and worthy of a place in a liberal education, and
fruitful in temporal benefits to the community, still they are not,
and cannot be, *the instrument* of an ethical training; that physics
do not supply a basis, but only materials for religious sentiment;
that knowledge does but occupy, not form the mind; that apprehension of the unseen is the only known principle capable of
subduing moral evil, educating the multitude, and organizing
society; and that, whereas man is born for action, action flows not
from inferences, but from impressions,—not from reasonings,
but from Faith.[3]

The debate concerning the role of moral education at the university
made its way to the United States, and it was by and large the Catholic
institutions that defended Newman's vision. Historian James Burtchaell
tells a story that captures the clash of these two visions in the early 20th
century.[4]

In his *Dying of the Light*, Burtchaell describes an exchange between the
then presidents of Boston College and Harvard over the merits of the elective system of education for undergraduates. Boston College, founded by
the Jesuits in 1863, was, at the time of this exchange, still located rather
conspicuously directly across the Charles River from Harvard University.
Harvard professors and indeed presidents took a certain delight in berat-
ing what they perceived as their intellectual and moral inferior across the
river. In the words of one Harvard professor: "To those who, like ourselves,
look upon the Romish system as a system of dangerous and fatal error, as a
monstrous incubus, stifling and oppressing the Gospel of Christ, no place
can be so dangerous to the young as the Jesuit college, every exercise of
which is made to assume a religious aspect, and to exert a religious influence."[5] For Harvard president Charles Norton Eliot, the problem with religious education was its undue authoritarianism. In *The Atlantic Monthly*,
Eliot deplored any "system of education that treated certain subjects as
obligatory" and went so far as to equate Muslim and Catholic education.
He noted with derision that Jesuits had hardly changed their educational
system in 400 years.

In his response, which *The Atlantic Monthly* refused to print, then
president of Boston College Timothy Brosnahan, SJ first corrected Eliot

on a factual matter: The *Ratio Studiorum* was only 300 years old, not 400. He then argued that "if the Jesuits were out of date, it was not by 400 years or 300, but by 15, for it was only that long since President Eliot had persuaded his colleagues that studies must be entirely elective."[6] President Brosnahan then identified the real weakness in an entirely elective system: namely that the student, without the proper knowledge of self or moral truth, has to determine his own course of studies at the outset of his education. In Brosnahan's words,

> The young man applying for an education is told to look out on the whole realm of learning, to him unknown and untrodden, and to elect his path. To do thus with judgment and discrimination, he must know the end he wishes to reach; he must moreover know himself—his mental and moral characteristics, his aptitudes, his temperaments, his tastes; and finally he must know which of the numberless paths will lead him to the goal of his ambition... He must also distinctly understand that it is no longer the province of his Alma Mater to act as earthly providence for him. Circumstances have obliged her to become a caterer. Each student is free to choose his intellectual nourishment, and must assume in the main the direction of his own studies. If he solves the problem wisely, to him the profit; if unwisely, this same *Alma Noverca* (stepmother) disclaims the responsibility.[7]

Boston College's curriculum was based on a different vision of education. As stated in the Boston College student handbook:

> Education is understood by the Fathers of the Society, in its completest sense, as *the full and harmonious development of all the faculties that are distinctive of man*. It is not, therefore, mere instruction or the communication of knowledge... Learning is an instrument of education, not its end. *The end is culture, and mental and moral development*.[8]

Thus, at the beginning of the 20ᵗʰ century, Catholic institutions were willing to defend the integration of moral and intellectual education while the wider academy was moving away from it. In the latter case, the abandonment of moral education was complete by the 1970s. According to one dean of Harvard from those days, Harvard, like most colleges, by that time "had withdrawn from the last vestiges of the regulation of the personal lives of students."[9]

Catholic colleges' proud resistance to this trajectory in the leading American universities began to weaken in the middle of the 20th century. This was largely due to the fact that Catholics themselves had lost confidence in Catholic education.

In 1955 John Tracy Ellis published his influential essay "American Catholics and the Intellectual Life." This critique of the then-reigning mode of Catholic higher education by the leading Catholic intellectual in the United States launched an enduring conversation among Catholics about the limitations of their own system of education. The critique was codified by Thomas O'Dea in his 1958 book, *The American Catholic Dilemma*.[10] O'Dea identified four basic characteristics of the American Catholic milieu that inhibited the development of mature intellectual activity:

1.   Formalism: the tendency to view the world in general as already grasped and conceptually classified. This was an attack on the version of Scholasticism then predominant in Catholic colleges.

2.   Authoritarianism: According to this critique, the Church's teaching authority, the Magisterium, was too involved in academic matters.

3.   Overemphasis on vocations: O'Dea argued that too many Catholics were worried about religious and priestly life and not, strictly speaking, academic life.

The fourth, the most relevant to our discussion, is moralism. Catholic education, O'Dea claimed, was too concerned with the moral education of its students, hindering the development of true Catholic scholars. He claimed that Catholics viewed the world not as filled with intellectual challenges, but with spiritual perils. The Catholic mentality, he wrote, is basically "neo-Jansenism grafted onto a lower-middle class mentality." In conclusion, as historian Phil Gleason puts it, "The overall impression conveyed by the discussion was that practically everything historically associated with American Catholic life, intellectual and otherwise, would have to be scrapped."[11]

These critiques are not entirely absent of reason and merit. That there were not enough homegrown Catholic scholars in the mid-1950s to supply the needs of growing institutions is simply true. And most scholars agree on the limitations of scholastic manualism. Still, as David Solomon has argued, the moral education that students received in these institutions may not have been as ineffective as some have claimed. Whatever the case, Catholic educators were experiencing increasing pressure and incentive to change their approach in a number of matters, including the role of moral education. Also, surrounded by deeply Catholic environments, many could not imagine that such changes in theology or the curriculum or the approach to moral education could ever threaten the Catholic identity of their institutions.

Catholic educators thus faced a choice. They could join with the wider trajectory of higher education in the United States and abandon or diminish the importance of moral education in order to correct their moralism, or, through a process of recovery and development, they could choose to create a wider intellectual culture—free, yet firmly rooted in the truth—that did away with the formulaic and simplistic moralistic approach to education. Ultimately, through a process of abdication, they settled for a considerable compromise. James Burtchaell describes this process:

> One of the social forces that came to distinguish and to divide administrators from faculty professionally was the way the latter soon left responsibility for student piety and morality in the hands of the former. It was later, when the administrators in their turn created a class of religious functionaries—chaplains, secretaries, deans of students, et al.—to relieve them, too, of those responsibilities, that ecclesial piety and discipline were shown to be only loosely and incoherently bound to the central purposes of the colleges.[12]

Without entirely abandoning the idea of moral education, administrators and professors settled for the very position Newman a hundred years earlier had criticized: the creation of two circles of influence, one for the study of science (intellectual formation), the other for religion (religious and moral formation). But whereas in Newman's configuration we see two horses contending head to head, in the latter half of the 20th century the religious "circle of influence" was significantly outdistanced.

Given the wider cultural trajectory, this has proved to be a radically insufficient and temporary solution. Today, the deans of students at many Catholic universities are trained much like their peers in non-Catholic institutions and often embody the same view of moral education. The dominant contemporary paradigm for moral education is nicely summarized in a 2007 Report on General Education by Harvard College. The report was the culmination of a process of review that began in 2002. In the words of the report:

> The aim of liberal education is to unsettle presumptions, to defamiliarize the familiar, to reveal what is going on beneath and behind appearances, to disorient young people and to help them to find ways to re-orient themselves. A liberal education aims to accomplish these things by questioning assumptions, by inducing self-reflection, by teaching students to think critically and analytically, by exposing them to the sense of alienation produced by encounters with radically different historical moments and cultural formations and with phenomena that exceed their, and even our own, capacity fully to understand.... Ethical awareness ... is achieved by exposing students to beliefs and values that have shaped others' lives ... so that they are put in a position from which they can choose for themselves the principles that will guide them.[13]

In short, the contemporary ideal of moral education requires that the student be provided with a morally neutral environment filled with as many ethical alternatives as exist in the world, so that, having been stripped of his assumptions, the student can freely choose which moral path best suits him. Of course, this ideal has found its way into many, perhaps most, of our Catholic institutions to a high degree as well. Is a neutral space possible? What vision of the human person does this create? At what cost?

WHY A MORALLY NEUTRAL EDUCATION IS PROBLEMATIC

Before turning to some practical recommendations that address this rupture in education, it is important to consider briefly three issues that, together, reveal the fundamental flaw in the current pursuit of "moral neutrality" at modern universities.

First, without asking whether the goal of turning a university into a morally neutral space is a good one, we ought to reflect for a moment on whether it is even possible. There are serious reasons to doubt this. As Newman pointed out in his *Idea of a University*:

> [A] youthful community will constitute a whole, it will embody a specific idea... it will furnish principles of thought and action... Here then is a real teaching, whatever be its standards and principles, true or false; ... it does a something, which never will issue from the most strenuous efforts of a set of teachers, with no mutual sympathies and no inter-communion... who are teaching or questioning a set of youths who do not know them, and do not know each other.[14]

A university will inevitably have a moral culture whether or not it is an intentional one. Newman's claim would seem to find support from current concerns about the lack of tolerance for certain moral positions at secular universities, concerns driven by some version of political correctness. Even if they lack a campus ministry or counseling program devoted to advancing service as a moral imperative, or condemning racism or advocating non-judgmentalism in sexual matters, universities have nonetheless effectively inculcated these same moral principles and suppressed opposing viewpoints. The life of universities, from the classroom through the dorm room, will shape a student for good or ill. It means that the choice is not will we or will we not have a university that is morally educative of our students, but rather, will the moral education our students receive be clear and true and rational, or will it be haphazard and arbitrary and dominated by sentiment, fashion and ideology?

Second, it is important to recognize that at the root of the two different visions of moral education we considered are two different anthropologies. For the authors of the Harvard report, the human being is an autonomous choosing individual, with no inherent end, whose will and intellect are unrelated to one another. Ethical choices are purely a matter of rational argumentation. How you live has no effect on how you think. The best thing one can do for such a being, therefore, is to question assumptions and multiply choices, lest one risk the possibility of coercion. For President Brosnahan, the human being not only has an inherent end, but the pursuit of that end requires a moral education that addresses both will and intellect, because they cannot be separated in action. According to St. Thomas Aquinas: "The will moves the intellect as to the exercise of its act. ... But as to the determination of the act ... the intellect moves the will."[15] It follows that if the will is habituated to choosing evil, it will cloud the intellect. On the other hand, if the intellect is incapable of seeing truth, the will becomes habituated to choosing evil. (And this is not to mention the moral significance of the passions in relation to both intellect and will.) Yes, what you do in your dorm room does affect your moral view of the world, and what you learn in the classroom does affect your choices and actions.

Third, as universities no longer offer a coherent moral view, the serious question raised by Christopher Dawson—among others—comes to the fore. Namely, on what basis will contemporary society organize itself? Today, as Cardinal Ratzinger had asserted in his famous debate with Jürgen Habermas, "the basic question of what is good, and why one should do what is good even where this is to one's own disadvantage, remains largely unanswered in the public domain."[16] This constitutes a crisis. Without a shared vision of the good, all "freedom... is anarchy and therefore destructive of freedom."[17] Without a shared vision of the good, man becomes the subject, not the master, of his own scientific power. As Ratzinger said further: "Man is now capable of making men ... [man] has become a product."[18] One is reminded of C.S. Lewis' account of the "abolition of Man," when history reaches a point where some men, the "Conditioners," guided by nothing more than their own whim, will through scientific power determine what human beings ought to be.[19]

This is all simply to say that the abandonment of moral education in the university produces consequences that extend beyond its walls. The incoherent state of our moral discourse "after virtue," combined with a lack of a coherent, integrated education of intellect and will, puts at risk our very ability to function as a free society oriented to a common good: Humanity itself is thus put at great risk.

RECOMMENDATIONS FOR THE REINTEGRATION
OF MORAL AND INTELLECTUAL EDUCATION

In this second half of the paper, I wish to turn to six recommendations essential to the reintegration of moral and intellectual formation. As a preliminary comment let me insist that the way forward is not simply backward, returning to the way things were before the rupture. That is to say, my purpose in recounting the history of the relationship between intellectual and moral education in the university has not been to assert that the Boston College of 1900 or Newman's Oxford is a perfect model for us to imitate or impose today. I hope to make it clear that the ways in which we recover the integration of intellectual and moral education in Catholic universities will often need to be as innovative as they are faithful to the tradition. Furthermore, I have no perfect "one-size-fits-all" model of an integrated education to propose. Different circumstances dictate different models. My goal below is to offer recommendations at a level of generality applicable to various situations. Nevertheless, Catholic Studies is, it seems to me, one of these simultaneously "innovative" and "faithful" models for holistic formation. Catholic Studies incorporates each of the following six elements to a high degree into its integrative philosophy and practical approach to education. This, I venture to say, is one major reason for its present flourishing, at least where this approach has actually been done. Catholic Studies offers the Catholic university of today a coherent vision of formation and a corresponding interrelated set of principles and practices that could powerfully assist any efforts the university undertakes toward the broad reintegration of the moral and intellectual life of its students.

1. Maintaining the Distinction Between Intellectual and Moral Education within an Integrated Vision

First, any attempt to reintegrate moral education and intellectual education in the modern university will nevertheless need to maintain the distinction between the moral and the intellectual. Even in Newman's day, this integration was not achieved by a single institution but, rather, by an institution within an institution, which remained relatively autonomous. Neither was it achieved by a single individual (e.g., the professor). Rather, it was the college, under the care of a tutor, where this integration principally occurred, not in the professor's university lecture hall. But the professors and all administrators of Newman's day realized and often took personal interest in the fact that the way a student behaves when not studying or hearing lectures nevertheless makes a great difference in the quality of the student's intellectual, not just moral, character.

Newman believed that the Church helped to guarantee the integrity of the university:

> The university is a place of teaching universal knowledge. This implies that its object is, on the one hand intellectual, not moral ... Such is the university in its essence, and independently of its relation to the Church. But, practically speaking, it cannot fulfill its object duly ... without the Church's assistance; or, to use the theological term, the Church is necessary for its integrity.[20]

Yes, theology had a uniquely important role in securing universal knowledge, since neglecting the reality of God would certainly leave knowledge horribly deficient. But the Church's assistance to the university was especially felt in and through her work in the colleges, for the colleges "are the direct and special instruments, which the Church uses in a University [for] the attainment of her sacred objects."[21]

On the other hand, the college was a place of "careful catechetical training, [that also allowed for] a jealous scrutiny into [the students'] power of expressing himself and of turning his knowledge to account."[22] Thus the person in the college central to the process of integrating intellect and will in the life of the student, of learning and morals, was the tutor.[23] The tutor to whom the student was assigned was responsible for making sure that the content of academic subjects was understood sufficiently and internalized deeply. Moreover, he was given the task of making sure the student under his tutelage developed the proper discipline of study and behaved morally and well, i.e., in such a manner that his way of life and activities apart from study would not undermine his intellectual formation.[24] Regarding the distinct but complementary roles of college and university, Newman concludes, "Colleges constitute the integrity of the University. A university embodies the principal of progress, and a College that of ballast; each is insufficient in itself for the pursuit, extension, and inculcation of knowledge; each is useful to the other."[25] Thus, while the object of each is distinct, the work of the university in advancing and transmitting knowledge is rounded off and becomes formative of the whole student only when this learning is inserted and integrated into the student's broader "collegiate" life.[26]

Maintaining the integration of moral and intellectual education while respecting their distinct objects is somewhat difficult in the American setting. In most cases, dormitories at the contemporary university are structurally very different from Newman's colleges and deliberately omit moral education as their object, instead making student safety and comfort their primary therapeutic ends. Furthermore, as noted earlier, contemporary dorm life is completely separate from the intellectual life of the wider institution. Thus we need new models of student living and association, as well as new means of religious and moral instruction. When done well, these models will also help us avoid a potential pitfall in efforts to reintegrate moral and intellectual education: namely, that of trying to force moral formation directly into the classroom. A "How-to-Be-Moral 101" course that some very adventurous students may even be willing to take as a pass/fail cannot achieve the objective. We are not made moral by listening to lectures and taking written tests on our personal lives. Such false steps would also undermine the intellectual object of the university, because the mind cannot develop "under the lash."[27]

In the end, intellectual education without moral education is prone to the vice of pride, serious intellectual and moral error and, ultimately, skepticism.[28] On the other hand, a university education that emphasizes the moral to the detriment of the intellectual will fail in properly training the mind, and risks moralism: the reduction of the moral life to a set of rules or sentiments that may not sustain rational assault later in life. Thus, there is a need for integration but with the proper distinctions.

2. The Prudential Balance of Freedom and Regulation

Second, effective moral education requires the prudent balance between the demands of freedom and the imposition of rules for the sake of the proper moral development of young men and women.

Virtue to be such must be freely chosen. Indeed, an overly coercive environment not only will not help students mature morally, but will likely produce young Pharisees or rebels—that is, fundamentalists or relativists.

It might also produce what David Brooks calls the "organization Kid": the passive rule-follower who is "eager to please, eager to jump through whatever hoops ... eager to conform" because conformity always yields acceptable outcomes.[29] An overly permissive environment, on the other hand, creates a different set of problems, which hardly needs comment here.

There is a third problematic environment created by improper application of rules, what we might call the "nanny university." As Harry Lewis explains:

> Because we strive to make students happy, we cannot say that they are wrong. Because students' vision is crowded with immediate demands that we try to satisfy, we do not tell them to lift their eyes toward distant horizons. Because students—and their parents— struggle for flawlessness, we do not make them responsible for their mistakes. As a result, colleges now are holding students in childhood rather than helping them to grow up.[30]

All three of these environments extend adolescence. In the case of the nanny university, some are even now arguing that we are creating a serious psychological problem for students. By not allowing students to fail in anything while at the same time demanding flawlessness, some would argue that our institutions are producing polished and accomplished but also very insecure and emotionally fragile young people.

The goal of moral education, alternatively, will be achieved when we set high ideals for our students and then hold them to their own aspirations. This in part requires rules and other elements of campus culture that encourage the pursuit of virtue yet permit consequences for vice in order to help students grow into individual responsibility and self-mastery. In this way, the university can foster authentic freedom in which the students come to interiorize "rules" as a call to responsible and virtuous action as mature and confident adults issuing more from within themselves than from others.

3. Teaching Virtue Ethics and the Importance of Magnanimity

Third, in order to effectively educate students morally, there needs to be a clear presentation of Christian anthropology and the life of virtue, which will inspire students generously to answer the call to greatness.

Even very simple accounts of the nature of the human person as a being made for happiness and of virtue as a power that can be increased through practice are extremely helpful to young men and women. It is not uncommon for college students to whom I have presented a basic Christian anthropology and an account of the virtues to respond as though I had explained everything about their lives to them. Desiring, as many students do, to live a better life, and sensing that the worldly allurements around them will not make them happy, they experience as liberating the knowledge of what constitutes true happiness and the road map for its attainment.[31]

There is one virtue in particular that I would like to briefly highlight: magnanimity. In an age that tells young people that they are their own gods and the authors of their own happiness, we sometimes encounter an interesting mixture of pride and insecurity in our students. A false view of their own importance only opens students to the insecurity that comes from experiencing, time and again, that they in fact make rather poor gods—especially in terms of determining what will make them happy. This admixture can lead to pusillanimity, fleeing from great things, and the despair and sorrow that come from it. Feeling they have no mission and that life is something that simply happens to them, some students simply give up and run after distractions or trivial things. Students need to know of their high calling in Christ and the virtues they need for living up to it. I have thought this for a long time, which is why I was so taken by an observation of Pope Francis to the bishops of Brazil on the occasion of World Youth Day:

> Many [people] have sought shortcuts, for the standards set by Mother Church seem to be asking too much. Many people think: "the Church's idea of man is too lofty for me, the ideal of life which she proposes is beyond my abilities, the goal she sets is unattainable, beyond my reach. Nonetheless—they continue—I cannot live without having at least something, even a poor imitation, of what is too lofty for me, what I cannot afford. With disappointed hearts, they then go off in search of someone who will lead them even further astray. The great sense of abandonment and solitude, of not even belonging to oneself, which often results from this situation, is too painful to hide.[32]

Magnanimity, the courage to pursue great things in accord with right reason, is the antidote to this despair. This is why all attempts to make the Gospel more attractive by lessening its demands ultimately fail. It is important that we present the Catholic vision of the human person in its fullness so that students have the opportunity, with their eyes wide open, to make a decision regarding the high call they are offered in Christ. This is essential to any education that is equal to the dignity of men and women made in the image and likeness of God and destined to share in His divinity. Such moral education, inspired by magnanimity, will naturally lead to a renewal and increase of vocations in the Church, religious, priestly and marriage vocations, as we've seen in Catholic Studies.

4. Forming Communities of Virtue

Fourth, effectively educating students morally must include a strong communal dimension with an ordered way of life.[33]

At the most basic level, the life of virtue needs to be learned through practice. That being said, in order to learn to love one's neighbor, one needs an actual neighbor or neighbors. Many contemporary living situations on campus do not provide one. Sharing a space is not the same as sharing a life. In order to learn virtue and love, we need environments of shared life. Regular prayer is also best learned with others: Even the most basic rules of courtesy, often lost in our increasingly barbarized age, need to be practiced with others in a community that values them.

Pope Benedict, in an appeal to St. Benedict, argued for the importance of community in the modern world: "Our culture is on the verge of being out of balance ... Time and again, our world could so easily find its corrective in the Benedictine rule, since it offers the fundamental human attitudes and virtues needed for a life of inner balance, those that are requisite for social life—and for the maturity of the individual."[34] The monastery and the university are different institutions. Still, as Benedict asserts, we should seriously consider and apply successful models of communal life in the Church in this relativistic age because, as we stated earlier, the way we live influences the way we think.

Communal life at the university is also important because so many of our students have not experienced it. Smaller and sometimes fragmented families, the isolated living of suburbs, the ease of transportation that makes the majority of our social engagements voluntary and therefore chosen in conformity with our preferences—all make for a highly individualized and individualistic set of habits. These habits, confirmed by a powerful rhetoric of individual identity and self-assertion, coupled with the experience of being full-time consumers, make for self-oriented, egocentric people. The way out of this self-orientation is in part by living a common life while going to college, which often requires us to set aside our personal preferences for the sake of the common good. This will involve a commitment to some shared activities, such as meals, recreation or cultural outings. Further, if community is centered on prayer and the liturgy, this also combats selfishness by taking the focus away from the self and putting it on God and the needs of others.[35] As Don Briel points out (and as I've witnessed myself), to sponsor and encourage various forms of intentional community of friendship based on virtue is a hallmark of Catholic Studies and is a factor most definitely contributing to its flourishing.

At the same time, we should be careful not to allow communal environments to become overbearing, or to insist on uniformity. There is difference between uniformity and solidarity. The former asks that everyone do the same thing. Solidarity recognizes all that is shared—foundational truths that orient one's life and a love of Christ and desire to be like Him—but also allows for a breadth of expression and a healthy freedom of thought and action. I mention this because a desire for uniformity that undermines the freedom of solidarity is not uncommon among idealistic, dedicated and intelligent college students. It has been my experience that as students begin to appreciate the value of communal environments and the joy that comes from sharing life and mission, they can be tempted to construct living situations that demand too much conformity in matters that are either inessential or where real diversity is not only permissible but actually mutually enriching (e.g., devotional practices, pastimes, hobbies, etc.). The net result can be a somewhat stilted moral education. These environments can become too insulated and can undermine the purpose of a university. "A University is a direct preparation for this world," Newman writes. "It is not a Convent, it is not a Seminary; it is a place to fit men of the world for the world."[36]

5. Encountering the Poor

Fifth, an effective moral education will include the opportunity for a regular encounter with the poor. Indeed, a proper moral education simply *requires* sustained encounters with the poor.

In order to be effective, though, encounters with the poor should be personal. Pope Francis gives a beautiful description of what it means to have a personal encounter with the poor in a speech he gave to thousands of pilgrims in Buenos Aires on the feast of St. Cajetan:

> Sometimes, I ask people, "Do you give alms?" They say, "Yes, father." "And when you give alms, do you look into the eyes of people you are giving alms to?" "Ah, I do not know, I don't really think about it." "Then you have not reached out to those people. You just tossed them some charity and went away. When you give alms, do you touch their hands or just toss them the coins?" "No, I toss them the coins." "Then you have not touched them. And if you have not touched them, you have not reached out to them." We must be able to reach out to each other. We must build, create, and construct a culture of encounter.[143]

Dorothy Day was fond of saying that this kind of encounter is about the reform of the person offering help more than the reform of the one receiving it.[38] Pope Benedict XVI offers an interesting reflection on this point:

> For young people, this widespread involvement [in volunteer work] constitutes a school of life which offers them a formation in solidarity and in readiness to offer others not simply material aid but their very selves. The anti-culture of death, which finds expression for example in drug use, is thus countered by an unselfish love which shows itself to be a culture of life by the very willingness to "lose itself" (cf. Lk 17:33 et passim) for others.[39]

When a group of us founded a program called "Christ in the City" in Denver, we made the personal encounter with people living on the streets a central element of the program. The college students who participate year after year—many of whom are Catholic Studies students or alumni—would confirm Dorothy Day's assertion.

In addition, in order to be efficacious, opportunities to encounter

Christ in the poor need to be combined with serious intellectual reflection. Students can treat service opportunities that lack intellectual content as mere tasks to be accomplished, something to check off of a list, or a good emotional experience and nothing more. And despite the common assertions that Catholic Social Teaching is "dynamite" or the best-kept secret of the Church, and despite even entire courses on Catholic Social Teaching, terms like "the common good," "human dignity," "subsidiarity and solidarity" and "the preferential option for the poor" have a tendency to remain mere buzzwords or abstractions for many students, unless combined with a genuine encounter. Service of the poor, a good in itself, can thus also provide an excellent means of integrating moral and intellectual education. And while many opportunities for service to the poor and "volunteering" already exist on our campuses, there is often no robust educational rationale or coherent philosophical or theological vision behind them. Catholic Studies on university campuses will promote such regular and sustained encounters with the poor, both because Catholicism upholds the "preferential option" for the poor and because it is committed to a unified moral and intellectual formation of its students.

6. Defining and Teaching Leadership

Sixth, moral education should train students in leadership. This should be explicit. It is not enough simply to assume that training in the liberal arts or a particular field produces leaders as a natural by-product. This may have been true in a different time, when a young person was learning how to take on responsibility and see that tasks were accomplished and goals achieved with others in various day-to-day settings. Today's ambient culture and the experience of daily life allow many young people to evade the demands of leadership and responsibility for others entirely. Many of our students come to college with very little experience of taking responsibility in matters of high importance.

The situation is perhaps made worse by the fact that many of the activities called "leadership" in a university setting amount to little more than the oversight of relatively inconsequential tasks or club management. There are of course exceptions, but we should intentionally seek to provide meaningful leadership opportunities for students. For a number of years now, the Center for Catholic Studies at the University of St. Thomas has offered many students leadership formation in its Leadership Intern program, which has become a venue for many of the other recommended elements outlined above to be implemented and experienced.

Given demographic shifts in the Church and society in this country, I also believe that Catholic efforts in higher education have a responsibility to educate Latino leaders. By this I mean that the university should cultivate leaders for the Latino communities themselves, but also for our country and the Church. Here again there is something to be said for the forward-looking vision of Catholic Studies and its Latino Leaders program at St. Thomas.

Finally, we need to be explicit and clear about what we mean by "leadership." Given the innumerable books on leadership and the ubiquitous use of the word, it is important to teach the Catholic vision of leadership and give students access to exemplary leaders of the past and present, many of whom have integrated holiness and political prudence.[40] Leadership needs to be understood as being rooted in discipleship to Christ and carried out as an exercise of responsibility for the good of others, with their Ultimate End in view. It starts with following Christ and taking on His mind and His character. Not every student will be Christian, but for those who are, it is important that this be the first principle of leadership.

CONCLUSION: MORAL EDUCATION, HOLINESS AND APOSTOLIC WORK

Although the primary object of a university is not necessarily to evangelize, it is inadvisable and perhaps impossible to completely separate the mission of Catholic institutions from this fundamental mission of the Catholic Church and all of its members. This is of particular importance in this post-Christian age. We live at a time when the Gospel does not come to modern ears as something new and extraordinary, but instead as something old and failed, perhaps even as something evil. This is no cause for great alarm for the Church. It has lived through many predictions of its death. It has faced grim persecution as well as the sometimes more dangerous temptations inherent in cultural and political ascendancy, and it has survived both.

When the Church is marginalized and increasingly pressed by the wider culture, the disparity between the way Christians live and the "lifestyles" of those around them is more evident, and fidelity to the Gospel comes at a higher cost. In a post-Christian age, then, perhaps one intentional goal of a Catholic university or a Catholic educational center, such as Catholic Studies, at a larger institution is to be "apostolic." We are faced with increasing numbers of students who themselves have not been evangelized, even if they come from Catholic homes. Thus we should be especially concerned with presenting the Truth about reality in a way that is inviting and convincing. We should expect that in teaching Truth, hearts may be opened to an encounter with Christ. The Truth, when presented clearly and in its fullness, presents every person with a choice. The Catholic vision of the world is not something one studies like the migration pattern of birds. It evokes a response at the deepest level of the soul.

Further, our educational efforts should allow room for, encourage and help foster a life of discipleship for those students who desire it. Perhaps this goes beyond the object of the university as Newman conceived it (as distinct from the "college"), but given the times, I think we should deliberately make room for it in today's university. This does not necessarily mean that we should create special programs as part of our educational efforts or provide a course on evangelization and discipleship, although either may be a good response in some situations. Perhaps this object is better attained by allowing outside groups, religious and otherwise, that are devoted to evangelization and deepening Christian life to simply meet our students or partner with us in our work.

The Church's mission of evangelization in this historical moment needs plausible witnesses, and while the university is not primarily ordered to the formation of saints, perhaps in our Catholic educational efforts we should make every appropriate effort to serve that end. In a sermon titled "Personal Influence, the Means of Propagating the Truth" (1832), Newman asks how it was that the Gospel spread from being an obscure eastern religion to become the official religion of the Roman Empire. Having acknowledged God's providential hand, he further concludes: "[The Truth] has been upheld in the world not as a system, not by books, not by argument, nor by temporal power, but by the personal influence of [holy] men ... who are at once the teachers and the patterns of it.[41] The power of this personal influence is rooted in the majesty virtue, Newman continues, but not

> virtue in the abstract,—virtue in a book. Men persuade themselves, with little difficulty, to scoff at principles, to ridicule books, to make sport of the names of good men; but they cannot bear their presence: it is holiness embodied in personal form, which they cannot steadily confront and bear down: so that the silent conduct of a conscientious man secures for him from beholders a feeling different in kind from any which is created by the mere versatile and garrulous Reason."[42]

In Pope Paul VI's words: "Modern man listens more willingly to witnesses than to teachers, and if he does listen to teachers, it is because they are witnesses.[43]

The mission in the university, to educate the whole human person—both intellect and will—thus finds a natural affinity with the mission of the Church. In fulfilling the first, we serve the latter. Our efforts to reintegrate moral and intellectual education have consequences beyond the university and even beyond our political and social order.

NOTES

[1] Harry Lewis, *Excellence without a Soul: How a Great University Forgot Education* (NY: Public Affairs, 2006), 255.

[2] John Henry Newman, *Sermons Preached on Various Occasions* (London: Longmans, 1908), 12-13.

[3] John Henry Newman, *Discussions and Arguments on Various Subjects* (London: Longmans, 1907), 304.

[4] The following is taken from James T. Burtchaell, *The Dying of the Light: The Disengagement of Colleges and Universities from Their Christian Churches* (Grand Rapids: Eerdmans, 1998), 568-72.

[5] Ibid., 566.

[6] Ibid., 570.

[7] Ibid., 571.

[8] Ibid., 568. Emphasis added.

[9] James Fox cited in Lewis, *Excellence*, 150.

[10] Thomas O'Dea, *American Catholic Dilemma* (Chicago: University of Chicago Press, 1958).

11 Philip Gleason, *Contending with Modernity: Catholic Higher Education in the Twentieth Century* (NY: Oxford University Press, 1995), ch. 13.

12 Burtchaell, 821.

13 Stephen M. Kosslyn et al., "Report of the Task Force on General Education," 2007, http://isites.harvard.edu/fs/docs/icb.topic830823.files/Report%20of%20the%20 Taskforce%20on%20General%20Education.pdf, 1-2, 6.

14 John Henry Newman, *Idea of a University* (London: Longmans, 1907), 148.

15 *Summa Theologica,* I-II, q. 9, a. 1, ad 3 (Fathers of the English Dominican Province translation).

16 Joseph Ratzinger, *Values in a Time of Upheaval* (San Francisco: Ignatius Press, 2006), 32.

17 Ibid., 33.

18 Ibid., 36.

19 This is, of course, a reference to C.S. Lewis' *Abolition of Man*, first published in 1943.

20 Newman, *Idea*, ix.

21 Newman, *Historical Sketches*, vol. 3 (London: Longmans, 1903), 179.

22 Ibid., 190.

23 This is true at least in Newman's earlier Oxford days. Later, at Catholic University of Ireland, he seems to place moral and religious formation more in the hands of the collegiate residence rector and the chaplain. See "Discipline and Influence" in *Historical Sketches*. "Professors and Tutors" gets at the idea as well. See *My Campaign in Ireland* (Aberdeen: A. King & Co., 1896), 98 and 114-19 on the role of the dean of the collegiate residence. Also, see *Letters and Diaries*, vol. 17, Charles Stephen Dessain and Thomas Gornall, eds. (Oxford: Clarendon Press, 1973) 199-200. I owe this insight to David P. Fleischacker.

24 This can be found in some of his letters during his years as tutor at Oxford, especially in some of his disagreements with the provost Edward Hawkins. See vol. 2 of the *Letters and Diaries*.

25 Newman, *Historical Sketches*, vol. 3, 182.

26 Also key in all of this is the university church and chaplain. See Newman's essay on the University Preacher in *The Idea of a University*, his letters at the time that he was building the first chapel at CUI, and *My Campaign in Ireland*.

27 John Henry Newman, *Apologia Pro Vita Sua* (London: Longmans, 1908), 268.

28 See, for example, Newman's reflections on Peter Abelard in the *Historical Sketches*, "Strengths and Weakness of University: Abelard."

29 David Brooks, "The Organization Kid," *Atlantic*, April 1, 2001. https://www.theatlantic. com/magazine/archive/2001/04/the-organization-kid/302164/

30 Lewis, *Excellence*, 147.

31 A course like "The Search for Happiness," containing Christian anthropology and the study of the virtues within the natural order and elevated by grace, reinforces this dimension of moral education.

[32] Pope Francis, "Meeting with the Bishops of Brazil: Address on the Occasion of the XXVIII World Youth Day," July 28, 2013 (Libreria Editrice Vaticana, http://w2.vatican.va/content/francesco/en/speeches/2013/july/documents/papa-francesco_20130727_gmg-episcopato-brasile.html).

[33] Another way of saying this is that moral education requires settings and opportunities where friendships based on virtue, not merely on pleasure or utility, may arise, for such friends not only mutually strive for virtue but their good character makes them good for each other.

[34] Joseph Ratzinger, *God and the World: A Conversation with Peter Seewald* (San Francisco: Ignatius, 2003), 392.

[35] I should note an exception to what I have just said about the lack of communal experiences for modern young people. Some of our students, such as Hispanics, come from very communal backgrounds. My father is Mexican. In this case it is a service to provide communities in which the very things they believe important to life are available to them and lived well.

[36] Newman, *Idea*, 233.

[37] Pope Francis, "Video Message to the Faithful of Buenos Aires on the Occasion of the Feast of Saint Cajetan," August 7, 2013 (Libreria Editrice Vaticana, http://w2.vatican.va/content/francesco/en/messages/pont-messages/2013/documents/papa-francesco_20130807_videomessaggio-san-cayetano.html).

[38] For an excellent introduction to the thought of Dorothy Day and the mission of the Catholic Worker movement, see Mark and Louise Zwick, *The Catholic Worker Movement: Intellectual and Spiritual Origins* (NY: Paulist Press, 2005).

[39] Benedict XVI, *Deus Caritas Est*, §30.

[40] A refreshing account of leadership appealing to a broad audience is found in Alexandre Havard's "Virtuous Leadership" approach. See *Virtuous Leadership: An Agenda for Personal Excellence*, 2nd Edition (New Rochelle, NY: Scepter, 2007) and *Created for Greatness: The Power of Magnanimity*, 2nd edition (New Rochelle, NY: Scepter, 2014).

[41] Newman, *Oxford University Sermons* (London: Longmans, 1909), 92.

[42] Ibid., 92.

[43] *Evangelii Nuntiandi*, §41.

5

Revitalizing and Institutionalizing Mission: Business Education at Catholic Universities

Michael J. Naughton

Catholic Studies developed over 20 years ago to foster the ongoing renewal of Catholic higher education.[1] Shaped by the principles of the unity of knowledge and the complementarity of faith and reason, Catholic Studies seeks to bring into relationship the various elements of the university in a way that illuminates and strengthens its mission and identity. From its inception, Catholic Studies has engaged the professions in relation to mission and identity. It never saw itself as simply a liberal arts project, but as a program that might animate the whole university, including professional schools.

As a part of this engagement with the university as a whole and in particular with professional schools, Catholic Studies has been addressing the question of how to *institutionalize* the university's mission, especially in relationship to the curriculum, hiring and recruiting, development and formation, evaluation, tenure and promotion, research, and student life. The task of institutionalizing mission and identity is "to infuse with value beyond the technical requirements of the task at hand."[2] In his book *On Thinking Institutionally,* Hugh Heclo explains that this value or core conviction "points toward the distinction between strictly instrumental attachments needed to get a particular job done and the deeper commitment that expresses one's enduring loyalty to the purposes that lie behind doing the job in the first place."[3] One of the important roles of Catholic Studies is to continue to remind the university of these fundamental convictions and find creative and productive ways to make these convictions part of its day-to-day operations.

To institutionalize, then, is to incarnate the institution's core convictions into the practices and policies of the organization. The history of institutions points to the difficulty of this task. From monasteries to states to corporations to universities, the core convictions are easily lost over time. There is a bureaucratic force within institutions that can lose sight of their deeper commitments. External goods such as getting things done efficiently, rewards, growing faster, increasing margins, expanding market share, climbing rankings, etc., too often squeeze out the moral and spiritual convictions of an institution.

In light of this bureaucratic force, one of the most significant dangers of all organizations is "mission drift," and Catholic universities are not exempt from it. This drift occurs when the institution's policies, practices and processes are not linked to its deepest commitments.[4] This is why the process of institutionalizing is so important, and why those who run the organization must move, in the words of Philip Selznik, from "administrative management" (dominated by the logic of functionality and efficiency) to "institutional leadership" (governed by logic of integration of function and principle).[5]

One common story line of this mission drift and bureaucratic force for Catholic universities is the following narrative. Most Catholic colleges and universities were started by religious orders or dioceses. While never perfect, the priests, brothers and sisters of these orders and dioceses created a Catholic culture on campus that gave the institutions their unique mission and identity. As these founding orders and priests declined in number in the 1960s and '70s, the institutional environment became more complex and challenging than any of the founders could have imagined in virtually every dimension: administrative, economic, legal, technical, cultural. Priests and religious still lead many Catholic universities (although in decreasing numbers), but most of the leadership below the president passed to new lay leaders, chosen for their abilities to manage increasingly complex organizations and to navigate the "permanent whitewater" of organizational and societal change. This environment emphasized finance, accounting, marketing, operations and expertise in critical administrative skills, while muting knowledge of the founding tradition and commitment to its religious vision except in the vaguest of terms, such as "values" and "heritage." At this stage, universities assumed their distinctive mission but failed to cultivate or institutionalize it. Legitimate concerns for leaders' character and administrative abilities superseded concerns for their knowledge of the faith and traditions that previously animated the founders and the tradition they represented. Universities selected new leaders with an almost naïve hope that they could simply pick up the Catholic "thing" as they worked.

Mission drift is rarely intended; rather, it is often an unintentional movement away from the core religious vision of the institution, a movement powered by incremental and subtle changes arising from a series of decisions over time. A culture not institutionalized becomes a culture in decline. This mission drift has had serious implications for professional schools and in particular for business education. In the past, a general openness in the culture of business programs helped to address the questions of Catholic social thought, liberal education, ethics and interdisciplinary explorations. Unfortunately, when this cultural openness fails to institutionalize recruiting and hiring, faculty development, tenure and promotion, curriculum and so forth, the culture declines, losing its vital link to mission.[6] For example, as a matter of mission, policy or strategy, few business schools in Catholic universities make a commitment to the integration of the Catholic social tradition in research and curriculum, or even to the integration of liberal education and business. While some individual professors may do so as a matter of personal choice, few schools have engaged the particular tradition on which their university was founded and strategically shaped the policies and processes of the institution and the content of the curriculum with this tradition.[7]

In order for business programs to participate more meaningfully in the university's Catholic mission and identity, I will address three important questions related to institutionalizing mission. First, what is the "value" or indispensable convictions of a Catholic university and the implications for business programs? Business schools embedded within Catholic universities need to be informed by their convictions, otherwise they will default to the homogenizing forces of the instrumental and utilitarian tendencies of business. Second, what is the status of this vision in Catholic universities and their business programs? How well are Catholic business schools doing in light of these core convictions? Third, what effective levers do faculty and administrators have to institutionalize the mission and identity of Catholic business education? This three-stage process is simple: Know your end or purpose, evaluate your current state in light of this purpose and find ways to close the gap between your purpose and current operation. Although simple, it will take leaders with vision, prudence, courage and above all charity to deepen mission-driven business education in today's environment.

I. AN INTEGRATING VISION OF BUSINESS EDUCATION AT CATHOLIC UNIVERSITIES: TWO INDISPENSABLE CONVICTIONS

Catholic universities and their business programs speak of the importance of ethics, service, diversity and pluralism as mission-driven activities, but while these characteristics are important to any institution that calls itself Catholic, they are not unique or distinctive to Catholic institutions.[8] If Catholic universities genuinely hope to add to the pluralism necessary for business education to flourish, they and their business schools must fully engage the depth of their Catholic mission and identity and speak from their center, which draws upon the best their tradition has to offer. At the heart of this center are two major convictions of the Catholic intellectual tradition that need to animate Catholic business education: unity of knowledge and the complementarity of faith and reason.[9]

1. The Unity of Knowledge and the Integration of Liberal and Business Education[10]

Concerning the unity of knowledge, John Henry Newman explains that a university is concerned with the cultivation of the intellect to see things whole (as opposed to seeing things merely functionally and specifically). He uses the metaphor of the curriculum as "a circle of knowledge," where all the disciplines serve each other in a relationship of mutual correction and completion.[11] The exclusion of one portion of the circle of knowledge leaves not merely an absence of a particular intellectual claim but creates a disorder within the entire circle for the mutual relations among the disciplinary perspectives. The unity of knowledge reminds us that each discipline is not an isolated set of facts leading only to more specialized explorations. The "uni-versity," which by its very name implies unity of knowledge, should enlarge the mind's capacity to connect different disciplines in search of a more holistic view of the world. The minds of students need cultivation to develop an integration of knowledge, which, though a noble end in itself, also prepares them to make intelligent judgments that lend to their own transformation and that of the world. As Alasdair MacIntyre explains, a Catholic education should provide for the student "an integrative vision of the human and natural orders, as well as of the supernatural order, one that could inform not only education, but the subsequent lives of the educated, by providing them with a standard for identifying and criticizing the inadequacies of the social orders that they inhabited."[12]

Within this tradition, liberal education is not an exploration of one more technical skill to be achieved, but of a deepened and matured receptivity of the world's wonders and humanity and of the transcendent. If it has not lost its coherence, if it has not lost its center, if it is not closed off to the practical, a liberal education can create the soil in which the business student may think imaginatively, philosophically, theologically and spiritually about the world, humanity and business.

In many respects, this vision of liberal education, which serves as the soil in which business education can take root, is the most challenging curricular dimension of an authentic Catholic business education. Liberal education in many Catholic universities has lost sight of an education that nurtures an experience of wonder about the being of things; instead, it has become a "general education," a prescribed number of units in a prescribed distribution of disciplines that provides a multicultural tourism of discrete and specialized forms of knowledge that are unconnected from each other.[13] Without an understanding of liberal education based on a unity of knowledge, the reality of a holistic education with deep moral and spiritual roots within business remains unrealized.

Unity of knowledge serves as a significant formation to the study of business within the context of a liberal education. As an extension of liberal education, business education is first and foremost a serious engagement with reason. It seeks a reasonable way to do things and creates in the student the habit of discerning why things are done. Within business education at a Catholic university, reason will indeed be concerned with the instrumental rationality of how to get things done, but in its curriculum it should also be concerned, precisely because of its liberal education context, with an encounter with a moral rationality, engaging the business student in the deeper questions of business: the nature of the human person, work and profession, property and capital, the difference between wants and needs, the role of business within society and its impact on the poor. A Catholic business education should never merely be a training in the "how" of things but an education exploring "why" they are done, and it should also examine the relationship between the "how" and "why."[14] Newman had similarly warned that if professional education became severed from the liberal arts within the university context, its inclination would always tend to focus on the particular and instrumental at the expense of the universal and moral, and as a result would "undermine the broader pursuit of the unity of knowledge at the heart of the university's mission."[15]

A liberal education within the Catholic intellectual tradition provides an interdisciplinary experience for the business student, which opens him or her up to a more comprehensive vision of the unity of knowledge. Within the student, this interdisciplinary frame of mind fosters an understanding of life and a set of habits that create a view of business that is both noble and good. These habits are:

- The theological habit of wonder and a sacramental/ incarnational vision of life.

- The philosophical habit of "pushing things up to their first principles" (of the person, property, work, contracts, language and so on).

- The historical habit of time and recovering the tradition of their professional practice.[16]

- The literary habit of imagination.

- The scientific habit of discovery.

- The business habit of innovation, creativity, and effectiveness.

These habits help us to see the insight of Newman's dictum: "Who has been trained to think upon one subject or for one subject only, will never be a good judge even in that one."[17] Specialization in business without the broader engagement of a liberal education disorders business, usually in terms of a fixation on financial goals. The integration of a business and liberal education will help foster within students the habit of seeing things whole, which increases the probability of students being able "to come to the full measure of their humanity."[18]

2. Dialogue of Faith and Reason and the Vocation of Business

The second conviction of a Catholic university is the dialogue and complementarity between faith and reason. A Catholic university's privileged task is "to unite existentially by intellectual effort two orders of reality that too frequently tend to be placed in opposition as though they were antithetical: the search for truth [reason], and the certainty of already knowing the fount of truth [faith]."[19] Within the Catholic intellectual tradition, faith enhances reason; it does not replace or subtract from it. Or in the more traditional language, "grace perfects nature, it does not destroy it." Faith without reason tends toward superstition, fundamentalism and fatalism. Reason without faith tends toward an inhuman efficiency, instrumentalism and lack of community. Both distort reality. The more significant danger in the academy, however, is the marginalization of faith and theology from intellectual discourse. As Bill Byron S.J. put it, a Catholic university that fails to engage in this conversation of faith and reason and is closed to the search for God is an incomplete university."[20] The unique character of the Catholic university is to nurture reason's inquiry toward Christian faith's desire for a "comprehensive experience in understanding."[21]

When faith and reason fail to operate within business education, it fosters what *Gaudium et spes* has called one of the more serious errors of our age: "[t]he split between the faith which many profess and their daily lives," especially their professional lives.[22] We live in an age that fosters rather than resists this split. In the very language and categories we use to describe our lives, we no longer see distinctions but separations or walls between public and private, faith and work, spirituality and religion, church and state. Alasdair MacIntyre describes this particular modern division as "compartmentalization":

By compartmentalization I mean that division of contemporary social life into distinct spheres, each with its own highly specific standards of success and failure, each presenting to those initiated into its particular activities its own highly specific normative expectations, each requiring the inculcation of habits designed to make one effective in satisfying those particular expectations and conforming to those particular standards. So what is accounted effectiveness in the roles of the home is not at all the same as what is so accounted in the roles of the workplace. What is accounted effectiveness in the role of a consumer is not so accounted in the role of a citizen. The detailed specificity in the multiplicity of roles is matched by the lack of anything remotely like adequate prescriptions for the self which is required to inhabit each of these roles in turn, but which is itself to be fully identified with none of them. Yet it is this now attenuated core self, which in the compartmentalization of the distinctively modern self has become a ghost.[23]

What MacIntyre makes clear is that our culture not only fails to challenge this compartmentalization, but that it also works particularly hard at avoiding its confrontation. One contributory dimension to this compartmentalization is a departmental structure within universities and the isolation of disciplines from each other, equipping students for what Gustavo Gutierrez criticizes as "a peaceful coexistence of privatized faith within a secularized world."[24]

If this privatization of faith is to be avoided by our business students, Catholic universities must draw upon resources that are robust enough to engage students in a discernment of their state of life (which should qualify and condition every other role) and their vocation to business (understanding business more as a "calling" than merely a "job" unrelated to the rest of their life).[25] While courses in ethics and service-learning are helpful, they are often not strong enough by themselves to challenge this human and particularly modern problem of compartmentalization.

An institution that strives to act on such serious convictions as the two above will always experience collisions, tensions and confusions. At Catholic universities, there is a confidence that this unity of knowledge and dialogue of faith and reason will, at the end of the day, produce a higher synthesis of knowledge and deeper wisdom that is at the heart of a mission-driven Catholic business education. For students, this higher synthesis expresses itself in their experience of the following:

- An imaginative encounter of the wonder of the world.
- An interdisciplinary engagement within the curriculum, especially between theology, philosophy and business.
- A deep emphasis on spiritual meaning and the vocation of business.
- A constant experience of ethics across the business curriculum, especially the integration of virtue, technique and principles from the Catholic social tradition, such as human dignity, common good, dignity of work and its subjective dimension, the social nature of property, just wages, fair prices, etc.
- An encounter with the poor through service-learning.
- An emphasis on social businesses and their role in alleviating poverty.
- An experience of various non-curricular activities such as retreats, liturgies, prayer, mission trips and volunteerism.

The question now is whether the university has a faculty that can provide such experiences for students.

II. The State of Business Education at Catholic Universities

In his encyclical *Caritas in veritate*, Pope Benedict XVI called for "a profoundly new way of understanding the business enterprise."[26] Throughout the encyclical, he writes of rethinking in terms of the "logic of gift," which "requires a *deeper critical evaluation of the category of relation*."[27] He explains that "[t]his is a task that cannot be undertaken by the social sciences alone, insofar as the contribution of disciplines such as metaphysics and theology is needed if man's transcendent dignity is to be properly understood."[28] Yet where can such a theological and interdisciplinary exploration and conversation on the business enterprise take place?[29] Such an understanding of business could be developed within Catholic universities and, in particular, through collaboration with their theology and philosophy departments and business schools. With over 200 Catholic universities in the U.S. alone, most of which have some kind of business program, one would expect that such places would afford the greatest amount of resources for such a conversation. Unfortunately, in light of our current analysis, both the business schools and theology departments have struggled to generate a robust conversation. Catholic Studies, by nature an interdisciplinary program, can play an indispensible role in fostering this conversation.

Many Catholic business schools get nervous when theological and, in particular, ecclesial language is introduced. For the most part, they tend to ignore or suppress it. Steve Porth, John McCall and Joseph DiAngelo surveyed Catholic business schools and found that most had mission statements, many had references to ethics, but very few connected such missions and their understanding of ethics to the Catholic character of the university.[30] When ethics was mentioned, it was an understanding of ethics that was secular in nature and, for the most part, tended to be utilitarian.[31]

Theologians, for their part, have ignored business questions, leaving it to their philosophy colleagues to engage the field of business ethics. While there is a strong interest in Catholic social thought among theologians, there is a tendency to focus that interest on either political questions or macroeconomic issues. As a discipline, theology tends to see politics as an instrument to economic justice rather than educating business leaders to change their own institutions.[32] This is particularly unfortunate because business majors often make up the highest percentage of students in theology classrooms.

While there are many positive dimensions of Catholic universities and their business programs, they have not, in relation to their resources, contributed to the workings and advancement of the Catholic social tradition in business. This tradition has grown from a complementary relationship among authoritative teachers (Catholic social teachings), insightful scholars (Catholic social thought) and effective and principled practitioners (Catholic social practice). It is a tradition constantly developing, purifying and readjusting itself as it seeks to discern the good in social life. And yet, Catholic business programs and Catholic universities have not developed a robust relationship between Catholic social thought and business. Popes and bishops continue to speak about principles of Catholic social teachings. Business people, unionists and a variety of practitioners have responded as they ought—according to their lights, out of their various and concrete concerns—and they continue to respond. Yet, the Catholic university—the place where (as Rev. Theodore Hesburgh of Notre Dame put it) the Church does her thinking—and, in particular, the business schools that have lately come to prominence within the contemporary Catholic university, have been relatively silent on questions that, peculiarly, seem to be concretely *theirs*.[33]

Moreover, disengagement of Catholic business education from Catholic social teaching contributes to an unhealthy uniformity in the necessary plurality of management education. Various voices have complained of the homogeneity of higher education and particularly of business education. They have argued that a "cookie-cutter mentality" exists in many U.S. schools of management, which discourages a diversity of approaches to management education and to solving pressing business challenges. Lyman Porter and Lawrence McKibbin's argument was taken most seriously by the American Assembly of Collegiate Schools of Business (AACSB) when its accreditation standards were reformulated in the 1980s and '90s. Today, the standards are mission-driven and process-oriented.[34] A school of business' mission must be consistent with the mission of the university, and management processes must continually reflect the mission and its accomplishments. Unfortunately, most AACSB accreditors have little sense of what business education at a Catholic university should look like; thus, they rarely take its implications seriously.

III. Building Culture and Institutionalizing Mission-Driven Business Education

In 1978, the Association of Catholic Colleges and Universities (ACCU) Committee on Purpose and Identity asked James Burtchaell, then provost at the University of Notre Dame, to prepare a document on the specific mission and identity of Catholic higher education. In the resulting document he insisted that:

Every quality that a college or university desires as an institutional characteristic must be embodied in its faculty; they are what most make it what it is. To seek academic excellence would be in vain, for instance, unless at every evaluation of faculty and in every personnel decision this excellence were a quality openly sought after. If an institution professes to be Catholic, not just nominally but in ways that are *intellectually inquisitive and morally committed*, then it is similarly imperative that faculty and administrators unabashedly pursue and articulate those interests and those commitments in the recruitment and the advancement of colleagues. Neither intellectual excellence nor religious commitment nor any other positive value will exist within an institution unless each of those qualities is candidly recruited and evaluated and preferred in the appointments of its faculty.[35]

Burtchaell makes clear that if we are serious about the Catholic mission and identity of business education, we need to evaluate the way its commitments are institutionalized and operationalized. While there are many conditions to make this happen, Burtchaell's point is that if universities do not institutionalize the way faculty are 1) recruited and hired, 2) formed and developed and 3) promoted and evaluated, Catholic mission and identity will be marginalized and often relegated to contained spheres within the university, such as theology requirements, campus ministry, mission trips and service projects. There are other issues to consider, such as the curriculum, research, administrative leadership, non-curricular activities of students, board of trustees, alumni, accrediting organizations, donors, recruitment of students and so forth, but these items become peripheral where there is not a faculty that is "intellectually inquisitive and morally committed" to its Catholic mission.

1. Faculty Recruitment and Hiring [36]

Without a critical mass or at least a creative minority of faculty in both the colleges of arts and sciences and business to drive a mission-centered business education, "Catholic" will be simply in name only. It is the faculty who ultimately express and define a university's deepest convictions, which is why mission-driven recruitment and hiring is one of the most important policies to institutionalize within an organization. If the recruitment and hiring process at a Catholic university only engages candidates' academic credentials, and nothing is expected in terms of their contribution to the university's religious identity, the secularization of the university is inevitable.

One of the crucial questions for recruitment and mission-based hiring is at what level faculty participate in the mission of a Catholic business education. There are several such levels to consider: methodological rigor, research creativity, pedagogical excellence, ethical reflection, engagement with the religious mission of the institution, identification with the Catholic mission of the university, etc. Below is one way to think through a recruitment/hiring strategy for a Catholic university that considers various levels in which people participate in the mission of the institution. The following levels will entail a variety of initiatives, each of which is "incomplete in isolation from the others" and which, if not taken as a whole, can cause serious distortions and ill will.[37]

Hiring teachers and scholars of excellence

A hiring strategy or mission plan should seek to attract professors to the university who have either a distinguished record of teaching and scholarship or the promise for developing such a record. Faculty should have a demonstrated respect for and understanding of the distinctive claims of the university's Catholic identity, even if they have no commitment to any faith tradition. As John Paul II indicated, such scholars can make a real and essential contribution to the University's mission in the light of their own disciplinary competence and commitment. Many Catholic universities tend to hire on this level and this level alone, however. An increasing number of universities will ask interviewees to respond to the mission-driven character of the university, and if the answer is not hostile to its Catholic character, most responses are accepted.

Hiring and recruiting scholars from other religious and philosophical traditions

Catholic universities should seek scholars and teachers from other Christian denominations and faith traditions who have a respect for and knowledge of the fundamental distinctiveness of the Catholic mission of the university, and who can make a contribution to that mission in the light of their own faith and philosophical tradition. It is commonly heard that

Lutherans, Jews, Mormons, Hindus and others are often more engaged in ethical and spiritual questions, and even in Catholic social thought, in departments of accounting, economics, management and finance than many Catholics within those departments. Faculty who take their religious tradition seriously make an indispensable contribution to Catholic business education precisely in terms of their engagement as non-Catholics. They bring to the university both a fresh set of eyes to its mission and their own distinct insights with which to engage the Catholic tradition.[38]

For the most part, Catholic universities do not recruit and hire for this type of plurality of religious and philosophical traditions, but because they are the largest single denomination of universities, Catholic universities attract people of a wide variety of faith traditions who are interested in ethical and spiritual questions. Such faculty find themselves freer at Catholic universities to raise spiritual, moral and social questions in their research and teaching precisely because of the universities' mission. Yet, because this kind of hiring and recruiting is not intentional, attracting people of faith can be and is easily lost when it is not institutionalized in the university's hiring strategy.

Hiring seriously committed and intellectually accomplished Catholics who seek a dialogue between faith and reason[39]

Catholic faith is not merely a historical phenomenon, but a reality to live as well as to die for. It is not merely an emotive reality, but it has an intellectual dimension that gives a vision of the world. The ecclesial identity, sacramental participation and familiarity with the Catholic intellectual and social tradition of Catholic faculty are indispensable expressions of the commitments of a Catholic university.[40] When Catholic faculty take their faith seriously in an academic context, they foster conversations on faith and reason, business as a vocation, the social nature of property and capital, the role of the theological and cardinal virtues in leadership, the just distribution of wealth, etc. A Catholic university should provide the freedom and space for Catholic intellectuals to explore the unique contributions of their own tradition. This exploration does two things simultaneously. First, as Don Briel explains: "Catholic faculty members can fully commit to the Catholic university's distinctive claim not only to pursue a free and open search for truth, but also to express with integrity and conviction, a commitment to the Catholic university's claim to possess and disclose the fount of truth."[41] Precisely because they are Catholic, they freely commit to the fullness of a Catholic vision of university life. Second, Catholic priests, religious and laypeople who are seriously committed intellectuals and who draw upon their faith within their academic pursuits provide an indispensable and unique contribution to further their own discipline by taking a tradition seriously that otherwise would not be engaged.

To some, the idea that Catholic universities should have a critical mass of Catholic faculty appears exclusive, sectarian and full of religious discrimination. An analogy might help to see the reasonableness and necessity of such a goal for the identity of a Catholic university. In order for the NAACP to carry out its mission, most people would not have a problem with a critical mass of African Americans involved with such an organization. Without such a critical mass, there is a good chance that the NAACP would lose the distinctiveness of its mission. In a similar way, a Catholic university and its programs cannot be Catholic without Catholics who take their faith seriously in relation to their respective academic disciplines.[42]

Such a multifaceted strategy reflected in these three levels allows the university the freedom to judge, based on the variables of who is available, which person would be best, what is needed at the university and so forth. If university leadership does not have a clear picture of the kind of faculty needed to translate the mission into the wide variety of disciplines, it will have a difficult time achieving its mission as a Catholic university.

Besides adopting a more comprehensive recruitment/hiring policy, as implied in this section, Catholic business schools should have at least one chair in Catholic social thought and business. Institutionalizing such a chair would guarantee a presence of its deepest held principles, and if all Catholic business programs went in this direction, research in the area of Catholic social thought and business would increase. Among their specific contributions, such chairs could facilitate interdisciplinary work that enhances the Catholic mission of the business school.

2. Faculty Development and Formation[43]

The mission of business education at a Catholic university is a complex project. Once hired, faculty need to have regular opportunities to examine and reflect upon the specific implications of the university's mission and their own responsibility to it. Such opportunities must be serious and purposeful, as well as free and exploratory. The university must seek its commitment to its common tradition, one that should be regularly translated and affirmed as well as explored and debated.

The university needs to create a variety of faculty development programs that help to form and sustain faculty as they develop their own roles within the university's Catholic mission. Such initiatives, many of which could be organized by Catholic Studies, might include the following:

- New faculty seminars on the Catholic intellectual tradition and the mission of the Catholic university.[44]

- Mission-driven seminars on business education and the Catholic university.[45]

- Curricular seminars that help faculty to integrate Catholic social tradition across the liberal arts and business curriculum.[46]

- Summer School seminars and courses on Catholic social thought and business-related issues.

- Leadership faculty forums that serve to develop future leaders of the university.[47]

- Annual lectures and workshops on a wide variety of issues that highlight the university's distinctive mission and identity.

3. Faculty Evaluation, Tenure and Promotion

Ken Goodpaster explains that there are two languages of ethics in institutions: espoused values driven by mission statements, and values in action driven by rewards, incentives and promotions.[48] When the two come into conflict, the second one inevitably prevails. Within Catholic universities, faculty evaluation, tenure and promotion are increasingly based on scholarship, especially scholarship in highly specialized discipline-based journals. By itself, this type of specialized and empirical scholarship within a university's research portfolio will repress a unity of knowledge and a dialogue of faith and reason.

Unless administrators recognize these distorted incentives, they will not be able to prevent the inevitable result of mission drift. Since research is an increasingly important part of the reward structure within Catholic universities, faculty and administrators will need to discern the mission-driven character of their research portfolio. A larger portion of Catholic business schools' research should have a focus on ethics, poverty, interdisciplinarity, spirituality and Catholic social thought. This may mean certain tier-one journals may not find moral and spiritual research of interest. Catholic universities that want mission-driven research cannot then turn around and punish faculty whose research is not acceptable to higher ranking journals that only want empirical studies. This does not mean restricting the research program of business faculty to only ethical, social and spiritual issues in the Catholic tradition, but it does mean that such research has an absolutely essential presence at a Catholic university.[49]

CONCLUSION: REASONS FOR HOPE

There are significant pressures that undermine the core convictions of a Catholic university: The increasing specialization of disciplines re-presses avenues to explore the unity of knowledge; the increasing secularization marginalizes faith and theology in academic discourse; and the sheer bureaucratic force of the institution loses sight of its deeper commitments. To think that Catholic business education is an easy task is naïve and dangerous.

Yet, despite the challenges, there are reasons to hope. 1) While the financial crisis has caused significant pain and suffering in people's lives, it has, at least temporarily, deflated our overconfidence in the market's ability to achieve the good and in financial engineering's ability to rule corporations. 2) Despite the problems of a postmodern world, it provides new opportunities to consider where faith and religion can engage business disciplines. There has been a serious critique of modernity, and one can only suspect it will increase in the context of our technologically driven world. People speak of a post-secular period that may become more hospitable to religious traditions. 3) Faculty at Catholic business schools tend to understand the importance of institutional mission and identity better than their liberal arts colleagues, making them more open to the question of mission. They also tend to be less ideological than their liberal arts colleagues, which tends to create more openness to the discussion of mission. 4) There is an increasing interest in Catholic social thought and its relationship to business and economics. It is difficult to know where any of these trends will lead and what new realities will appear in the future, but they are opportunities for Catholic universities and their professional and business programs to deepen their mission to educate highly principled business leaders.

Catholic Studies programs, which are by nature dedicated to the integration of faith and the professions, will increasingly be needed by the university to take full advantage of these opportunities, hosting and fostering the integration of business and professional education into the deepest convictions of the university. As an interdisciplinary program, Catholic Studies serves as a meeting ground to, in the words of John Paul II, "work towards a higher synthesis of knowledge, in which alone lies the possibility of satisfying that thirst for truth which is profoundly inscribed on the heart of the human person." Without Catholic Studies, or something like it, the centrifugal forces of the departmental structure of the university will default into fragmented pieces of highly specialized and disconnected disciplines. Catholic universities can play an important role in the future of higher education, but they need vision from leaders, innovative programs such as Catholic Studies and mission-driven practices and policies to effectively institutionalize the unity of knowledge and the complementarity of faith and reason in business programs and elsewhere.

NOTES

1   A version of this paper served as a background document for the 8th International Conference on Catholic Social Thought and Management Education, University of Dayton, June 18-20, 2011, http://www.stthomas.edu/cathstudies/cst/research/conferences/dayton/. I am indebted to my graduate assistant, Sarah Lippert, who was invaluable in revising the paper.

2   Philip Selznick, *Leadership in Administration: A Sociological Interpretation* (New York: Harper & Row, 1957), 17.

3   See Hugh Heclo, *On Thinking Institutionally* (Boulder, CO: Paradigm Publishers, 2008), 101.

4   See James Burtchaell, *The Dying of the Light: The Disengagement of Colleges and Universities from Their Christian Churches* (Grand Rapids: Eerdmans, 1998), 842. On top of this bureaucratic force is a secular logic or bad theology that runs like this: religious and specifically Catholic and Christian identity is fine so long as it does not

animate the decision-making process of the university in relation to policies and strategies of hiring, of designing a core curriculum, of choosing institutes and centers, budgeting for research projects, advertising, student life, etc. Burtchaell explained that this theology, which he defines as pietism, has a particularly destructive role within Protestant universities in the U.S. One of Burtchaell's insights is that the failure of mission is not principally caused by outside forces such as secularism, but is already internal to the church: "It was the churches themselves and their theology of pietism that are responsible for the slide. The pietist view eventually shared by these various denominations and churches was that religious endeavors on campus should be focused upon the individual life of faith, as distinct from the shared labor of learning. Religion's move to the academic periphery was not so much the work of godless intellectuals as of pious educators who, since the onset of pietism, had seen religion as embodied so uniquely in the personal profession of faith that it could not be seen to have a stake in social learning.

5 See Selznick.

6 See Warren Bennis and James O'Toole, "How Business Schools Lost Their Way," *Harvard Business Review* 83, no. 5 (2005): 96-104. They chronicle the increasing specialization that is occurring in business schools in general.

7 See Stephen J. Porth, John J. McCall, and Joseph A. DiAngelo, "Business Education at Catholic Universities: Current Status and Future Directions," *Journal of Catholic Higher Education* (2009) 28:1, 3-22. There are, of course, several dangers with institutionalizing mission, particularly at this time. The current culture of Catholic higher education may view attempts at institutionalizing as threatening. They may appear coercive and imposed, especially if the failure to institutionalize mission has created a highly secularized culture that sees religion as merely a private affair. There are examples of well-intentioned administrators who have attempted to operationalize mission-driven policies, only to have such attempts backfire and cause more harm than good.

8 Thomas Mengler, "Why Should a Catholic Law School Be Catholic?" *Journal of Catholic Social Thought* 7, no.2 (2010): 211-29.

9 Using Newman, Don Briel points out that the Church plays a critical role with these convictions for the Catholic university. He explains that "Newman predicted that in the absence of the Church the university would shift from its traditional emphasis on knowledge for its own sake to a pursuit of power or aesthetic taste, what he often called mere sentimentality. Of course the modern university has tended in both directions at once. For, without a comprehensive and coherent intellectual tradition which can secure the tensions at the heart of a claim to a unity of knowledge, the circle of knowledge will break down into isolated and autonomous disciplinary guilds and with the removal of a vibrant ecclesial theology, the ultimate complementarity of faith and reason will be equally undermined." Don Briel, "The Idea of a University: A Contemporary Reappraisal" (unpublished lecture, last modified August 29, 2014, http://www.donbriel.org/articles/).

10 Many of the ideas in the following section come from various conversations I have had with Don Briel.

11 See John Henry Newman, *The Idea of the University*, "Discourse 3. Bearing of Theology on other Branches of Knowledge," http://www.newmanreader.org/works/idea/discourse3.html.

[12] Alasdair MacIntyre, "Dangers, Hopes, Choices," in *Higher Learning & Catholic Traditions*, ed. Robert E. Sullivan (Notre Dame, IN: University of Notre Dame Press, 2001), 16.

[13] See Ernest Pierucci, "Restoring the Broken Image: The Centrality of the Subjective Dimension of Labor and Liberal Education in Catholic Business Education," paper presented at the 7th International Symposium on Catholic Social Thought and Management Education, University of Notre Dame, Notre Dame, Indiana, June 11-13, 2008, https://www.stthomas.edu/media/catholicstudies/center/johnaryaninstitute/conferences/2008notredame/Pieruccipapersummary.pdf.

[14] See also Josef Pieper, who explains that "[t]raining is distinguished by its orientation toward something partial, and specialized, in the human being, and toward some one section of the world. Education is concerned with the whole: whoever is educated knows how the world as a whole behaves. Education concerns the whole human being, insofar as he is *capax universi*, 'capable of the whole,' able to comprehend the sum total of existing things." *Leisure the Basis of Culture* (South Bend, Indiana: St. Augustine's Press, 1998), 23-24. As Benedict XVI stated to European university professors on the theme of a "new humanism" and the role of universities, reason needs "to be 'broadened' in order to be able to explore and embrace those aspects of reality which go beyond the purely empirical." "Address to the Participants in the First European Meeting of University Lecturers," June 23, 2007, Libreria Editrice Vaticana, http://w2.vatican.va/content/benedict-xvi/en/speeches/2007/june/documents/hf_ben-xvi_spe_20070623_european-univ.html.

[15] See Don Briel's essay on Newman's understanding of professional education, http://www.stthomas.edu/media/catholicstudies/center/johnaryaninstitute/facultydevelopement/documents/briel.pdf.

[16] See S.A. Zeff, "Does Accounting Belong in the University Curriculum?," *Issues in Accounting Education* 4, no. 1 (1989): 203-10.

[17] John Henry Newman, *The Idea of a University* (Notre Dame, IN: The University of Notre Dame Press, 1982), Discourse VII, 9.

[18] John Paul II, *Ex Corde Ecclesiae*, §5.

[19] Ibid., 1.

[20] Bill Byron, "Commentarii de Constitutione Apostolica *Ex corde Ecclesiae*," *Seminarium*.

[21] Michael Buckely, "The Catholic University and Its Inherent Promise," *America* 168, no. 19 (1993): 14-16.

[22] Vatican Council II, *Gaudium et Spes*, §43.

[23] Alasdair MacIntyre, "Moral Philosophy and Contemporary Social Practice: What Holds Them Apart?," in *The Tasks of Philosophy: Selected Essays* (Cambridge: Cambridge University Press, 2006), 117.

[24] Gustavo Gutierrez, *A Theology of Liberation* (New York: Maryknoll, 1973), 224.

[25] See Pontifical Council for Justice and Peace, *Vocation of the Business Leader*, http://www.pcgp.it/dati/2012-05/04-999999/Vocation%20ENG2.pdf.

[26] Pope Benedict XVI, *Caritas in Veritate* (Vatican: Libreria Editrice Vaticana, 2009), §40. This theological and interdisciplinary rethinking is not Benedict's alone. In the U.S., several businesspeople and academics have called for this rethinking. Back in the

1970s, Robert Greenleaf also noted the important role of theology in engaging this "category of relation" to institutions. He coined the phrase a "theology of institutions," arguing, "[w]e have much *science* of institutions, but little *theology* of institutions." In 1990, Michael Novak called for "theology of the corporation," recognizing the dearth of theological reflection upon the growing influence of the corporation. More recently, Gary Hamel, a leading business scholar in the U.S., wrote in the *Harvard Business Review* that an important challenge for management is to "reconstruct management's philosophical foundations." This "will require hunting for new principles in fields as diverse as anthropology, biology, design, political science, urban planning and theology." See S. A. Cortright and Michael Naughton, eds., *Rethinking the Purpose of Business* (Notre Dame, IN: University of Notre Dame Press, 2002); Robert K. Greenleaf, *The Institution as Servant* (Cambridge, Mass.: Center for Applied Studies, 1972); Michael Novak, *Toward a Theology of the Corporation* (Washington, D.C.: AEI Press, 1990); Gary Hamel, "Moon Shots for Management," *Harvard Business Review* (2009): 93.

[27] Benedict XVI, *Caritas in Veritate*, §53.

[28] Ibid.

[29] This is one of Benedict's contributions to the Catholic social tradition—reconnecting us to the theological ground that is the fundamental resource, not only to its intellectual understanding, but to its affective connection and willful acts. It is a tradition that does not merely add one more level of motivation to economic life, but rather it reorders this life to its deepest roots in God's gift of love mediated through vocation, virtues, prayer, discernment, etc. "In a word, the Christian difference, as it affects the economic and political order, is one not merely of *additional motivation* but of *inner transformation.*" David Schindler, "The Anthropological Vision of *Caritas in veritate* in Light of Economic and Cultural Life in the United States," *Communio* 37 (2010): 564.

[30] Stephen J. Porth, John J. McCall, and Joseph A. DiAngelo, "Business Education at Catholic Universities: Current Status and Future Directions," *Journal of Catholic Higher Education* 28 (2009): 3-22. Of those schools with undergraduate learning goals, over 80 percent of the respondents "measured student outcomes with respect to ethics education but only 6 percent assessed learning with respect to religious identity."

[31] Benedict explains that a utilitarian and contractual approach poses serious problems for the world, let alone a Catholic university. "In the face of these imbalances it is necessary to re-establish an *integral reason* that regenerates thinking and ethics. Without moral thought capable of overcoming the structure of secular ethics, such as the neo-utilitarian and neo-contractual, that are based mainly on skepticism and on a prevalently immanentistic view of history, access to knowledge of the *true human good* becomes difficult for contemporary man. It is necessary to develop *humanistic cultural syntheses* open to the Transcendent through a *new evangelization*—rooted in the new law of the Gospel, the law of the Spirit." See "Address to Participants in the Meeting on the 50th Anniversary of the Encyclical *Mater et magistra*," Vatican Web site, May 16, 2011, http://www.vatican.va/holy_father/benedict_xvi/speeches/2011/may/documents/hf_ben-xvi_spe_20110516_justpeace_en.html.

[32] See James Davison Hunter, *To Change the World: The Irony, Tragedy, & Possibility of Christianity in the Late Modern World* (New York, Oxford University Press, 2010).

[33] Quoted in Richard McBrien, "What Is a Catholic University?" *The Challenge and Promise of a Catholic University*, ed. Theodore M. Hesburgh, C.S.C. (Notre Dame, Indiana: University of Notre Dame Press, 1994), 156. There are of course notable

exceptions to this silence but that Catholic business schools as a whole have failed to engage Catholic social thought seems an indisputable fact. When, for example, Edwin M. Epstein, who is Jewish, came from the University of California's Haas' School of Business to take over as dean of the School of Economics and Business Administration at St. Mary's Moraga in California, he thought he would find a robust and dynamic conversation on the relationship between Catholic social thought and management. He was moved to note that while it seemed obvious that Catholic social thought should inform business education at a Catholic university, he has been "struck by the paucity of discussion devoted, in Catholic sources, to business and economics education in Catholic institutions." "Catholic Social Teaching and Education in Business and Economics," *Educational Perspectives* 14 (1996): 26.

[34] Lyman W. Porter and Lawrence E. McKibbin, *Management Education and Development: Drift or Thrust into the 21st Century?* (New York: McGraw-Hill Book Company, 1988). See also Michael Naughton and Thomas Bausch, "The Integrity of an Undergraduate Catholic School of Management: Four Integrating Characteristics," *California Management Review* (1996): 38.

[35] James T. Burtchaell, CSC, "Catholic Institutions of Higher Learning: Dutiful yet Free in Church and State," *Current Issues in Catholic Higher Education: Commitments and Communities* 9, no. 1 (1988): 20. Emphasis mine.

[36] See James L. Heft, S.M. and Fred P. Pestello, "Hiring Practices in Catholic Colleges and Universities," *Current Issues in Catholic Higher Education,* 20, no. 1 (1999): 89-97.

[37] The following material is adapted from Don Briel, "Mission and Identity: The Role of Faculty," *Journal of Catholic Higher Education* 31 (2012): 169.

[38] In 2004, Joseph Ratzinger (later Pope Benedict XVI) wrote that "The tree of the Kingdom of God reaches beyond the branches of the visible Church, but that is precisely why it must be a hospitable place in whose branches many guests find solace." This image of a tree fed by the Catholic intellectual tradition that provides a home and a nesting place for guests of many traditions who share in the life of the tree is a helpful way to think of the identity *and* the diversity of a Catholic university. Ratzinger contended that schools face a new challenge, that of "the coming together of religions and cultures in the joint search for truth." This means, he said, on the one hand, "not excluding anyone in the name of their cultural or religious background," and on the other "not stopping at the mere recognition" of this cultural or religious difference. *Without Roots: The West, Relativism, Christianity, Islam,* trans. Michael F. Moore (New York: Basic Books, 2006), 122.

[39] In *Ex Corde Ecclesiae,* John Paul II states that "the future of Catholic Universities depends to a great extent on the competent and dedicated service of lay Catholics. The Church sees their developing presence in these institutions both as a sign of hope and as a confirmation of the irreplaceable lay vocation in the Church and in the world," [is this the end of the quotation?] confident that lay people will, in the exercise of their own distinctive role, "illumine and organize these (temporal) affairs in such a way that they always start out, develop, and continue according to Christ's mind, to the praise of the Creator and the Redeemer" (sec. 25).

[40] Regarding faculty sacramental participation, Steve Cortright explains that "What is radically Catholic is not a code of morals nor even a credal statement, but an action: the Passover of the Lord. What is proposed for faith is not proposition, but event." Cortright speaks of the importance of "sacramental identification" as the defining

center of a Catholic university. When this center is marginalized, the university's ecclesial commitment is not far behind. "Sacramental Identification," paper presented at the 7th International Symposium on Catholic Social Thought and Management Education, University of Notre Dame, Notre Dame, Indiana, June 11-13, 2008, accessed January 10, 2015, http://www.stthomas.edu/media/catholicstudies/center/johnaryaninstitute/conferences/2008-notredame/Cortright-final-pape.pdf.

41 Don Briel, "Mission and Identity," *The Don Briel Blog*, January 10, 2015, http://www.donbriel.org/mission-and-identity-the-role-of-faculty/. See *Ex Corde Ecclesiae,* §9, where John Paul II speaks of "the Christian mind" and "advancing higher culture."

42 In *Ex Corde Ecclesiae,* John Paul II states the following: "In order not to endanger the Catholic identity of the University or Institute of Higher Studies, the number of non-Catholic teachers should not be allowed to constitute a majority within the Institution, which is and must remain Catholic" (II:4.4). Corroborating the mandates of *Ex Corde*, D. Paul Sullins found that Catholic faculty at Catholic universities showed "higher support for Catholic identity in latent structures of aspiration for improved Catholic distinctiveness, a desire for more theology or philosophy courses, and longer institutional tenure." "The Difference Catholic Makes: Catholic Faculty and Catholic Identity," *Journal for the Scientific Study of Religion* 43 (2004): 83–101.

43 Recruiting and faculty development are connected. Bill Brinkman, former Vice President of Leadership Formation from Ascension Health, once told me that hiring is 50 percent of development and formation. If you hire the right people, 50 percent of your faculty development is accomplished. If you hire the wrong people, faculty development could be an exercise of deep frustration. Without significant formation and development among faculty concerning an engagement of the Catholic intellectual and social tradition, mission drift will occur.

44 For an example of such general faculty development seminars, see http://www.stthomas.edu/media/catholicstudies/center/johnaryaninstitute/facultydevelopement/documents/BACKCOVERScheduleRev.pdf.

45 A sample of a mission-driven seminar in business education context can be found at http://www.stthomas.edu/media/catholicstudies/center/johnaryaninstitute/facultydevelopement/documents/BackCoverSCHEDULE201.pdf.

46 See http://www.stthomas.edu/cathstudies/cst/curriculum-dev/biz-ed/.

47 See Andre Delbecq's Santa Clara's Ignatius Faculty Forum "A Leadership Perspective on Catholic Business Education" (paper presented at the 7th International Symposium on Catholic Social Thought and Management Education, University of Notre Dame, Notre Dame, Indiana, June 11-13, 2008, accessed January 10, 2015, http://www.stthomas.edu/media/catholicstudies/center/johnaryaninstitute/conferences/2008-notredame/Z2-Delbecq.pdf).

48 Ken Goodpaster, *Conscience and Corporate Culture* (Malden, MA: Wiley-Blackwell, 2006), ch. 6.

49 Lee Tavis, "Professional Education in a Catholic University." In *The Challenge and Promise of a Catholic University,* ed. Theodore M. Hesburgh (Notre Dame: University of Notre Dame Press, 1994): 329-38.

Part II

The Transformative
Pedagogy of Catholic Studies

6

Poetic Knowledge, Catholic Studies and the Formation of Culture

R. JARED STAUDT

The reality that God has become flesh stands at the center of Christian belief. For Catholicism, this reality remains ever-present in the Church through the Eucharist, the Body and Blood of Christ, which in turn provides an ongoing incarnational principle for Catholic thought. Catholics can take this reality for granted, but the prayer of an Episcopalian woman in Italy shows how profoundly this belief stood out in her first, prolonged encounter with Catholicism:

> My Sister dear how happy would we be if we believed what these dear Souls believe, that they possess God in the Sacrament and that he remains in their churches and is carried to them when they are sick, oh my—when they carry the Blessed Sacrament under my window while I face the full loneliness and sadness of my case I cannot stop the tears at the thought. My God how happy would I be even so far away from all so dear, if I could find you in the church as they do.[1]

And when she later accepted this reality as a matter of faith, she exclaimed at her first Communion: "At last—God is mine and I am His—Now let all go its round. I have received Him."[2] These words of St. Elizabeth Ann Seton powerfully testify not only to Catholic belief, but to its tangible and sacramental manifestation in the world.

This essay explores how the sacramental reality of Catholicism, as experienced by Seton, translates to the university. I contend that the examination of Catholicism from an incarnational and sacramental perspective serves as the foundation for Catholic Studies as a field of study at the university. In particular, I argue that approaching Catholic Studies from the vantage of poetic knowledge provides the best entry into its sacramental character. I will proceed with four major sections. First, I present the nature of poetic knowledge. Second, I look at how Catholic Studies explores the incarnational dimension of Catholicism in the world. Third, I will relate the importance of poetic knowledge for Catholic Studies. Fourth, I will examine how the poetic encounter with Catholicism provides a foundation for the formation of Christian culture within the university.

POETIC KNOWLEDGE

What is poetic knowledge? The word poetic immediately conjures thoughts of poetry and the arts. Though these have an important place in poetic knowledge, the poetic as a way of knowing embraces a broader meaning, reflecting the most fundamental way of encountering something through direct contact with it. Poetic knowledge could be defined as "not strictly speaking a knowledge of poems, but a spontaneous act of the external and internal senses with the intellect, integrated and whole, rather than an act associated with the powers of analytic reasoning."[3] Cardinal Joseph Ratzinger, commenting on the thought of the Orthodox theologian Cabasila, makes a similar distinction between "two kinds of knowledge." He outlines these distinct forms as "knowledge through instruction which remains, so to speak, 'second hand' and does not imply any direct contact with reality itself. The second type of knowledge, on the other hand, is knowledge through personal experience, through a direct relationship with the reality."[4] The ultimate meaning of the poetic consists in knowing directly from experience rather than from second-hand mediation.

Hylomorphism, the principle establishing that human nature exists in a body-soul unity, provides the ultimate foundation for the importance of poetic knowledge. All knowledge begins in the senses, and from this foundation we ascend to higher forms of understanding. According to John Senior, "the ancients distinguished four degrees of knowledge," building upon the primary encounter of reality by the senses. This first degree, "the poetic," occurs when "truths are grasped intuitively." The second, "rhetoric," follows when "we are persuaded by evidence ... next the dialectical mode in which we conclude to one of two opposing arguments beyond a reasonable doubt ... and finally, in the scientific mode ... we reach to absolute certitude."[5] Aristotle points toward this progression of knowledge in Book 1 of the *Metaphysics*, as he moves from experience, which is rooted in the "delight we take in the senses;" to art, "when from many notions gained by experience one universal judgment about a class of objects is produced"; and finally to science, through which we have "knowledge about certain principles and causes."[6] According to this theory, the natural way of knowing comes first by encountering what is known through the senses, having direct contact with it. The poetic is foundational, as Aristotle states, for art and science must build upon experience: "Really science and art come to men through experience; for 'experience made art,' as Polus says."[7] Learning has a natural progression, beginning with sense experience.

In *Poetic Experience*, an early 20th-century work on poetic knowledge, Thomas Gilby describes this form of knowledge as a "direct way ... real things can be immediately and nobly experienced in themselves, without the go-between of abstraction, representation and argument."[8] Aquinas describes knowledge as the conformity of the mind with the thing known.[9] Direct contact with the reality under study protects against abstraction and superficiality. Jacques Maritain, in *Creative Intuition in Art and Poetry*, explains how poetic knowledge fundamentally brings the soul into conformity with the truth of things: "By Poetry I mean, not the particular art which consists in writing verses, but a process both more general and more primary: that intercommunication between the inner being of things and the inner being of the human Self which is a kind of divination .... Poetry, in this sense, is the secret life of each and all of the arts."[10] The poetic draws upon intuition: "When it comes to poetry, the part of intuitive reason becomes absolutely predominant ... an intuition of emotive origin."[11] Maritain describes this, drawing from Aquinas, as a "knowledge through connaturality," by which something is "embodied in ourselves, and thus ... in accordance with it or connatured with it in our very being." This "knowledge through union or inclination" provides a foundation for all other knowledge by placing the knower in intimate union with the reality of things.[12]

James Taylor's *Poetic Knowledge: The Recovery of Education* presents a more contemporary articulation of the importance of the poetic. Taylor critiques the predominance of abstract ideas in education flowing from Descartes' insistence on "clear and distinct ideas" and his distrust of the senses: "The Cartesian view is one of the great disintegrating philosophies of all time with its tendency to set the mind against the sensory and intuitive powers of the body-soul harmony."[13] In response to this modern epistemological turn, Taylor articulates a vision of the poetic as one that "reverberates ... throughout the body and mind as a kind of real *experience* of the concept."[14] It "sees in delight," "gets us *inside* the thing experienced" and "derives from the *love* of a thing."[15] This may sound overly sentimental, yet Taylor quotes Socrates' vision of education in Plato's *Republic* for support: "But to love rightly is to love what is orderly and beautiful in an educated and disciplined way ... for the object of education is to teach us to love what is beautiful."[16]

Taylor's account moves beyond a mere description of poetic knowledge by describing its embodiment within a collegiate program of studies, the Integrated Humanities Program (IHP) at the University of Kansas. The IHP has been described as a Great Books program, but Taylor says "it was never the plan of the IHP to simply teach the books of Western culture, but rather to discover the roots of that culture and give, to the extent possible, the actual experience of that civilization." The IHP did not simply teach the ideas of the great books, but rather it sought to engage the whole person and to bring wonder and enthusiasm to study in a way that transformed many lives. Taylor uncovers the program's success within the philosophy of the program: "There can be no real advancement in knowledge unless it first begins in leisure and wonder, where the controlling motive throughout remains to be delight and love."[17] The poetic encounter with a reality in itself, rather than simply an idea of reality, brings about greater wonder and joy, initiating the learner into the subject rather than approaching it abstractly from a distance.

As the most foundational way of knowing, the poetic itself does not provide the culmination of learning but the necessary foundation for it. Learning must follow the natural patterns of human development and take the body and emotions seriously. Taylor describes the way in which the IHP achieved this: "Literally and figuratively, in this way the IHP was a musical education, observing in poetry, dance, song, star gazing, and calligraphy, an understanding of what Socrates, Aristotle, [and] Aquinas ... all called for as preliminary and prerequisite music and gymnastic for humanizing the student prior to any advanced study."[18] Thus, poetic knowledge serves as a means of awakening the student to the wonder of reality so that a transformational encounter with the truth may occur as a gateway for further learning.

Catholic Studies

In order to relate poetic knowledge to Catholic Studies, we must first ask, "What is Catholic Studies?" The name has been used broadly to incorporate academic chairs, departments and centers at both secular and religious institutions. James T. Fisher and Margaret McGuinness, in their introductory essay to The Catholic Studies Reader, note that "there is no clear consensus as to what constitutes a Catholic Studies program."[19] They do relate some common characteristics such as the interdisciplinary nature of its courses, which include but are "not limited to, theology, history, literature, political science, economics, sociology, fine arts, music, and social work."[20] David O'Brien, in the same volume, synthesizes three key foci for Catholic Studies programs: "Catholicism as an object of study .... Catholicism as a perspective on human experience .... Catholicism as a source of inspiration and integration for the academic vocation, either the learning experience of undergraduate students or the intellectual life of faculty and staff."[21] Each particular instantiation of a Catholic Studies program includes its own distinctive combination of these elements within its courses, degree or concentration offerings, scholarship and formation opportunities.

The diversity of conceptions and programs leads inevitably to the question of whether Catholic Studies can have any definite meaning. John

Cavadini asks fundamentally in relation to Catholic Studies, "What is the formal object of study?" He poses two options, either "all things Catholic ... as a cultural artifact" or "God as understood from the perspective of revelation."[22] This implies that Catholic Studies must present either a model akin to religious studies or a competing paradigm to theology. In what follows in this section, I propose a third option, which combines the two: approaching all things Catholic, but from the vantage point of faith. In this sense, Catholic Studies will draw from and complement theology, without offering a competing paradigm.

One can define Catholic Studies simply as the study of what is Catholic. In this sense, it would be an objective study open to anyone who wanted to study the phenomenon of Catholicism. In this sense, as Cavadini suggests, Catholic Studies would be a segment of the broader discipline of religious studies. This approach would be legitimate, but Catholic Studies can, however, penetrate more deeply into the living reality of Catholicism when it is not simply studied from an objective or neutral point of view (if this is possible), but when it is seen from the inside—when its essence is not perceived abstractly from afar but experienced directly. This does not discredit an approach of Catholicism from the outside, but rather recognizes that to understand Catholicism more fully one must see into its heart. Indeed, Catholicism claims to convey a supernatural and divine reality and, if this claim is taken seriously, to approach this reality fully one must look with the eyes of faith to recognize what exceeds the ordinary glance.

A Catholic vision of reality requires an entry point through what Aquinas calls *sacra doctrina*. Aquinas' understanding of sacred doctrine has always been nearly impossible to define, relating to revelation, Scripture and theology all at once. At its heart, though, stands a participation in the very knowledge of God, knowledge of himself and other things through this knowledge: "So it is that sacred doctrine is a science because it proceeds from principles established by the light of a higher science, namely, the science of God and the blessed."[23] The claims of Catholicism are supernatural claims. These claims are subject to study and thus can be organized as a science, but faith provides access to the principles of this science, sharing in God's own knowledge or science of them.

Ultimately, the study of the realities that lie at the heart of Catholicism entails a poetic encounter with God. The International Theological

Commission makes this clear toward the end of its document reflecting on the nature of theology, *Theology Today: Perspectives, Principles, and Criteria*:

> The intellectual contemplation which results from the rational labour of the theologian is thus truly a wisdom. Mystical wisdom or "the knowledge of the saints" is a gift of the Holy Spirit which comes from union with God in love. Love, in fact, creates an affective connaturality between the human being and God, who allows spiritual persons to know and even suffer things divine (*pati divina*), actually experiencing them in their lives. This is a non-conceptual knowledge, often expressed in poetry. It leads to contemplation and personal union with God in peace and silence.[24]

Even the rational contemplation of the faith in theology has its limits. Note the connection to poetic knowledge in this quotation: "connaturality," "love," "actually experiencing" and "expressed in poetry." To understand Catholicism as a divinely inspired and formed reality, there must be an interior encounter with the one who reveals himself that exceeds the limits of rational comprehension. Ratzinger insists upon this, building upon his distinction of the two forms of knowledge quoted above: "True knowledge is being struck by the arrow of Beauty that wounds man, moved by reality ... . Being struck and overcome by the beauty of Christ is a more real, more profound knowledge than mere rational deduction ... . We must rediscover this form of knowledge; it is a pressing need of our time."[25] Ratzinger recognizes the necessity of the poetic in a genuine knowledge of the reality of the Catholic faith.

At this point, we must ask, following Cavadini, if Catholic Studies offers a competing paradigm to theology. In my opinion, a full understanding of Catholic Studies should indeed rely upon theology to provide access to the study of what lies at the heart of Catholicism: a supernatural revelation of faith. Catholicism, however, as a living reality in history includes much more than theology. A full understanding of Catholic Studies must bring theology into relation with a wide range of concerns and disciplines, which impinge upon the life of Catholicism. The Word of God, which has been revealed, is a Word that has become flesh (Jn 1:14), and the flesh of Catholicism must be given its own proper attention.

To view Catholicism in a holistic fashion, which accounts for both its interior core and its exterior manifestation, requires a sacramental understanding. *Lumen Gentium* described the very nature of the Church "as the universal sacrament of salvation," which acts as a "sign and instrument" of Christ in the world.[26] Archbishop Michael Miller extends this principle further, noting that the incarnational or sacramental vision infuses the Catholic understanding of the world more broadly: "The Incarnation, which emphasizes the *bodily* coming of God's Son into the world, leaves its seal on every aspect of Christian life. The very fact of the Incarnation tells us that the created world is the means chosen by God through which he communicates his life to us. What is human and visible can bear the divine."[27] The study of Catholicism extends beyond the content of faith to include the way in which the divine life of faith expresses itself in and through the world.

An integrated approach to Catholicism examines its embodiment in culture and history, paying close attention to its cultural artifacts and achievements beyond the confines of theology. Christopher Dawson's call for the study of Christian culture, in particular, provides a compelling vision for Catholic Studies. Dawson argued for the study of Christianity as a "social reality," devoting "more attention to the social institutions and moral values of Christian culture than to its literary and artistic achievements."[28] This is not to say that the literary and artistic should be neglected, but Dawson placed the focus on Christian culture as a lived reality, which has shaped and can shape life. He states further that "what we need is not an encyclopaedic knowledge of all the products of Christian culture, but a study of the culture-process itself from its spiritual and theological roots, through its organic historical growth to its cultural fruits."[29] It is necessary to study Catholicism in a holistic and integrated fashion to understand it as a historical force, which has drawn upon its supernatural principle and spiritual vision to produce an organic and complete way of life in the world.

The sacramental understanding of Catholicism as a living force that extends to all aspects of culture and life embraces the full spectrum of university studies, including professional programs. The Second Vatican Council supplies the rationale for the extension of Catholic Studies to professional areas of the university by teaching that the Church expresses its mission in two main ways. The Council's Decree on the apostolate of the laity, *Apostolicam Actuositatem*, relates this twofold mission:

> Christ's redemptive work, while essentially concerned with the salvation of men, includes also the renewal of the whole temporal order. Hence the mission of the Church is not only to bring the message and grace of Christ to men but also to penetrate and perfect the temporal order with the spirit of the Gospel. In fulfilling this mission of the Church, the Christian laity exercise their apostolate both in the Church and in the world, in both the spiritual and the temporal orders.[30]

This understanding of mission, which embraces every aspect of human life by relating it to the Gospel, provides yet a further opportunity for Catholic Studies to reflect on the relation of the Catholic faith to fields beyond the liberal arts.

In sum, Catholic Studies embraces the living reality of the Catholic faith within history and culture. It is possible, though incomplete, to study Catholicism simply from an empirical perspective. To understand its essence, one must approach it in light of the supernatural realities of faith and grace. The supernatural and inner reality of the Church incarnates itself in the life of believers in the world. Also, the Church claims a universal mission that influences every aspect of life. Therefore, the organic study of Catholicism requires a coordination and integration of a large number of disciplines. First, theology and philosophy provide an entrance into the vision of Catholicism, rooted in the relationship of faith and reason. Next, history and the other human sciences, as well as the arts, provide access to the life of Catholicism in the world. Finally, relating faith to the professions enables the Catholic vision to enter into the life of Catholics in the world today.

Catholic Studies, therefore, is not one single or simple thing. It cannot be reduced to one single discipline, such as theology, or one particular methodology, as it requires the cooperation of a great many. To cover the breadth of the Catholic tradition, vision and reach, Catholic Studies requires a diverse faculty, committed to working together in a coordinated fashion to impart upon their students the unity and breadth of Catholicism, in all of its various dimensions. The living reality of Catholicism within the world provides unity to these diverse approaches. Without direct contact with this reality, the study of Catholicism will become abstract and cut off from its vital source. For this reason, Catholic Studies requires an emphasis on poetic knowledge to uphold its sacramental and incarnational vision.

POETIC KNOWLEDGE AND CATHOLIC STUDIES

As seen above, poetic knowledge in no way comprises a complete methodology. It is only one aspect of education, the most elementary aspect at that; but because it is elementary, it is also the most fundamental and largely overlooked. Poetic knowledge is fundamental to human learning in general, but I would argue that it also is particularly suited to a holistic study of Catholicism, due to its incarnational and sacramental nature.

One poignant example of a poetic approach to Catholicism can be seen in Robert Barron's documentary series and book *Catholicism: A Journey to the Heart of the Faith*. In the introduction to the book, Barron describes his methodology of using art, music, the saints, and the great sites and churches of Christendom to teach the Catholic faith:

> Essential to the Catholic mind is what I would characterize as a keen sense of the prolongation of the Incarnation throughout space and time, an extension that is made possible through the mystery of the church. Catholics see God's continued enfleshment in the oil, water, [and] bread ... of the sacraments; they appreciate it in the gestures, movements, incensations, and songs of the Liturgy; they savor it in the texts, arguments, and debates of the theologians; they sense it in the graced governance of popes and bishops; they love it in the struggles and missions of the saints; they know it in the writings of Catholics poets and in the cathedrals crafted by Catholic architects, artists, and workers. In short, all of this discloses to the Catholic eye and mind the ongoing presence of the Word made flesh, namely Christ.[31]

Reflecting back on Taylor's critique of Descartes and modern epistemology, we can say that Barron recognizes that clear and distinct ideas cannot accurately portray Catholicism. Catholicism is not a concept that can be imparted by words alone. Words become flesh in Catholicism, and this reality is essential to a methodology that would convey its significance in human life.

The poetic approach to Catholicism does not leave words and ideas behind, however. Barron continues: "The Incarnation is one of the richest and most complex ideas ever proposed to the mind, and hence it demands the space and time of the church in order fully to disclose itself."[32] Reading retains its importance in approaching the word. "This is why, in order to grasp it fully we have to read the Gospels ... , St. Augustine ... , Aquinas ... , Dante... among many other texts."[33] Reading is not enough, however, for "we also have to *look and listen*. We have to consult ... Chartres, the Sainte-Chapelle, the Arena Chapel, the Sistine Chapel ... , the soaring melodies of Gregorian chant, the Masses of Mozart, the motets of Palestrina." This leads to the crucial distinction that "Catholicism is a matter of the body and the senses as much as it is a matter of the mind and the soul, precisely because the Word became *flesh*."[34]

Barron makes another key connection with poetic knowledge in the need for sympathy, an affective inclination, for full understanding. In poetic knowledge, reality is known, or should we say experienced, from the inside. He says that he intends to take his reader "on a guided exploration of the Catholic world, but not in the manner of a docent ... showing you the artifacts of Catholicism as though they were dusty objets d'art in a museum of culture."[35] Rather, Barron understands his role more profoundly, using a traditional catechetical term, "as a mystagogue, conducting ... ever deeper into the mystery of the Incarnation," because "the truth of Catholicism is best appreciated from within the confines of the church, just as the windows of a cathedral, drab enough when seen from the outside, shine in all of their splendor when viewed from the inside."[36] Catholicism, as the complex idea Barron mentions above, unites the inner word with outer enfleshment.

To appreciate the fullness of Catholicism, an inner approach of the word is not enough without the outer experience of the flesh, the concrete instantiation. Likewise, the phenomenological or objective approach falls short without the inner word that gives life to the flesh. Simply focusing on the exterior expression falls short of the vision and spiritual dynamism that has propelled the Catholic tradition throughout space and time. It is the full experience, interior and exterior, that does justice to Catholicism as a whole. Poetic knowledge ensures that the study of Catholicism will not remain incomplete or un-incarnational.

Though poetic knowledge provides an essential and foundational way of knowing, it obviously has to be integrated with the other modes of knowledge. From a Catholic perspective, Bl. John Henry Newman has provided the most intriguing account of how the poetic relates to what he describes as the scientific and the practical. Newman describes the history of Christian education as a progression of "three great masters of Christian teaching .... To St. Benedict ... let me assign, for his discriminating badge, the element of Poetry; to St. Dominic, the Scientific element; and to St. Ignatius, the Practical."[37] Newman offers a perfect vision of the fullness of approaching Catholicism—the lived encounter in the poetic, which progresses to the reflective study of the scholastic method, which then sheds light on action, responding to what has been experienced and understood.

The poetic provides the foundation precisely because the formal study of science and the practical application presuppose an encounter with reality, which moves naturally to these further steps. Newman describes this foundational role of the poetic as follows:

> It demands, as its primary condition, that we should not put ourselves above the objects in which it resides, but at their feet; that we should feel them to be above and beyond us, that we should look up to them, and that, instead of fancying that we can comprehend them, we should take for granted that we are surrounded and comprehended by them ourselves. It implies that we understand them to be vast, immeasurable, impenetrable, inscrutable, mysterious; so that at best we are only forming conjectures about them, not conclusions, for the phenomena which they present admit of many explanations, and we cannot know the true one.[38]

The poetic, for Newman, is the age of youth—a time of romance and dreams, which is not primarily concerned with logic or the wisdom that comes from experience. Just as in human life, we must move through the stages of "Imagination, Reason, and Sense."[39] The beginning of one's study lies in the imagination, with an appreciation of what is studied that borders, according to Newman, on the mysterious. This is why, for Newman, the poetic relates intrinsically to the Christian faith.

> Revealed Religion should be especially poetical—and it is so in fact. While its disclosures have an originality in them to engage the intellect, they have a beauty to satisfy the moral nature. It presents us with those ideal forms of excellence in which a poetical mind delights, and with which all grace and harmony are associated. It brings us into a new world—a world of overpowering interest, of the sublimest views, and the tenderest and purest feelings. The peculiar grace of mind of the New Testament writers is as striking as the actual effect produced upon the hearts of those who have imbibed their spirit. At present we are not concerned with the practical, but the poetical nature of revealed truth. *With Christians, a poetical view of things is a duty,*—we are bid to colour all things with hues of faith, to see a Divine meaning in every event, and a superhuman tendency.[40]

It is just this understanding—the condition of standing in awe before the subject matter, of appreciating the mystery of an overpowering greatness—that lends the poetic to Catholic Studies. Catholic Studies must approach Catholicism with a rigorous, academic study, but this should be positioned within a more general receptivity to a reality that exceeds the limits of this study. The poetic disposition enables the student to encounter the sacramental and incarnational dimensions of Catholicism.

CATHOLIC STUDIES AND THE FORMATION OF CULTURE AT THE UNIVERSITY

The Catholic Church has identified the formation of culture as a key goal for education. The Second Vatican Council's Declaration on Education, *Gravissium Educationis*, in particular, stresses the necessary connection between education and culture:

> No less than other schools does the Catholic school pursue cultural goals and the human formation of youth. But its proper function is to create for the school community a special atmosphere animated by the Gospel spirit of freedom and charity, to help youth grow according to the new creatures they were made

through baptism as they develop their own personalities, and finally to order the whole of human culture to the news of salvation so that the knowledge the students gradually acquire of the world, life and man is illumined by faith.[41]

Education, therefore, should illumine all of life so that it can be lived as a unified whole through faith. Catholic Studies, therefore, can form the person completely by teaching students how to understand the various aspects of life from a Catholic perspective and how to draw them into a living synthesis. It should be noted, however, that "tension exist[s] between those promoting Catholic Studies solely as an intellectual discipline and those who believe it should be used as one of many vehicles by which the faith can be handed down to future generations."[42] If the higher truths of the faith are taught without integration, however, it is unlikely that faith will take root in life to become a culture.

Catholic Studies' emphasis on integration will help its students to recognize how faith relates to life in its fullness. Like the IHP, Catholic Studies can provide an opportunity not simply to learn Catholicism, but to encounter it within a living culture. Speaking to participants at a diocesan convention in Rome, Pope Benedict XVI summarized this task: "Catholic schools should therefore seek to foster that unity between faith, culture and life which is the fundamental goal of Christian education."[43] This commitment reflects the very nature of the Catholic school itself. The Congregation for Catholic Education has also made clear that "its specific pastoral service consists in mediating between faith and culture."[44] Catholic Studies is uniquely positioned to contribute to this task by communicating the content of Catholic faith along with the cultural and artistic legacy that has arisen out of this faith.

Catholicism exists within the world as a reality embodied in culture, which is why Catholic Studies must approach it within this context. In their thorough study of Catholic universities in America, *Catholic Higher Education: A Culture in Crisis*, Melanie Morey and John Piderit note that "knowledge of Catholic culture is not gained most effectively through purely intellectual means ... . The relationship between the imaginative and conceptual components of the faith is circular ... . It is through ... living theological experience that the content of Catholic culture is integrated, experienced, and lived."[45] The integrated, experienced and lived contact with the reality of Catholicism as a culture, or a way of life, only strengthens the central role of the poetic for Catholic Studies. Daniel McInerny points out that the poetic translates the Catholic vision concretely, helping students to recognize its living dimensions: "When it comes to a loving appreciation of how the essentials of happiness might plausibly be lived out, then poetry is the more adequate mode of expression."[46] The poetic translates the reality of faith to life in a tangible way, assisting students in applying the content of instruction to their lives.

In providing both an intellectual and personal synthesis in faith, Catholic Studies will prepare students to transform culture more broadly. Archbishop Miller clarifies this point: "A second principle governing all Catholic education from the apostolic age down to the present is the notion that the faithful should be engaged in transforming culture in light of the Gospel. Schools prepare students to relate the Catholic faith to their particular culture and to live that faith in practice."[47] Pope John Paul II recognized that universities can serve this purpose, stating that in them he found "hope for a new flowering of Christian culture in the rich and varied context of our changing times, which certainly face serious challenges but which also bear so much promise under the action of the Spirit of truth and of love."[48] Culture, understood as a way of life, is a key aspect of the life and mission of the university. Stratford Caldecott notes education's relation to culture generally: "Ideally, Catholicism fulfills and brings to perfection the natural educational process, which is the transmission in creative freedom of a cultural tradition."[49] While this cultural initiation applies to education in general, it applies even more directly to the university. The university system itself approaches a culture more closely than any other educational system. It involves a communal passing on of knowledge and ways of thinking about life. It embodies a tradition, drawing upon relations between scholars, scholars and students, and students to one another. It focuses on key aspects of human life and forms one to enter into both coherent thinking and practice in how to respond to these questions. It also requires a serious commitment of time and energy and uniquely in our world is a place of focus, where one steps out of the ordinary rhythms of life and commits to deeper formation for life. The university system is profoundly cultural.

Catholic Studies, with its interdisciplinary approach, can model the integration across the university, especially by exploring the relationship of theology to other disciplines. Studying Christian culture, or Catholicism as a living reality, necessitates a unified approach that goes beyond theology to include the social and human sciences, the arts, and the integration of faith and the professional fields. The connection between these various fields manifests the harmonious relationship of faith and reason, providing the foundation for Catholic Studies' integrated approach. Presenting a unified view of the whole of university studies and human life more broadly enables students to live coherently with the university by integrating faith, academics and personal life, modeling Christian culture in a way that can be maintained after graduation.

In addition to illuminating the relationship of faith and culture on campus, Catholic Studies also provides strength for institutional identity.[50] Catholic Studies programs can serve as forums for faculty and students to explore the implications of their institution's identity and mission. Morey and Piderit confirm the central importance of forming a clear understanding and actualization of mission for the life of a university, particularly in the formation of a culture:

> There is no single way for a Catholic college or university to understand and actualize its Catholic mission. How *mission* is understood and implemented, however, will be greatly affected by the culture from which it emerges and the depth and breadth of the Catholic character of that culture. Culture is the medium from which organizational identity grows and mission flows. Effective management of the mission of a Catholic college or university requires attention to all dimensions of Catholic culture.[51]

Morey and Piderit point out that culture requires both *inheritance* in receiving Catholic identity and *actions* in living this out in the present. One particular challenge comes from the lack of distinguishability of Catholic institutions from secular ones: "In those circumstances, it is legitimate to have doubts about whether a Catholic culture that educates and forms students actually exists at the Catholic college or university."[52] The authors note that there is a general "Catholic cultural illiteracy," which summarizes the situation of many Catholic universities today:

The Catholic tradition is not being received or handed on to the new generation.[53]

As Catholic Studies programs mediate the cultural heritage and living reality of Catholicism inside and outside of the classroom, they provide opportunities for the formation of Catholic culture on campus. For a university to foster a Catholic culture, it is necessary for the experience of Catholicism to extend beyond academics in poetic fashion. On a college campus, the clearest way in which Catholicism can be encountered poetically is in the sacraments. The sacraments, especially in the Eucharist, transmit a living and vital contact with the Word, which is the fullness of truth. This encounter is a poetic one, engaging the senses and drawing one into a living encounter with the spiritual reality transmitted materially. The sacraments also provide the moral and spiritual strength that enables the student to live out the truth that is learned in Catholic education.

The sacramental life at the university also reveals a crucial aspect of the renewal of culture. The interior dimension of culture lies at its very roots. As Jacques Maritain points out, "culture is essentially the inner forming of man."[54] John Paul states the case even more clearly, specifically in relation to the university:

> Culture and holiness! We must not be afraid, when saying these two words, of pairing them unduly. On the contrary, these two dimensions, if well understood, meet at the roots, they unite with naturalness on their journey, they join together in the final goal. *They meet at the roots!* ... Therefore, cultural commitment and spiritual commitment, far from excluding one another or from being in tension with each other, mutually sustain one other.[55]

There is a reciprocal relation between holiness and culture, as holiness lies underneath genuine Christian culture while culture embodies and expresses this holiness in the world. If a Catholic Studies program does not celebrate the sacraments itself, it must nonetheless point toward the sacramental expression of Catholicism as the center of culture and the highest expression of the divine life in the physical world. The sacraments provide an opportunity for the subject matter taught concerning Catholicism to come alive and to shape the lives of students and the campus culture.

Conclusion

Christopher Dawson provides a central thread from which to grasp the unity of the claims put forth by this essay, touching on the importance of direct contact with the incarnate reality of Catholicism and the culture-building task that flows from this encounter:

> The essential function of education is "enculturation," or the transmission of the tradition of culture, and therefore it seems clear that the Christian college must be the cornerstone of any attempt to rebuild the order of Western civilization. In order to free the mind from its dependence on the conformist patterns of modern secular society, it is necessary to view the cultural situation as a whole and to see the Christian way of life not as an isolated set of precepts imposed by ecclesiastic authority but as a cosmos of spiritual relations embracing heaven and earth and uniting the order of social and moral life with the order of divine grace. Christian culture is the Christian way of life. As the Church is the extension of the Incarnation, so Christian culture is the embodiment of Christianity in social situations and patterns of life and behavior. It is the nature of Christianity to act as a leaven in the world and to transform human nature by a new principle of divine life.[56]

Flowing from the Incarnation, Catholicism embraces the whole of human life, both interiorly and exteriorly. Catholic Studies, in its attempt to grasp the essence and cultural manifestation of Catholicism, must have an approach suited to its sacramental nature. Poetic knowledge could serve Catholic Studies not only by emphasizing the ideas and beliefs of Catholics, but by fostering an encounter of Catholicism within a living culture, which can be entered into and transmitted within the college campus and the world.

NOTES

1 Elizabeth Bayley Seton, *Collected Writings: Vol. 1, Correspondence and Journals 1793-1808*, eds. Regina Bechtle, S.C. and Judith Metz, S.C. (New York: New City Press, 2000), 292.

2 Ibid., 376.

3 James Taylor, *Poetic Knowledge: The Recovery of Education* (New York: State University of New York Press, 1998), 6. Even in attempting to define Catholic poetry, Angela Alaimo O'Donnell speaks in broad terms: "What defines a Catholic poet and Catholic poetry cannot be readily summed up in terms of content or technique; instead, Catholic poetry reflects and embodies a particular disposition towards the world. It is corporeal, perhaps even bloody-minded, in its insistence upon an embodied, incarnate faith" ("Seeing Catholicly: Poetry and the Catholic Imagination," in *The Catholic Studies Reader*, ed. James T. Fisher and Margaret M. McGuinness
[New York: Fordham University Press, 2011], 337).

4 Joseph Cardinal Ratzinger, *On the Way to Christ Jesus* (San Francisco: Ignatius Press, 2005), 35-36. The chapter, "Wounded by the Arrow of Beauty: The Cross and the New Aesthetics of Faith," in which this quote is found, derives from a lecture Ratzinger delivered to Communion and Liberation in 2002, entitled "The Feeling of Things, the Contemplation of Beauty."

5 John Senior, *The Restoration of Christian Culture* (Norfolk, VA: IHS Press, 2008), 115. In this division, it seems that Senior may be drawing upon Plato's distinction of four faculties: "Let there be four faculties in the soul—reason answering to the highest, understanding to the second, faith (or conviction) to the third, and perception of shadows to the last—and let there be a scale of them" (Plato, *Republic*, VI, 511d-511e, trans. Benjamin Jowett). For a succinct overview of poetic knowledge and its importance, see Stratford Caldecott, *Beauty for Truth's Sake: On the Reenchantment of Education*. Grand Rapids, MI: Brazos Press, 2009, ch. 2, "Educating the Poetic Imagination," 37-52.

6 Aristotle, *The Metaphysics*, trans. W. D. Ross, Bk. 1, part 1.

7 Ibid.

8 Thomas Gilby, O.P., *Poetic Experience: An Introduction to Thomist Aesthetic* (New York: Sheed & Ward, 1934), 1-2.

9 "For this reason truth is defined by the conformity of intellect and thing; and hence to know this conformity is to know truth. But in no way can sense know this" (*Summa Theologiae* I, q. 16, a. 2, corpus).

10 Jacques Maritain, *Creative Intuition in Art and Poetry* (New York: Pantheon Books, 1953), 3. Maritain cites Coleridge in support of the second sentence of the quotation: "Coleridge used the word poesy with the same universal meaning: 'poesy in general, as the proper generic term inclusive of all the fine arts as its species.'" *Lectures and Notes on Shakespeare and other Dramatists* (New York: Harper, 1853), pp. 181-82.

11 Maritain, 76.

12 Ibid., 117.

13 Taylor, 93.

14 Ibid., 21.

[15] Ibid., 6, 7.

[16] Ibid., 17.

[17] Ibid., 153

[18] Ibid., 150.

[19] James T. Fisher and Margaret M. McGuinness, "The Need for Catholic Studies," in *The Catholic Studies Reader*, 3.

[20] Ibid., 2.

[21] David O'Brien, "The (Catholic) Politics of Catholic Studies," in *The Catholic Studies Reader*, 102.

[22] John Cavadini, "Catholic Studies? A Cautionary Note," *The Idea of a Catholic University: Proceedings from the 30th Annual Convention of the Fellowship of Catholic Scholars*, ed. Kenneth D. Whitehead (Chicago, IL: University of Scranton Press, 2009), 95.

[23] St. Thomas Aquinas, *Summa theologiae* I, q. 1, a. 2, corpus.

[24] International Theological Commission, "Theology Today: Perspectives, Principles, and Criteria," (2011), §91. The document in footnote 150 points the reader to Pseudo-Dionysius to support its reference to *pati divina*: "Cf. Dionysius, *De divinis nominibus*, ch. 2, 9 (in *Corpus Dionysiacum*, 1. Pseudo-Dionysius Areopagita De divinis nominibus, Herausgegeben von Beate Regina Suchla, [Patristische Texte und Studien, 33], 134)."

[25] Ratzinger, 36.

[26] The Second Vatican Council, "Lumen Gentium" (Nov. 21, 1964), §48; §1.

[27] J. Michael Miller, C.S.B., *The Holy See's Teaching on Catholic Schools* (Manchester, NH: Sophia Institute Press, 2006), 39-40.

[28] Christopher Dawson, *The Crisis of Western Education* (Washington, DC: The Catholic University of America Press, 2010), 105.

[29] Ibid., 105-6.

[30] The Second Vatican Council, "Apostolicam Actuositatem" (Nov. 18, 1965), §5.

[31] Robert Barron, *Catholicism: A Journey to the Heart of the Faith* (New York: Image, 2011), 3.

[32] Ibid.

[33] Ibid., 3-4.

[34] Ibid., 4.

[35] Ibid.

[36] Ibid., 4-5.

[37] John Henry Newman, "The Mission of St. Benedict," in *Historical Sketches*, vol. 2 (London: Longmans, Green, and Co., 1906), 366.

[38] Ibid., 387.

[39] Ibid., 368.

[40] John Henry Newman, "Poetry, with Reference to Aristotle," in *Essays Critical and Historical*, vol. 1 (New York: Longmans, Green, and Co., 1907), 23, emphasis added.

41 §8. Stratford Caldecott expands on the relation of teaching to lived experience in the world: "The process of education certainly involves the communication of useful information and skills, but only in the context of an initiation into a community of relationships extending through time, the family first of all, then broadening to the lived experience of cultural tradition. The more human we become, the more our own lives and experience connect with different aspects of the culture into which we are progressively initiated by the school" (*Beauty in the Word: Rethinking the Foundations of Education* [Tacoma, WA: Angelico Press, 2012], 34).

42 Fisher and McGuinness, 8.

43 Pope Benedict XVI, "Address to the Participants in the Convention of the Diocese of Rome," June 11, 2007. Libreria Editrice Vaticana, 2007, http://w2.vatican.va/content/benedict-xvi/en/speeches/2007/june/documents/hf_ben-xvi_spe_20070611_convegno-roma.html.

44 The Congregation for Catholic Education, *The Religious Dimension of Education in a Catholic School: Guidelines for Reflections and Renewal*, §31.

45 Melanie M. Morey and John J. Piderit, S.J., *Catholic Higher Education: A Culture in Crisis* (New York: Oxford University Press, 2006), 151.

46 Daniel McInerny, "Poetic Knowledge and Cultural Renewal," *Logos* 15, no. 4 (2012): 29.

47 J. Michael Miller, C.S.B., *The Holy See's Teaching on Catholic Schools* (Manchester, NH: Sophia Institute Press, 2006), 49.

48 Pope John Paul II, *Ex Corde Ecclesiae*, §2. John Paul also states that the university is the "primary and privileged place for a *fruitful dialogue between the Gospel and culture*" (ibid., §43. Italics original). For more on Pope John Paul II in relation to culture, see Avery Cardinal Dulles, "John Paul II as a Theologian of Culture," *Logos: A Journal of Catholic Thought and Culture* 1, no. 2 (1997): 19-32.

49 Caldecott, *Beauty in the Word*, 9.

50 As David O'Brien points out, "the politics of Catholic Studies have emerged from sometimes bitter debates about the specifically Catholic responsibilities of Catholic colleges and universities" (93).

51 Morey and Piderit, 21.

52 Ibid., 69.

53 Ibid., 149.

54 Jacques Maritain, *The Education of Man*, eds. Donald and Idella Gallagher (Garden City, NY: Doubleday & Company, Inc., 1962), 154.

55 Pope John Paul II, "Address to the Catholic University of the Sacred Heart," April 13, 2000, (Libreria Editrice Vaticana, http://w2.vatican.va/content/john-paul-ii/en/speeches/2000/apr-jun/documents/hf_jp-ii_spe_20000413_univ-catt-sacro-cuore.html), §3-4.

56 Dawson, ibid., 115.

7

In Defense of Christian Art

ELIZABETH LEV

A rt historians have long debated whether or not there is such a thing as Christian art. Even the most prestigious museums clump Christian-themed subjects together with their secular counterparts under the same chronological umbrella such as "Late Antique" or "High Renaissance."[1] Thus, Leonardo's portrait of *Mona Lisa*, the wife of a Florentine merchant, holds court over *Christ Crowned with Thorns* by Titian in the Louvre. In the National Gallery of London, Caravaggio's *Supper at Emmaus* stands between Guido Reni's *Rape of Europa* and a raucous *Lute Player* by Hendrick ter Brugghen. In these contexts, the accident of the subject appears irrelevant for the classification of the work.

While some works may have a Christian subject or depict a sacred scene, one can fairly ask whether there is a real distinction to be made that justifies the creation of a specific discipline. After all, we don't speak of "floral art" as a proper category, despite the fact that there are enough paintings of flowers to justify this classification. Nor does portraiture enjoy a privileged status alongside Baroque or Renaissance art, even though portrait-painting occupies an important niche in the history of art. Moreover, between sacred and profane art the techniques employed remain the same: The same type of chisel carved the *Pieta* and the *Venus of Cnidos*, and the same fresco technique produced Michelangelo's Sistine Ceiling and The Villa of the Mysteries in Pompeii. As C.S. Lewis quipped in his essay on Christianity and literature, "Boiling an egg is the same process whether you are a Christian or a Pagan."[2]

So is it a fruitful investment of time for a student of Catholic Studies to focus on "Christian art"? If there is nothing unique or distinctive to be gleaned from a "Christian art," the student might be better served with a broad survey of global masterpieces to develop his or her aesthetic palate independent of subject matter. Furthermore, the brief semester a Catholic Studies student spends in Rome already offers full immersion into the papacy and a fair amount of contact with Roman theology, so why draw attention to Christian art?

Most teaching programs in Rome offer survey courses covering the art and architecture of Antiquity. Some span the breadth of Ancient Rome from the Republic to the fall of the Empire: about 1,000 years of art. Still others stretch back to the Etruscan age or era of Classical Greece, adding another 200 or 300 years to the mix. Studying these vast periods, students learn to recognize patterns in architectural orders and painting styles through the Hellenized world, which are rendered increasingly more complex as the Romans began to annex new territories and incorporate new styles into their Empire. One can witness how certain qualities and characteristics developed over time in the art of pagan Rome; this, in turn, offers insight into the various stages of the Empire. Few bother, however, to investigate the 1,000-plus years of artistic production of Christians in Rome, from the first hastily drawn images on a catacomb wall to the Sistine Chapel painted some 1300 years later. Could we learn specific lessons or discover particular qualities in the art produced by and for Christians, or are they indeed simply indistinguishable parts of the larger historical current?

The discipline of Art History, born in 1764 under Johann Winckelmann and carried forward a century later by Jacob Burkhardt, developed under an ideology that separated the subject matter from the formal qualities of a given work. Under this optic, the greatness of the *Last Supper* by Leonardo is solely the fruit of Leonardo's vast artistic talent and has little to do with the narrative that opens Christ's Passion. Similarly, Caravaggio's *Conversion of Saul* is thought to be extraordinary for its innovative use of chiaroscuro, but not for how it relates to St. Paul's missionary vocation. Yet one might ask whether this artificial separation of substance and form does justice to art. Were form and technical prowess, for instance, all that mattered to the artist at work, the patron who commissioned him and the viewers who stood in awe of his work? While Michelangelo may have used tools similar to those of the Greek sculptors, it is doubtful he would have considered his *David* the same as Praxiteles' *Hermes,* and he certainly was not producing art for the same audience. Indeed, Greek sculptors of the Classical age would have been quick to disassociate the Florentine from their ranks. The lack of proportion in the colossal work, the anxious expression on the face of the teenage hero and the awkward tensions in the muscles—all of this defied the ideal that the Greeks had striven to bring to art. It was the distance that Michelangelo knowingly put between himself and his pagan predecessors as well as his thematic continuity that first sowed the seed of developing a course that would survey a millennium of monuments in Rome, from the legalization of Christianity to the Renaissance, looking for patterns and characteristics that would distinguish Christian art.

After developing a course on Christian art over a decade ago and teaching it to Catholic Studies students for the last seven years, I have grown to believe that it is neither a particular brushstroke nor even a biblical theme that renders a work Christian. Two principal qualities emerge to define art as distinctively Christian: 1) the unique doctrine of the Incarnation that permeates Christian art irrespective of medium, style and technique, and 2) the purpose and function of art in the life of the Christian viewer, an aim pursued especially in the pilgrim city of Rome.

While stylistic similarities—whether *horror vacui* in sculpture or naturalistic garlands in mosaic and painting—tempt viewers to believe that all late Antique art is essentially the same, the Christians lived in an environment that made them constantly aware of their uniqueness, whether through social ostracism or outright persecution. From worshipping a "new" divinity to extolling the virtue of poverty, everything the Christians did went against the social grain, especially in art. In 220, Origen found himself defending the Christians against the attack of the pagan intellectual Celsus for *not* producing art. Origen writes: "Celsus accuses that we shrink from raising altars, statues, and temples; and this, he thinks, has been agreed upon among us as the badge or distinctive mark of a secret and forbidden society."[3] But Origen asserts that while indeed distinct, this is no secret cult, explaining that temples have little purpose since "there is no comparison even between the Olympian Jupiter of Phidias and the man who has been fashioned according to the image of God the Creator."[4]

Origen's disregard for art came in an age when Christians, having grown out of the Jewish tradition where images were discouraged, shied away from the use of imagery. The first commandment excluded "graven images," so subsequently the number of pictures in the ancient Jewish tradition is miniscule. Naturally, the earliest Christians tended to follow their elder brethren in eschewing anything that could be mistaken for idolatry, and they would have continued on this course if it hadn't been for one exceedingly important element: Christians proclaimed that the invisible, all-powerful God had become visible, knowable, touchable and relatable in the person of Jesus Christ. At the heart of all Christian art there is the fact of the Incarnation, the Word made Flesh, which elevates the dignity of the entire human experience but also indicates for all persons the ultimately divine destiny of man. Both of these Christian realities can be traced in the evolution of art, and often the creative tension between them has guided styles and typologies in the history of art. In studying images from the era of the Mendicants, for example, one sees the humanity of Christ placed at the forefront of art, whereas in the era of Byzantine influence on Roman art one witnesses a greater emphasis on Christ's divinity and transcendence.

The Christian understanding of the Incarnation pervades Christian art, far more in the early centuries than in the modern era. In the representation of God-made-Man in narratives or icons, the real, historical event of Jesus Christ is called to mind. Jesus Christ is God the Father's artistic masterpiece, the perfect icon or image of Himself, and the model or exemplar for the creation of man, as Aquinas reminds us.[5] Henceforth, when the Christian makes art, he imitates God himself.

This translates into architecture as well. Although the early Christian church can initially appear as no more than a derivative of the Greco-Roman basilica, Christians deliberately infused the building with elements that contrast pagan worship spaces, accentuating specific facets of the design to proclaim the unique nature of the Christian message. At first glance, the Roman cathedral of St. John Lateran, the first legally-built Christian church in the world, looks much like the Basilica Giulia in the Forum with its double row of columns and high clerestory windows, but several modifications decisively altered its character and made it a distinctively Christian building.

The exterior of the original church was coated in simple brick, anathema to Roman architects who adorned the exteriors of their religious structures with costly imported marbles.[6] The Christians, however, saved the precious veneer of imported yellow marbles for the interior, situating them alongside golden candelabras and silver altars.[7] The contrast would underscore the teaching of God-made-man, sturdy and humble on the exterior but glorious within. Size also distinguished the early Christian churches. While pagan temples were designed for worship *sub divos* in the open air, and other cults made small, dark and exclusive spaces, the Christians built for size and luminosity. "Obscurity and invisibility are not goals for Christians," points out historian Paul Corby Finney.[8] A basilica design could be expanded as far as capacity required, and the high windows flooded the space with light. Add to this the axiality demanded by the Christians with the apse in the west and the façade toward the east, and the resulting edifice evoked Christ's own words: "I am the way and the truth and the life. No one comes to the Father except through me" (John 14:6).

Architecture holds a privileged position in the Christian world, as worship spaces bring the people of God together on a common journey. In spite of the aforementioned implications of the Incarnation, painting and sculpture, however, would have to struggle to grow in a climate suspicious of imagery. In the "eyes of Christians," writes Marcel Laurent, "art had become an accomplice to idolatry," and, as a result, "warrens of errors and habitations of demons."[9] Art in the Christian tradition would be challenged over the centuries, from its inception to the iconoclast movement to the Reformation, and arguably even in the modern age. Yet the first and last line of defense in the Christian tradition, from St. John Damascene to the 25th session of the Council of Trent, was the proclamation of the Incarnation as the fount from which all Christian art springs.

The earliest image of Christ is found in the Catacombs of Priscilla and dates from the late second or early third century. This fresco, painted in an almost impressionistic style, with delicate tendrils of plaster to enhance the image, is one of the first images we visit in the Christian art course. Standing in a dark, narrow tunnel crowded with tombs, students crane their heads upwards toward what is believed to be a martyr's tomb, decorated with a man pointing toward a star who is standing in front of a woman embracing a child. That child turns from his mother's arms toward the viewer. As we look upon the first Madonna and Child, we see Christ already looking for us. The universality of this image illustrates the "visible God," knowable and paintable, or in St. John Damascene's words, "God made visible in the flesh."[10] It also resonates in contemporary culture. Pope Francis describes the personal encounter with Christ as "treasuring in my heart the living memory of that call, when Jesus passed my way, gazed at me with mercy and asked me to follow him."[11] A few steps later, students see a mural of the Epiphany, the most repeated Christological scene in early Christian art. In those three silhouettes, painted in three separate colors and wearing the peaked caps recognizable from Imperial art as those of a freedman, the visible God becomes universal in his Epiphany, as does his mission to save all who turn to Him from the slavery of sin. This theme enjoys continuity throughout the history of art, even when Byzantine influences produce more regal images of Mary as *Theotokos*, shrouded in precious gold mosaic tiles or painted in lapis lazuli blue: She always engages the faithful with wide-open eyes and long fingers to direct the viewer's gaze to her Son the Savior. Ultimately, students find that this same theme guided the hand of Michelangelo in the Sistine Chapel, as the seemingly odd juxtapositions of Genesis scenes, prophets and pagan sibyls draw the eye inevitably from the Creation of Man through the stories of Noah only to return to the altar, completing this cycle of the Father's act of creation and the Son's act of salvation.[12]

By the Renaissance era, the understanding of God-made-man had taken on greater richness, so that the poet Petrarch could rhapsodize that "God came to us so that we could go to Him, and at the same time our God was mixed with men, when 'having been found clothed as a man' he dwelt in us." Artistically, this invites the artist—whether poet or painter—to raise man to glory, as "a marvelous aggregation of wholly unequal things."[13] Giotto's focus on common human actions and reactions and Michelangelo's heroic figures fit comfortably under the same umbrella of the

Incarnation. Even the rough taverns and humble personages of Caravaggio, Velasquez and Gerrit van Honthorst continue to illustrate the endless artistic fruits of Christ's arrival into human history. Up until the contemporary era, when abstraction removed even form and legibility from many religious images, Christian art remained rooted in the theology of the Incarnation.

Along with the doctrine of the Incarnation, which suffuses the entirety of Christian art and distinguishes it from all other art forms, the *purpose* and *function* of art in the life of the Christian viewer are also defining characteristics, especially in the city of Rome. Like other forms of communication, art involves both a communicator and a receiver of the message, as well as a particular medium through which the message is conveyed.

In the digital age, wherein one can obtain virtually any image and enjoy its contemplation in the quiet of a classroom or library, the idea of on-site classes may seem counterproductive. In the age of online classrooms and the ease of accessibility offered by cyberspace, the insistence on place and setting could be described as outmoded. The expense of tickets and the haphazardness of opening hours can indeed be detrimental to serious study. As students swarm abroad, often to enjoy lax drinking laws or to take advantage of facilitated travel with few academic expectations, one can easily look askance at the on-site experience as an obstacle to real understanding. Even in the academic community it is not an unheard-of phenomenon that the tenured residents of well-resourced institutions look down at their country cousins abroad.

And yet, although baseball broadcasting offers virtual spectators a bird's-eye view from behind home plate and instant replays, sports fans nonetheless continue to fill stadiums in order to enjoy the immediate experience. Sitting in the stands, side by side with fellow aficionados, they share an irreplaceable community experience. Even in our cyber era, there is a real distinction between seeing something on television and "being there." Somewhere between the private study of the game—with the privileged images of replays and slow motions—and the experience of listening to the crowd cheer and gasp lies an understanding not only of the technical rules and statistics of the game, but also of what draws people to the sport, what makes a player great in the eyes of fans and what makes baseball so quintessentially American. In Christian art as well students benefit from time in the classroom, which enables them to make comparisons with other images and to get more context through written sources, but it is the site visit that fixes the lesson in the memory and allows the student to understand, in a way that cannot be duplicated, when and how the form suits the purpose of the artwork and the Christian mission itself.

As a religion of community, Christianity and its art benefit from the shared experience of discovery and wonder. Standing at the narrow orifice of the Holy Sepulcher amid myriad faces and languages, one knows distinctly the universality of Christ's salvific sacrifice; entering the shimmering space of the Hagia Sophia with Muslims, Jews, atheists and others illustrates the vast impact of beauty. Experience is part of the Incarnation, and its pale relative, the visual arts, works within the confines of man's abilities and gifts to proclaim that "what we have heard, what we have seen with our eyes, what we looked upon and touched with our hands: this is what we proclaim to you." [14]

One of the field trips for Catholic Studies students has as its destination Ravenna, which for a brief period in the fifth and sixth centuries was the capital of the Roman Empire. Students take a long bus ride to the northern edge of the Adriatic coast and emerge in a small town that bears the nondescript hallmarks of postwar rebuilding. They walk from one end of town to another, finally arriving at what looks like a poorly-tended urban garden with a small brick structure plunked in the grass, looking more like a gardener's shack than a UNESCO monument. And yet after the unprepossessing exterior they step inside and fall into silent wonder. The interior, coated in blue mosaic tiles, invokes a somber peace. Large stone sarcophagi define the site as a place of burial. As the students look around the room, their eyes are led from an image of St. Lawrence, carrying a slender cross as he walks cheerfully toward his fiery grill, to the lapis night sky illustrated on the vault with golden stars orbiting a shining cross. Then, in the direction of the door and the light, they see Christ in a bucolic setting among His saved sheep. Their reading has told them about the mosaic technique; the classroom lectures give context to the patron, but the space illuminates the Christian belief in death, resurrection and salvation in a way that resonates even 1600 years after its construction. Many come, are awed and leave; the Christian art student understands and thus gains a richer understanding of the oft-used phrase "rest in peace."

When St. Paulinus of Nola decorated his shrine to St. Felix in the fifth century, he left explicit instructions on how to view his frescoes. "Crane your neck a little until you take in everything with face tilted back. The man who looks at these and acknowledges the truth within these empty figures nurtures his believing mind with representations by no means empty."[15] The shared experience of truth and beauty among the students speaks to all the other facets of their Catholic Studies education.

Paulinus even goes so far as to claim a moralizing influence over the shared experience of art, instructing the faithful to "point out and read over to each other the subjects painted ... In this way, as the paintings beguile their hunger, their astonishment may allow better behavior to develop in them."[16]

My own experience is that the students do spend a lot of time "guiding" each other through the art, and while the question of "better behavior" is beyond the scope of this essay, Catholic Studies students do share more edifying conversations and make a point of seeing more art together—even on their independent travels—than many of their peers. Christian art becomes more than a hurdle toward graduation or a diversion between meals, but a portal to a community of pilgrims, saints and sacred stories.

As the continuous home of a Christian community, not to mention the See of Peter for 2,000 years, with a corresponding influx of pilgrims and a central focus on the sacramental life of the Church, Rome has a very particular relationship with art. Visitors enjoying a *gelato* break or a photo op in front of the Trevi fountain rarely ask themselves why the continuous line of successors of St. Peter would shower the city with so many beautiful, useful and pleasurable monuments. This richness of postcard-worthy piazzas also tells a story—that of Rome, St. Peter and conversion. The papal art of Rome is driven by deep aims, and one of those purposes is to establish a visual emphasis on the ancient tradition of St. Peter's presence in Rome.

Within the first week of their arrival, Catholic art students are taken on a tour of the excavations under St. Peter's Basilica. They start in the wide space that once held the Circus of Nero, where St. Peter and his companions were killed in gruesome ways by the Roman emperor. St. Peter's body, they discover, was claimed by a few followers and carried for a hasty burial a few steps away in a pauper's grave consisting of a hole in the ground covered with bricks. They walk through proud monuments of pagan merchants and freedmen perched on the Vatican hillside until they reach the simple niche that concealed St. Peter's bones for almost 2,000 years. A flight of steps takes them from the germinating seed of St. Peter's body to the glorious flowering of the basilica. This scene sets the stage for the Christian art student: the triumph of the sacrifice of the martyrs celebrated not through memory of brutality and injustice, but through beauty.

Where the papacy did not commission monuments and decoration directly, the popes played a major role in preserving the vestiges of the ancient city. Despite the history of cruelty and persecution that the Forum and Coliseum represented, the papacy sponsored and restored Rome's most grandiose vestiges, from the Pantheon to the Coliseum. In the eyes of the papacy, these were the proud objects of a civilization of men-turned-gods that had fallen into ruin and was refounded for God-turned-man by the new Romulus and Remus, Saints Peter and Paul.

Pope Benedict XVI, speaking on the feast day of these "twin" patrons of Christian Rome, said, "It was through their martyrdom, that they became brothers; together they founded the new Christian Rome...; they are founders of a new sort of city that must be constantly rebuilt in the midst of the old human city that is threatened by the opposing forces of human sin and selfishness."[17]

It becomes evident to every Christian art student when visiting the excavation under St. Peter's Basilica that the concentration of visual beauty around the Vatican is no mere accident. Peter's tomb and the successive monuments that surround it are very much the epicenter of Christian art in Rome and tell the story of the underground religion, once relegated to hidden churches and catacombs, that was finally able to stand side by side with temples and altars only to continue to grow and transform long after these crumbled.

The faithful from near and far have also constituted a purpose for papal art commissions. Although visitors have been flocking to Rome since the age of the Republic, with the advent of the Christian era, pilgrims far outnumbered those who came to Rome driven by political, mercantile or even cultural motives. In the Vatican Museums, Christian art students have the opportunity to see the oldest Christian inscription in the world, a slab of stone from Turkey that reads:

> Abercius by name, and I am the disciple of the chaste shepherd who feeds flocks of sheep on mountains and on plains, who has great eyes that, from above, look on all sides. He [the shepherd] taught me in faithful Scriptures and he sent me to Rome, to behold a kingdom, and to see the queen with goldenrobe and golden shoes. There I saw a people bearing a splendid seal. But everywhere I had associates having Paul as a companion.... Everywhere Faith led the way. [18]

This object attests to the Bishop's pilgrimage to Rome in the late second century, and to the fact that he found others who did the same thing. The students that come to Rome every semester are yet another generation of a tradition that stretches back to the age of the apostles.

For the centuries that the papacy governed Rome, first in fact and then in name, they took pains to make the city a place in which pilgrims could see not only the resting places of Peter, Paul and the martyrs, but also in which the faithful could deepen their faith and understanding of the history of salvation. Surveying Christian art over a vast chronological expanse reveals the long-standing concern that art serve not only to delight the weary pilgrim, but to teach and persuade through beauty.

St. John Damascene explained the didactic function of art in the eighth century during the height of iconoclasm. He wrote that Christ, having

> lived upon the earth and dwelt among men, worked miracles, suffered, was crucified and rose again, and was taken back to heaven. Since all these things actually took place and were seen by men, they were written for the remembrance and instruction of those who were not alive at the time in order that though we saw not, we may still, hearing and believing, obtain the blessing of the Lord... for this reason the Fathers gave their sanction to depicting these events on images as being acts of great heroism. [19]

During the era of the Counter-Reformation, as the threat of iconoclasm returned, the role of painters increased in importance. Archbishop Gabriele Paleotti of Bologna wrote his *Treatise on Sacred and Profane Images* articulating the new, increased responsibilities of the artist toward the viewer. In writing of the "office and end of the painter," he explains that "just as orators have it as their office to delight, teach and move, so painters of sacred images, who are like mute theologians, must do the same, and that pictures will be more or less perfect to the degree they approach this mark."[20] Paleotti's treatise demonstrates not only how, over the centuries, Christian art grows in freedom of expression but also in awareness of its duties.

Students are never more aware of this than when on-site in Rome. Despite crowding and noise or cold and discomfort, the setting provides essential clues to the story. A Google Earth video may take us through the ancient catacombs, but until we feel the close space tightly packed with silent tombs, touch the damp walls and breathe in the earthy smells, the power of this Christian witness remains untapped. Furthermore, students see the limited repertoire and austere design of catacomb frescoes give way to splendid if distant icons shining in the golden apses of early churches. These expressions, in turn, undergo a further metamorphosis that engages the heart and the mind of those who view the art of the Renaissance and Baroque eras.

During the modern era, as art history developed as a discipline, the disconnect between substance and function grew. Purely formal qualities overshadowed both the content and the original placement of a work and particularly its role during the liturgy or personal worship. While formal analysis is an indispensable tool for examining a work of art's diagnostics, it can often result in a clinical understanding of art devoid of spirit. As essential as technical data is to the discipline, seeing an object in a Christian space and recognizing its Christian meaning and function provide a deeper and fuller understanding of a work of art than mere dimensions, precedents, contracts and technique.

Michelangelo's *Pieta* has garnered a fame that occasionally seems to suggest that St. Peter's Basilica is merely a backdrop for this masterpiece. But despite its incorrect placement in a larger space and the impediment of the glass shield, Christian art students can penetrate beyond the magnificent carving, the mastery of antique art and the personal achievement of the sculptor to delve into what really—day after day—draws thousands of people to stand before the work, often in tears.

Michelangelo's refusal to follow traditional conventions of the subject matter can be easily discovered in any good biography, and the triangular composition is textbook Florentine design. But the body of Christ, easily identified as deriving from a classical matrix, alerts all students of art history to the anomaly of the details of His lifeless body drawn from empirical observation, which adds poignancy to the scene. The Christian art student will be sensitive to the break with classical culture. Instead of the immortal gods posing among the porticoes, this is a God who died. The figure of Mary, too, has been interpreted in myriad ways depending on the sweeping winds of explanatory fads: from the psychological (Michelangelo mourning his lost mother) to the humanistic (imposing the classical ideal on the figure of a young Jewish girl). Again, here a Christian art student will have seen enough images to recall that Mary's face is identical to the endless depictions of the Annunciation in Florence, specifically as Mary acquiesces to the Angel's message with the words "Behold, I am the handmaid of the Lord. May it be done to me according to your word."[21] Through this lens, the stability of the triangle, the gentle expression and the lack of violence recorded on the body all point to the heroic fiat of Mary. Thus the work grows beyond an appropriation of antique elements and beyond a harmonious compositional grouping of bodies into a deeply challenging presentation of a Christian ideal. But while even this could be gleaned from study, one element can really only be understood on-site: Mary's lower body was carved disproportionately large in relation to the rest of her body, undoubtedly to increase the impression of vulnerability of Jesus in her lap. The Body of Christ, however, does not fit compactly but "seems poised to tumble from her knees despite their breadth. As an altarpiece, the destination of the body would be the altar, site of the transubstantiation of bread and wine into the flesh and blood of Christ."[22]

Several students in the Catholic Studies program are seminarians and on occasion have been invited behind the glass of the Pieta to assist the Pope before Mass. Standing at the altar, they experience the fullest understanding of the work, imagining the day that they will lift the Host above the altar, to the space occupied by the polished, luminous body of

Christ, here set off by the deep carving of Mary's robes, and say the words of consecration that are clearly illustrated by this work: "This is my body, which will be given for you; do this in memory of me."[23]

The Christian lens gives a new dimension to the history of art, adding texture and meaning to facts and phenomena, while the understanding of the site allows the work to reach out from its historical period and communicate with the present day.[24]

A class on Christian art distinguishes not only the uniqueness of the Christian message and experience in the painting, sculpture and architecture produced by and for its adherents, but also a uniquely Christian understanding of art and beauty themselves. Especially in the earliest examples, the art of the Christian community was dictated by its eschatological subject and its intended viewers. Therefore, in most cases the best way to understand the Christian nature of a work of art is by understanding its placement and function and how the stylistic choices made by the artist reflect these considerations.

Over the last 10 years of teaching Christian art in Rome, I have found that non-religious students also gained a greater respect for the history of art as a discipline through the study of Christian art. I have employed a methodology that takes into account the enormous weight that religious content carried for the society in which the work was produced. Simultaneously, Christian students grasp the critical contribution that faith and sacraments have made to art and beauty, but also learn how to apply a rigorous process to discern the spiritual content of a work of art and its relationship to technique and form, instead of simply imposing pious meaning to a Christian-themed image. This facile approach to art history, which bypasses analysis in favor of a spiritual stimulant, is a form of art historical "heresy" almost as problematic as the secularist narratives thrust upon sacred images in popular novels. In teaching students a more disciplined approach to art, this course takes its place among the other pillars of Catholic Studies, working to teach students to find harmony between faith and reason.

Though art has always existed outside of Christianity, within the faith it found its natural environment and true home, and not surprisingly produced some of its finest works. Christian art is not only a proper category unto itself; it is, in a very real sense, what art was meant to be.

NOTES

1   Many authors have questioned the legitimacy of a Christian art, especially in the late 19th century as more and more Christian frescoes and sites were coming to light in the rampant era of archeology. These were led by Ludwig Von Sybel's *Christliche Antike; Einführung in die altchristliche Kunst* (Marburg: N.G. Elwertsche Verlagsbuchhandlung, 1909). This tendency re-emerged in the 1970s with Peter Brown's *The World of Late Antiquity* (London: Harcourt Brace Jovanovich, Inc, 1971), and recently with Yukako Suzawa's *The Genesis of Early Christian Art: Syncretic Juxtaposition in the Roman world* (Oxford: Archaeopress, 2008).

2   C.S. Lewis, "Christianity and Literature," in *Christian Reflections* (London: Fount/Harper Collins, 1981), 15.

3   Origen, *Contra Celsum*, Book VIII, ch. 17.

4   Ibid.

5   Cf. *Summa Theologiae*, I, q. 35, a. 2; I, q. 44, a. 3; I, q. 93, a. 1.

6   Richard Krautheimer, *Early Christian and Byzantine Architecture* (New York: Penguin Books, 1970), 49.

7   Sible de Blaauw, *Cultus et decor: Liturgia e architettura nella Roma tardoantica e medievale*, 2 vols. (Studi e Testi, 355-56) (Vatican City: Biblioteca Apostolica Vaticana, 1994), 118.

8   Paul Corby Finney, *The Invisible God* (Oxford: Oxford University Press, 1994), 291.

9   Marcel Laurent, *L'Art chrétien des origines à Justinien.* (Bruxelles: Société Royale d'Archéologie de Bruxelles, 1956), 17.

10   "I am emboldened to depict the invisible God, not as invisible, but as he became visible for our sake, by participation in flesh and blood. I do not depict the invisible divinity, but I depict God made visible in the flesh" (John Damascene, *Three Treatises on the Divine Images*, trans. Andrew Louth [New York: St. Vladimir's Seminary Press, 2003], 82).

11   Pope Francis, "Easter Vigil Homily," April 19, 2014, Libreria Editrice Vaticana, http://w2.vatican.va/content/francesco/en/homilies/2014/documents/papa-francesco_20140419_omelia-veglia-pasquale.html.

12   Elizabeth Lev and Jose Granados, *A Body for Glory: Theology of the Body in the Papal Collections* (Vatican City: Edizioni Musei Vaticani, 2014), 69.

13   Petrach cited in Charles Trinkaus, *In Our Image and Likeness: Humanity and Divinity in Italian Humanist Thought*, vol. I (Notre Dame, IN: University of Notre Dame Press, 2009), 37.

14   1 John 1:1.

15   Cynthia Hahn, "What Do Reliquaries Do for Relics?," *Numen* 57 (2010): 303.

16   Ibid.

17   Pope Benedict XVI, "Homilies of His Holiness Bartholomew I Ecumenical Patriarch of Constantinople and His Holiness Pope Benedict XVI: Homily of the Holy Father," Libreria Editrice Vaticana, 2008, http://w2.vatican.va/content/benedict-xvi/en/homilies/2008/documents/hf_ben-xvi_hom_20080629_pallio.html.

[18] *The Engraved Word: The Bible at the Beginning of Christian Art* (Vatican City: Vatican Museums, 2005) catalogue of the eponymous exhibition at the Vatican Museums from September 29, 2005 to January 7, 2006, 72.

[19] St. John Damascene, "Exposition of the Orthodox Faith," in *Nicene and Post-Nicene Fathers*, eds. Philip Schaff and Henry Wace (Grand Rapids, MI: Eerdmans Publishing, 1963), Bk IV, ch. 18, 88.

[20] Gabriele Paleotti, *Discourse on Sacred and Profane Images*, trans. William McCuaig Getty (Los Angeles: Getty Research Institute, 2012), 309.

[21] Luke 1:38.

[22] Elizabeth Lev, "Reading Theological Context" in *Revisioning: Critical Methods of Seeing Christianity in the History of Art* (Eugene, OR: Cascade Books, 2013), 214.

[23] Luke 22:19.

[24] For a lengthier explanation of the original placement and function of the Pieta as altarpiece, see Lev, "Reading Theological Context," 207-22.

8

Between the Beatific Vision and a Record of Man in Rebellion: Catholic Literature Revisited

Joshua M. Hren

A Sinless Literature?

In 1854, when John Henry Newman, then rector of the Catholic University of Ireland, sat down to write the lectures that would become *The Idea of a University*, the newly christened St. Stephen's Green buildings showed nothing of the "deep dilapidation" that poet and fellow convert Gerard Manley Hopkins would describe to the aging Cardinal 30 years later.[1] In spite of this natural decay, this inevitable withering of stones and wood, Newman's *ideas* maintained in Hopkins' mind—and still today maintain—that "life" of which he writes in *An Essay on the Development of Christian Doctrine*:

> When some great enunciation, whether true or false, about human nature ... is carried forward into the public throng of men and draws attention, then it is not merely received passively in this or that form into many minds, but it becomes an active principle within them, leading them to an ever-new contemplation of itself, to an application of it in various directions, and a propagation of it on every side.[2]

It is my hope that Newman's *idea* of literature, defined and defended in *Idea of a University,* can be brought out from his desk drawer at the Catholic University of Ireland and become—*alongside* other dominant Catholic approaches to literature—an "active principle" by which we in Catholic Studies can teach, create and study literature, even if, since 1854, new dangers and hopes have emerged in the world of literature that necessitate that Newman's idea "changes ... in order to remain the same."[3]

Newman wrote long before the 20th century's literary-Catholic boom, which brought to the fore such great authors as Leon Bloy, Georges Bernanos, Paul Claudel and Francois Mauriac in France, Muriel Spark, Evelyn Waugh, J.RR. Tolkien and G.K. Chesterton in the U.K., and Flannery O'Connor, J.F. Powers and Walker Percy in the U.S., and therefore did not have at hand a broad body of literary works written by Catholics, a body of works charged with what Fr. Andrew Greeley would come to call the "Catholic imagination." What we can controversially name "the modern Catholic literary tradition" did not exist—although the first shoots of one were burgeoning not far from Newman himself. Twenty seven years before Newman's *Idea*, the once Voltairian anti-Catholic Italian author Alessandro Manzoni had composed the first great "modern Catholic" novel, *I Promessi Sposi (The Betrothed)*. In 1859, Francis Thompson, son of a doctor who converted to the Catholic faith under the indirect influence of Cardinal Manning, would be born into the world, and his age of innocence would soon fade into one of quite too much experience when, as a longtime homeless opium addict, pockets stuffed with William Blake and Aeschylus, he would come to dramatize the "labyrinthine ways" of his wrestling with God in the great Catholic long poem "The Hound of Heaven."[4] And of course, in the 1860s, several years after Thompson's birth, both Coventry Patmore and that penultimate "Catholic poet" Gerard Manley Hopkins converted to the Catholic faith. Buckling a bit under his parents' wrath over his recent conversion, the soon-to-be Jesuit would receive words of consolation from Newman himself: "It is not wonderful that you should not be able to take so great a step without trouble and pain."[5] Hopkins' own poetry is often cited for its exemplification of the Catholic "sacramental" comprehension of the world. Poems such as "God's Grandeur" or "Pied Beauty" speak of a natural world "charged with the grandeur of

God," even as they contain tacit critiques of industrialization that would find more explicit condemnation in Pope Leo XIII's *Rerum Novarum*. But Hopkins' work contains another vein, and one whose tributaries share a source much closer to the theory of literature Newman develops in *Idea of a University*. In "Carrion, Comfort," for instance, Hopkins writes of "the mind, mind [that] has mountains; cliffs of fall/ Frightful, sheer."[6] Here literature plumbs the horrifying abysses of our human nature.

Again, Newman does not directly consider a "Catholic" literary canon. His scope is vast. His consideration of literature's place in the world at large and in the republic of letters in particular begins with that "Apostle of Civilization" Homer, a "blind old man" who "wandered over the islands of the Ægean and the Asian coasts."[7] With an unflinchingly universal aim, Newman reasons out a distinct and—at least in terms of Catholic approaches—often minimized understanding of literature in *Idea of a University*. Literature, he writes, is a study of human nature, and therefore a "Christian literature" is impossible. By "literature," Newman, writing with the 19th-century university curricula in mind, would have had in mind primarily the great classical works of *literature,* those works that preceded or were written beyond the influence of Christian revelation: Homer, the Greek tragedians, etc. Still, his judgment concerning literature will rightfully unsettle those familiar with the Christian virtue of hope: "You cannot have a sinless Literature of sinful man."[8]

This approach finds a companionable argument in Pope Emeritus Benedict XVI's "Address to Artists," where he writes that "an essential function of genuine beauty, as emphasized by Plato, is that it gives man a healthy 'shock,' it draws him out of himself, wrenches him away from resignation and from being content with the humdrum—it even makes him suffer, piercing him like a dart, but in so doing it 'reawakens' him, opening afresh the eyes of his heart and mind, giving him wings, carrying him aloft."[9] Note that for Pope Emeritus Benedict the beautiful is—at least not first and foremost, and in a sense not even *intrinsically*—evangelical, Christian or doctrinal. Even as, toward the end of his address, the Holy Father references literary giants such as Dostoevsky and Hesse in order to establish the way in which literature can lead the reader to God, he nevertheless introduces a caution concerning the beautiful, noting that "too often ... the beauty that is thrust upon us is illusory and deceitful, superficial and blinding, leaving the onlooker dazed."[10] Rather than bringing man out of himself, failing to open him up "to horizons of true freedom as it draws him aloft, it imprisons him within himself and further enslaves him, depriving him of hope and joy."[11] Newman's definition removes us even further from those theories of "Catholic" or "Christian" literature that see fiction as the handmaid of doctrine, dogma and—more broadly— theology, and thus it seems to chafe a bit at these theories.

The Catholic literary tradition's dominant interpretive approach is rooted in the *via pulchritudinis,* "the way of beauty," for which literature is justified and even considered good because in its sacramental dimension it contains a foretaste of the Beatific Vision and the transcendentals. In its 2006 concluding document, *The* Via Pulchritudinis, *Privileged Pathway for Evangelisation and Dialogue,* the Pontifical Council for Culture pro- claims that

> the *Way of Beauty* seems to be a privileged itinerary to get in touch with many of those who face great difficulties in receiving the Church's teachings, particularly regarding morals. Too often in recent years, the *truth* has been instrumentalised by ideologies, and the *good* horizontalised into a merely social act as though charity towards neighbour alone sufficed without being rooted in love of God. Relativism, which finds one of its clearest expres- sions in the *pensiero debole,* continues to spread, encouraging a climate of miscomprehension, and making real, serious and rea- soned encounters rare.[12]

The PCC goes on to position Christ as the paradigmatic incarna- tion of Beauty. Christ the Beautiful "invites contemporary Augustines, unquenchable seekers of love, truth and beauty," to come to eternal Beauty by way of perceptible beauty.

This approach can be traced back to Augustine's "Late have I loved you, beauty so old, beauty so new," and it manifests as *one* of the four ways enumerated in Dante's "four-fold method" or "allegory of the theolo- gians," which he famously outlines in a letter to his patron and protector, Cangrande I, Lord of Verona:

> Rather, it may be called "polysemous," that is, of many senses. A first sense derives from the letters themselves, and a second from

the things signified by the letters. We call the first sense "literal" sense, the second the "allegorical," or "moral" or "anagogical." To clarify this method of treatment, consider this verse: *When Israel went out of Egypt, the house of Jacob from a barbarous people: Judaea was made his sanctuary, Israel his dominion* [Psalm 113]. Now if we examine the letters alone, the exodus of the children of Israel from Egypt in the time of Moses is signified; in the allegory, our redemption accomplished through Christ; in the moral sense, the conversion of the soul from the grief and misery of sin to the state of grace; in the anagogical sense, the exodus of the holy soul from slavery of this corruption to the freedom of eternal glory ... they can all be called allegorical.[13]

This interpretive apparatus, inherited from medieval biblical exegesis, trains the mind to see a given literary work as *saturated* with meanings—literal, allegorical, moral and anagogical. As Umberto Eco jocularly remarks, here Dante "tak[es] a way of reading the bible as an example of how to read his own mundane poem!"[14] Revolutionary as Dante's move may have been, his insistence that "mundane" or non-sacred literature can contain an *anagogical* sense continues to ripple through Catholic readers, writers and educational institutions today. Set apart from this we have Newman's *idea* of literature, in which literature is justified as an inevitably problematic record of man's sinfulness.

If in defining poetry as a record of human sinfulness Newman is not defending it merely as record of human sinfulness for its own sake, it is necessary that we probe the ways in which that record of human sinfulness has been interpreted, and to what teleological end study of this record of human sinfulness should strive.

A Record of Rebellion and Grace

In his *Confessions,* Augustine momentarily embarks on an analysis of poetics:

I was captivated by theatrical shows ... [because] they were full of representations of my own miseries and fueled my fire. Why is it that a person should wish to experience suffering by watching grievous and tragic events which he himself would not wish to endure? Nevertheless, he wants to suffer the pain given by being a spectator of these sufferings, and the pain itself is his pleasure.[15]

Augustine considers this "amazing folly" in that when one is moved by such scenes, she enslaves herself to similar passions. For Augustine, fiction (specifically theatrical, but—and I hope I am not here unduly taking his *particular* experience of Roman theater for the *whole* of fiction—we can expand his consideration) is problematic precisely *because* it represents sins, because it is an invented dramatization of passions and others' sufferings. When one suffers in *reality* this is called misery, and when one feels compassion for others this is called mercy. Beholding fictions of tragic human existence, however, the audience's own sinful appetites are piqued and fostered, and, crucially, *the audience is not excited to offer help*, for the object of their attention is fictional, but is simply *invited to grieve*. Augustine seems to close the door to the possibility of purgation of these passions, and thus departs from Aristotle, who, in his *Poetics*, infamously posits that fictional representation of tragedy, "through pity and fear," effects "the proper purgation [*catharsis*] of these emotions."[16]

Although John Henry Newman, like Augustine, is keen to articulate the problematic character of fictionalized representations, he sees more in its messiness than an occasion of sin. In *The Idea of a University*, he posits literature as related to man in the same way that science is related to nature. Literature, he argues, is man's *history*. He "thinks and he acts; he has appetites, passions, affections, motives, designs; he has within him the lifelong struggle of duty with inclination; he has an intellect fertile and capacious; he is formed for society, and society multiplies and diversifies in endless combinations his personal characteristics, moral and intellectual."[17] Literature is the expression of all of this, a sort of autobiography of man. Newman's definition of literature keeps the literary distinct from the theological. Although Hebrew literature is "simply theological," having, as it does, a character impressed upon it that is above nature, Newman is striving to account for *all* literature, not, say, works of fiction written by authors who are Catholic or Christian, or whose rendered characters and plots are steeped in the Judeo-Christian vision.[18] As literature is the record of man, and man is intelligent, sentient, creative, and operative independent of supernatural aid from heaven, independent of any religious belief or sanctifying grace, literature represents him as such. Literatures are "the voices of the natural man."[19] Newman establishes this account of literature *in part* in order to lay out its *disadvantages.* Because literature is the reflection of nature moral and social, and because nature moral and social is endowed with a will, is self-governed and never abides in a "mere state of innocence," he is "sure to sin, and his literature will be the expression of his sin, and this whether he is heathen or Christian."[20] Christianity has only converted certain specimens of man, Newman contends, and thus has not altered the character of his history or of his mind. Here we see most clearly that in developing his theory of literature, Newman is not merely referencing those works written before revelation or written in traditions outside of the influence of Revelation. Because literature can only reflect man as he is "in proportion as there has been an abuse of knowledge granted and a rejection of truth," literature is the science or history "partly of man in rebellion."[21] Whereas physical science is dangerous because it is intrinsically indifferent to the idea of moral evil, literature is even more perilous because it is inclined to understand and recognize evil too well, to become excessively focused upon the abyss, and, as Nietzsche observes in *Beyond Good and Evil,* "And when you gaze long into an abyss the abyss also gazes into you."[22]

Again, as literature is a study of human nature, a "Christian literature" is impossible. In Newman's infamous formulation, "you cannot have a sinless Literature of sinful man."[23] This is not to say that it is impossible for a maker of literature to represent something grand, something great, but that when one achieves such a thing, this thing, whatever it may be, is not literature. Such an author or artist will have departed from the delineation of man *as such* in favor of *possible man* or *purer man,* in favor of man as he might be under particular vantages. Newman asks that one who undertakes such a task should "not say that you are studying him, his history, his mind and his heart," but something else. "If you would in fact have a literature of saints, first of all have a nation of them."[24] Implicit in this ordering of literature and political-historical reality is a stubborn insistence that literature, as literature, cannot and should not articulate the *possible*—that it is more mimetic than prescriptive; it can only imitate what already exists in reality. If a nation of saints should arise, *then* literature could record this redeemed Man spoken of in eschatological Scripture. Of course, Newman's own novels—*Callista* and *Loss and Gain*—are nothing if not conversion stories that take as their subject matter the lives of "saints," not canonized saints, but also not people outside the history of nature. Does this mean that Newman excluded from his definition of literature the modern novel, being as it was a form not fit for university study? Perhaps, but this in no way detracts from our attempt to extract from Newman's general theory of literature *ideas* applicable to any literary form.

One might expect that Newman's rather bleak appraisal of literature would lead to his banishing it from the Republic of the Liberal Arts University's Letters, but, like a great artist, he concludes with a somewhat unexpected plot twist. Indeed, he insists that a Catholic university *should* and even *must* teach the sinful literature of sinful man. Why? Because most men are not destined for the cloister:

> We cannot possibly keep them from plunging into the world, with all its ways and principles and maxims, when their time comes; but we can prepare them against what is inevitable; and it is not the way to learn to swim in troubled waters, never to have gone into them. Proscribe (I do not merely say particular authors, particular works, particular passages) but Secular Literature as such; cut out from your class books all broad manifestations of the natural man; and those manifestations are waiting for your pupil's benefit at the very doors of your lecture room in living and breathing substance.[25]

We sense this Augustinian anxiety over fictionalized representation in "The Church and the Fiction Writer," as Flannery O'Connor approaches the problem of sinful literature from the vantages of both writer and reader. What leads the writer to the fruition of her work and even her salvation may, O'Connor contends, "lead the reader into sin, and the Catholic writer who looks at this possibility directly looks the Medusa in the face and is turned to stone."[26] Try as she might to purify the source, the writer will find that her work may still scandalize. Even though such scandal may be the fault of an ill-equipped reader more than her own, she may decide that such works are somehow sinful. This is complicated in that since modernity, at least in representation, at least in *mind,* nature and grace have been separated with severity. Grace, the supernatural, is often reduced to pious cliché, and nature is represented in two distorted forms: the obscene and the sentimental. Sentimentality is born of an excess emphasis on innocence. Some readers may be scandalized simply because the work is not pious enough, is not filled with a nation of saints, because it is not what O'Connor would call "pious trash." For O'Connor, the writer of literature, in order to avoid paralysis, sentimentality or an indiscriminate embrace of depravity, needs to represent "the presence of grace as it appears in nature," and it is this possibility that legitimates the creation and contemplation of literary works.[27] For all of the grotesque extremities of her fiction, in her theory O'Connor inhabits an Aristotelean mean between literature as a record of man in rebellion and the *via pulchritudinis.*

We find an extraordinary exemplification of this mean on the last page of Evelyn Waugh's *Brideshead Revisited.* Charles Ryder offers his own concentrated, couched criticism of the events that he has just narrated: the debauchery and the divorces, the affairs and the recourse to alcohol, the lapsed Catholics and the decadence, the life experienced "second hand"— all of this tangled up with a recurrent searching and striving after firm faith and the chastening of sin that comes with it. Ryder, possessor of a poetic soul, ruminates on Brideshead Castle, the natural fruits of man's natural labors, which, built for distinctly different purposes during an age still echoing monarchy, now houses an army during the Second World War:

> Something quite remote from anything the builders intended has come out of their work, and out of the fierce little human tragedy to which I played; something none of us thought about at the time; a small red flame—a beaten-copper lamp of deplorable design relit before the beaten-copper doors of a tabernacle ... It could not have been lit but for the builders and the tragedians, and there I found it this morning, burning anew amidst old stones.[28]

In spite of its clear stature as a "record of human sinfulness" (the "fierce little human tragedy"), *Brideshead Revisited* is also an account of grace building upon nature. It seems a worthy piece of evidence to submit to the court of Newman. For here we have a work of literature that is nothing if not a "study of human nature"—and yet it begs the question: Is *religio* intrinsic to human nature?

Jacques Maritain, too, wrestles with the problem of sinful literature, but, unlike Newman, his emphasis is on the artist, not the reader, and, unlike Newman, he makes a distinction between the different ways in which a Christian will grapple with evil and sin. In *Art and Scholasticism*, he portrays the question as not whether a fiction writer can or cannot represent this or that aspect of evil, but rather "*at what altitude* he is prepared to depict it and whether his art and his heart are pure enough and strong enough for him to depict it without complicity or connivance."[29] Should the novelist wish to probe the abyss of human misery and wish the work to avoid scandalous sinfulness, she would require superhuman virtues. This is especially true because the fiction writer has as its object not a thing-to-be-made that, as an *artifact,* would have as its end a sort of beauty-in-itself, and for which human life would comprise only the elements, but—and this distinction is terribly important, as here Maritain intersects with Newman—*life, human life in itself,* molded into fiction. Maritain then reaches the crescendo of his qualifications by noting the necessity for universality, authenticity and integrity in the novelist's realism. "Only a Christian" he claims, "nay more, a mystic because he has some idea of *what is in man,* can be a complete novelist."[30] Even this is problematic because the novelist needs some measure of *experimental* knowledge of the creature, and such knowledge can only come from the gift of understanding (which comes from the Holy Spirit) and man's experience of the sins of which he writes.

Unlike Augustine, who implicitly favors the engagement with *real* human sinfulness, and unlike Maritain and O'Connor, who defend literature on the grounds that *at a certain altitude* fiction can truthfully render human sin in all of its awfulness and the perfecting of (sometimes hellbent) human nature via grace, Newman finds in literary sinfulness and suffering a means of mediating the harsh world to the student. If good can come from literature, he seems to say, much depends upon the teacher's capacity to impart those virtues necessary to engagement with sinful literature, namely, "wit and humour" and imagination, "fastidiousness of taste," "rule[s] ... for discriminating 'the precious from the vile,' beauty from sin, the truth from the sophistry of nature, what is innocent from what is poison."[31] If the teacher does not, through literature, mediate the sinful world, the student will meet this world with all of the charm of novelty, "all the fascination of amiableness."[32]

Newman warns us against taking man "for what he is not, for something more divine and sacred, for man regenerate."[33] He cautions us to "beware of showing God's grace and its work at such disadvantage as to make the few whom it has thoroughly influenced compete in intellect with the vast multitude who either have it not, or use it ill."[34] Perhaps this is where Newman's limitation of living before the great Catholic boom in literary fiction comes forth most clearly. *Brideshead*—and we could say this about the fiction of Flannery O'Connor's short stories, Muriel Spark's *The Prime of Miss Jean Brodie*, J.F. Powers' *Morte D'Urban* and so many others in the Catholic literary tradition—does not show God's grace in a manner that distorts the incomplete, impoverished condition of human beings. For would not the "Record of Man" of which Newman speaks be amiss if it lacked some representation of grace? Surely grace is not beyond literary representation? "[T]ake things as they are, not as you could wish them," he counsels, with genuine Aristotelian realism.[35] But in accounting for things as they are, we need not do so in the manner of Hobbes, who, in the *Leviathan*, states that "there is no such *Finis ultimus* (utmost ayme), nor *Summum Bonum* (greatest Good), as is spoken of in the Books of the old Morall Philosophers."[36] In place of this *summum bonum,* Hobbes puts "for a general inclination of mankind, a perpetuall and restlesse desire of Power after power, that ceaseth only in Death."[37] Does not the record of man's sinfulness, lest it remain a Hobbesian or Calvinistic documentation not merely of sinfulness but of an unreal, hyperbolic depravity, also beg to become the record of grace built upon that sinful being?

CONVERSION

A realistic literary account of man's history, of human nature, should not lack the possibility of *conversion,* conversion of both characters and readers. Because he strove for a universal definition of literature, Newman could not posit one of literature's possible subjects—conversion—as a subject of major import in the Catholic approach to literature. However, as the possibility is embodied in Newman's own novel *Loss and Gain,* he so clearly would not discard it either. It seems, then, that he does not discard such a possibility—either in theory or fiction—but because the story of nature building upon grace would concern a comparatively small contingent of the overall literary corpus—Catholic literary boom or not—he does not incorporate the workings of grace into his firmly general definition. By Maritain's measurements, this is only possible if the maker of literature is operating from a sufficient *altitude,* a sufficiently vertical state of being. I would add to this the possibility that a sufficient altitude can be cultivated in the reader as well. *Conversion* is both horizontal, in that it is tied up with the hero's human interrelationships and thus his sinfulness, *and* vertical, in that it signifies a shift in the hero's relationship to God and thus to the beautiful. An approach to literature that emphasizes conversion allows us to avoid an undue emphasis upon beauty and the beatific vision (which would find its earthly parallel in a life spent in contemplation at best, and if corrupted by focus on an apparent beatific vision, an undue overemphasis on private devotion). For conversion is eschatological; its doctrinal corollary is the resurrection of the body. But if we are to discern conversion in a given work of literature, we need to come equipped with hermeneutical tools by which we can fruitfully analyze and theorize sin, for it is only by theorizing about sin that we can recognize and participate in conversion and thereby avoid the aporia of literature as *mere* record of human sinfulness.

We can locate another more generalizable literary wrestling with sin that is tied to a teleological movement toward conversion at the beginning of the Catholic literary tradition—in Dante's *Divine Comedy.* In each terrace of Purgatory, Dante witnesses the "whips"—graven depictions of both sinfulness and saintliness that purge the penitents of their cardinal vices. When first he encounters these "whips," Dante describes them as "[appearing] to us with such a lively ease/ Carved, and so gracious there in act to move,/ It seemed not one of your dumb images."[38] Perhaps the most memorable whip from the terrace of the proud is a depiction of the Emperor Trajan, riding upon his stately horse, surrounded by banners adorned with eagles, a "poor widow to his bridle clung."[39] She begs him to avenge her son's death, and Trajan first resists but then, moved to mercy by her surreptitious plea, promises that justice will be fulfilled for her before he leaves his office. The proud contemplate epic acts of humility as correctives to their earthly corruption. Metanoia is not achieved merely by penance, but by meditation upon virtue manifest. Importantly, virtue is here incarnated without Pollyannaish piety (Trajan's good deed comes only after his knot of indifference and pride is untangled). That "pious trash" that O'Connor declaims could never incite authentic purgation— not in the poor souls of Purgatory, and certainly not in the reader.

Later, in Canto XX, the covetous Hugh Capet explains the corollary of the "whip"—the "bridle." In the terrace of the covetous, these "bridles" consist of enumerated examples of cupidity. Pygmalion's gold-thirsty murder of his brother-in-law Sichaeus; Midas, whose granted wish to be able to turn everything to gold turns tragic when as a result all of his food becomes inedible so that he has to beg to be rid of this "gift"; Marcus Licinius Crassus, nicknamed "the Rich," once triumvir along-side Pompey and Caesar who, known for his cupidity, had molten gold poured down his throat: The covetous behold these bridles as aids to their conversion. Historical chronicle is interspersed with classical myth and Scripture both canonized and Apocrypha—all told through Dante's pen, and all enframed in the Catholic cosmos. Without chiseling out a mite of its greatness, an honest assessment forces us to see that these examples of sinfulness and virtue, amenable to conversion as they are, are so largely because they are woven into Dante's explicitly theological and moral drama of the soul. If he cannot be charged with unduly giving us a "nation of saints," he does not necessarily help us reckon with liter-ary depictions of sinfulness (and saintliness) unhinged from the ordered afterlife of *The Divine Comedy*.

CONCLUSION: CULTIVATING THE CATHOLIC —AND CATHOLIC—VINEYARD OF LITERATURE

Again, the greatness of Newman's formulation lies in its universal-ity. Regardless of the work—whether we are reading Homer's *Odyssey*, Joyce's *Ulysses* or David Foster Wallace's *Infinite Jest*—Newman insists that the Catholic University can "do for Literature in one way what she does for Science in another; each has its imperfection, and she has her remedy for each. She fears no knowledge, but she purifies all; she represses no element of our nature, but cultivates the whole."[40]

Whereas science is methodical, logical and grave, literature "declaims and insinuates; it is multiform and versatile; it persuades instead of convincing, it seduces, it carries captive; it appeals to the sense of honour, or to the imagination." Here Newman asserts that, in a teleological sense, the study of literature must aim toward a *purification* and a *remedy*. Still, although he defines the qualities specific to literary form—it persuades, it seduces, it is multiform and versatile—he leaves much work to be done in terms of *how* the Catholic University is to achieve this purification. In Pope John Paul II's *Letter to Artists*, Pope Emeritus Benedict XVI's *Address to Artists* and Dana Gioia's *The Catholic Writer Today*, we find a common insistence that literature infused with a Catholic vision contains distinct characteristics such as the dramatization of (at least some) suffering as redemptive and a conscious dramatization of the natural world's sacramental character.

Still, a Catholic Studies approach to literature needs to be intrinsically universal, and thus study of explicitly Catholic works should comprise but one part of a broader curriculum. In other words, I agree with Jared Staudt's adherence to Christopher Dawson's "study of Christian culture" as "the missing link which ... is essential to supply if the tradition of Western education and Western culture is to survive, for it is only through this study that we can understand how Western culture came to exist and what are the essential values for which it stands," but I do not think that Christian culture must be its sole object of study.[41] In brief, I recommend four modes of teaching literature. Catholic Studies programs may do well to turn primarily to number two:

1. Study of ancient Greek and Roman texts in order to obtain a greater understanding of natural law as it chastens man in rebellion as his story unfolds outside of a direct encounter with Christian revelation, and, in order to, using Christian metaphors, come to behold the truths contained in ancient literature according to the light of Christ.

2. Study of literature that is intrinsically Catholic. This can be undertaken through an examination of the presence of metanoia in great literary texts, through an examination of the way in which writers dramatize the workings of grace upon nature.

3. Study of the persistence, often in traces or in veiled form, of Catholic ideas, images and tradition, in purportedly modern, postmodern or humanistic texts; additionally, texts grappling with faith within an increasingly secularized literary canon.

4. Study of literature as the study of human nature, of man often in rebellion, in order to mediate the reality of sin and human nature to students in a manner that will help countenance real sin with learned virtue.

Notes

[1] *Further Letters of Gerard Manley Hopkins, Including His Correspondence with Coventry Patmore*, ed. Claude Colleer Abbot (London: Oxford University Press, 1956), 63-64.

[2] John Henry Newman, *An Essay on the Development of Christian Doctrine* (Notre Dame: University of Notre Dame Press, 1989), 36.

[3] Ibid., 40.

[4] A poem that would permeate the mind and heart of that early-20th-century convert to Roman Catholicism: Dorothy Day.

[5] *The Letters and Diaries of John Henry Newman*, ed. Charles Stephen Dessain, et al. (London: Nelson, 1961-72; Oxford: Clarendon Press, 1973), xxii, 289. Hereafter cited as LD.

[6] Gerard Manley Hopkins, "Carrion Comfort," *Poems and Prose* (New York: Penguin, 1963), 60-61.

[7] John Henry Newman, *Idea of a University*, September 2001. http://www.newmanreader.org/works/idea/.

[8] Ibid.

[9] Pope Benedict XVI, "Address to the Participants in the Meeting with Artists," November 21, 2009, Libreria Editrice Vaticana, 2009, http://w2.vatican.va/content/benedict-xvi/en/speeches/2009/november/documents/hf_ben-xvi_spe_20091121_artisti.html.

[10] Ibid.

[11] Ibid.

[12] "The *Via Pulchritudinis*, Privileged Pathway for Evangelisation and Dialogue," Pontifical Council for Culture, March 28, 2006, http://www.vatican.va/roman_curia/pontifical_councils/cultr/documents/ rc_pc_cultr_doc_20060327_plenary-assembly_final-document_en.html.

[13] *Polysemy: Flexible Patterns of Meaning in Mind and Language*, eds. Brigitte Nerlich et al. (Berlin: Walter de Gruyter), 59.

[14] Eco, Umberto, "History and Historiography of Semiotics," *A Handbook on the Sign-Theoretic Foundations of Nature and Culture* (New York: Walter de Gruyter, 1996), 741.

[15] Augustine, *Confessions,* trans. Henry Chadwick (Oxford: Oxford University Press, 2009), 33.

[16] Aristotle, *Poetics,* trans. S.H. Butcher, 2009. http://classics.mit.edu/Aristotle/poetics.html.

[17] John Henry Newman, *The Idea of a University.*

[18] Ibid.

[19] Ibid.

[20] Ibid.

[21] Ibid.

[22] Friedrich Nietzsche, *Beyond Good and Evil: Prelude to a Philosophy of the Future,* trans. Walter Kauffman (New York: Vintage, 1989), 88.

[23] Newman, *The Idea of a University.*

[24] Ibid.

[25] Ibid.

[26] Flannery O'Connor, *Mystery and Manners,* ed. Robert Fitzgerald (New York: Farrar, Straus, and Giroux, 1969), 149.

[27] Ibid., 147.

[28] Evelyn Waugh, *Brideshead Revisited* (New York, Back Bay Books, 2012), 402.

[29] Jacques Maritain, *Art and Scholasticism,* trans. Joseph W. Evans (New York: Charles Scribner's Sons, 1962), 222.

[30] Ibid., 223.

[31] Newman, *The Idea of a University.*

[32] Ibid.

[33] Ibid.

[34] Ibid.

[35] Ibid.

[36] Thomas Hobbes, *The Leviathan* (New York: Penguin, 1982), 160.

[37] Ibid.

[38] Dante, *Purgatory,* trans. Dorothy Sayers (New York: Penguin, 1955), X, 38-39.

[39] Ibid. X, 77.

[40] Newman, *The Idea of a University.*

[41] Christopher Dawson, *The Crisis of Western Education* (Washington, DC: The Catholic University of America Press, 2010), 103.

9

Catholic Studies and the Science of Culture

Joseph T. Stuart

The academic integrity of Catholic Studies has been attacked by some scholars. Theologian John Cavadini of Notre Dame, for instance, says it lacks a clear object of knowledge. He argues that the object of Catholic Studies must be one of two things: either Catholicism as a cultural artifact or divine revelation. He worries that either of these conclusions will call it into question: "If it is the former, it has no way ultimately of avoiding secularization, as it is, at least formally, the study of a cultural object and has no essential methodological distinction from Religious Studies or any other Area Studies discipline. If it is the latter, it is Theology without the name" and will exist in a competitive relationship to that field. Catholic Studies has no distinct object of knowledge and so cannot be extended to the doctoral level. Therefore, it is not a real discipline and cannot be a platform for long-term renewal generating an intellectual culture of depth.[1]

I disagree. As Don Briel, Jonathan Reyes and Michael Naughton outline in their essays, not only is Catholic Studies a forum within a university for engaging questions of institutional identity, the nature of education, the possibilities of student life and the professions, I argue that it is also an academic field (though not a single discipline with only one formal object) with a clearly defined material object of knowledge: Christian culture. Cavadini presents a false dichotomy, for Catholic Studies must examine Catholicism in its cultural artifacts *and* in relation to divine revelation together, as an integrated whole that is termed "Christian culture." The English historian of culture Christopher Dawson, whose writings have profoundly shaped the development of Catholic Studies programs, wrote: "As the Church is the extension of the Incarnation, so Christian culture is the embodiment of Christianity in social institutions and patterns of life and behavior."[2] This incarnation of faith in institutions and patterns of life and behavior—that is, the leavening process of Christianity in culture – is the epicenter of Catholic Studies.

To study this object, Dawson says that there are three levels of inquiry necessary: the Christian way of life (a field shared with the theologians), the pre-existing or co-existing forms of non-Christian cultures (fields shared with the historians and anthropologists) and the interaction of the two, which is the field of study specific to the student of Christian culture. Practicing Catholic Studies does not mean only thinking about "Catholic" things; nor does it mean striving for encyclopedic knowledge of the artifacts of Christian culture or mastering the Great Books. Rather, it is predicated on the sociological and epistemological link between religion and culture: One cannot understand a culture without understanding how its religion (its highest allegiances) has shaped its formation. This is why the study of culture requires theology and philosophy in combination with the social sciences. Thus, one can practice Catholic Studies by studying the formation of culture "from its spiritual and theological roots, through its organic historical growth to its cultural fruits. It is this organic relation between theology, history and culture which provides the integrative principle in Catholic higher education," Dawson writes, not theology alone, which Cavadini insists is the case.[3]

The study of Christian culture obviously involves the study of *culture*, and my argument is that there is a science of culture essential to the practice of Catholic Studies. I do not claim that Catholic Studies is the same thing as the science of culture—hence my title "Catholic Studies *and* the Science of Culture"—for culture belongs to the order of nature as a human construct and Catholic Studies must study this human construct in relation to the Christian faith that is transcendent to, even if enshrined in, culture. But such a science is indispensable, I will argue, for it to carry out its mission of examining the interaction of Christianity and culture. Others may respond to Cavadini's challenge by focusing specifically on the integration of Christianity and culture from a theological or philosophical point of view; my contribution will be to examine Catholic Studies from the point of view of the science of culture that makes the study of such an integration possible.

By "science" I mean the classical sense of an ordered body of knowledge of causes that make something intelligible (in this case, culture). Culture is so complex, however, that no single formal object is sufficient to understand it, though scholars have tried to reduce it to such. Since the 19th century the social sciences have monopolized the scientific study of culture. I argue that this empirical, socio-historic tradition of studying culture cannot fully account for the complex reality of it. The authentic science of culture that serves as an indispensable foundation of Catholic Studies must be broadened to include the humanistic (contemplative) perspective on culture too. In this view, people are more or less "cultured" according to a hierarchy of spiritual and intellectual values, whereas in the socio-historic view all people are equally "cultured." Studying Christian culture according to the socio-historic and humanistic culture-study traditions *together* illuminates this object much more truly. This dual method reveals some of the methods, limits and goals of Catholic Studies that can serve as reference points in hiring decisions and faculty development programs for future professors of Catholic Studies. It also brings clarity to the dual usage of the word "culture" according to its socio-historic and humanistic senses in major documents of the Catholic Church on education and the modern world.[4]

The socio-historic and humanistic traditions are not exclusive categories imposed on the word "culture" by me. They will be treated separately here, but they overlap. They are interweaving strands in the historical meanings of "culture" revealed in its etymology. One of the Latin roots of culture is *cultus* or "worship," so the connection of the word to the practice of religion occurred early. The other Latin root of culture means "tending" or "cultivating," so the idea of culture really rests on a metaphor: the tending of natural growth. Culture is not a forest growing up naturally; rather, it is artificial because human minds and spirits reshape nature according to its possibilities. This distinction between nature and culture is common to many human societies, such as the Yanomamo, a large tribe of tropical South America: The things of their village and garden are "of the village" (culture) and all other things are "of the forest" (nature). The village is made of natural things (trees, leaves), but they become cultural through the transformation of human effort. Romano Guardini thought that in the modern world these roots of culture in nature should not be cut off. The integrity of a culture weakens the further people are removed from nature by technology, abstraction and artificiality. However that may be, the idea of tending natural growth was applied to the human mind, so that by the 17th century "culture" (in English) referred to the improvement and refinement of the mind, manners and faculties of the person by education and training.[5]

This humanistic view of culture was developed in important ways in the 19th century English-speaking world with Matthew Arnold's 1869 book *Culture and Anarchy* and Edward Tylor's 1871 book *Primitive Culture*. Both men reoriented a humanistic view of culture as the cultivation of the mind and soul of individuals to encompass society as a whole. Nevertheless, these works popularized two different views of culture. Tylor's proto-socio-historic view focused on culture as a common way of life, on those learned characteristics that people already have (a descriptive view of culture). Arnold's humanistic view of culture focused on those learned intellectual qualities that people *should* have, toward which they need to strive to better themselves and their society (a prescriptive view of culture). These two different extensions of the humanistic tradition responded to a common problem: the growing individualism of industrial English society and the need to comprehend the social order as a whole.[6]

In order to teach effectively, the Catholic Studies professor must at least attempt to answer questions about culture from both points of view: not only about how religion has shaped exotic cultures remote in time and place, but also about some ways it *should* shape our own in the present; not only about what kinds of architectural styles have dominated the American Catholic landscape over the past 40 years, but about some of the principles that *should* inform a humane architecture today; not only about how Catholics have viewed social problems in different times and places, but about how they *should* view some of them here and now. In my experience, it is the attempt to join these descriptive and prescriptive approaches to culture that creates the energy and the excitement of Catholic Studies. Teachers and students examine not just facts but what they mean and how one should live in response to that meaning. These dual sets of questions both seek to integrate two kinds of reasoning: *ratio*, the active observation and empirical analysis of an object, and *intellectus*, the pure, receptive contemplation of an object from the inside, so to speak.[7] These dual sets of descriptive and prescriptive questions about culture are the basis of the science of culture I propose in this essay that integrates the socio-historic and humanistic traditions.

CULTURE: THE SOCIO-HISTORIC ACCOUNT

As noted above, a new way of thinking about culture arose in the late 19th century, and the young discipline of anthropology can take much of the credit for this. Edward Tylor, one of the pioneers of this new way, was born in London in 1832 to a wealthy Quaker family that owned a brass factory. He traveled in Mexico and Central America and later wrote the book *Primitive Culture*. His definition of culture as a "complex whole" would be one of his most enduring contributions to the field, so that one studies the "knowledge, belief, art, morals, law, custom and any other capabilities and habits acquired by man as a member of society" together.[8] This powerful, synthetic insight encouraged the rise of an empirical science of culture in the 20th century that created fields such as cultural studies, *Kulturwissenschaft*, and cultural history.

However, among some anthropologists and historians today, the idea of culture as a synthetic concept seems passé because it imposes categories of meaning on others and it may not be possible to study "cultural wholes" without making false assumptions about cultural homogeneity. "Culture" is criticized as emphasizing too much the unity of a people, and neglecting diversity, ambiguity and relationships of power in human life. In fact, the idea of power, some suggest, should take culture's place in anthropology. Rather than make generalizations about such and such a "culture," some define culture narrowly as the human ability to conceptualize the world and communicate those conceptions symbolically. Due to these recent ideas, one could question whether "Christian culture" even exists at all as a thing in itself.[9]

However, other social scientists today define culture broadly as "the whole way of life of some group of people," and it is this broad approach that is defined as the socio-historic view of culture in this essay. It is still accepted by many anthropologists.[10] One prominent anthropologist, the late Eric Wolf, wrote that this concept of culture remains serviceable today because "it is precisely the shapeless, all-encompassing quality of the concept that allows us to draw together...material relations to the world, social organization, and configurations of ideas. Using 'culture,' therefore, we can bring together what might otherwise be kept sepa-rate."[11] *Bringing together what might otherwise be kept separate* is a central function of the idea of culture in anthropology as it continues to be prac-ticed and taught today. In this sense, "Christian culture" as a social way of life animated by Christian faith has existed in the past and does exist now just as much as Islamic culture or Yanomamo culture or any other common way of life of a people exists that one can study. The continued confidence in culture—in spite of the limitations of the concept—at the undergraduate and professional levels of the social sciences helps main-tain a living connection between them and Catholic Studies.

While Tylor's definition of culture as a "complex whole" has endured to the present day, by the early 20th century uncertain anthropologists won-dered what the science of anthropology should look like. Should it study general laws of development as Tylor did? Or should it emphasize detailed analysis of empirical facts? Should it focus on the universal or the partic-ular? Tylor neglected fieldwork and, influenced by the theory of evolution, he posited a universal culture that progressed according to a fixed law of stages. According to this view, one could rank societies according to their level of cultural development. For him, reasoning toward general laws demonstrated proper scientific method in anthropology as Darwin had shown in biology. But later anthropologists rejected this approach under the influence of a different scientific ideal that came from Germany.

This alternative scientific ideal rejected universal laws in the study of particular, unique cultures—plural. The 18th century German thinker Johan Gottfried Herder spoke of "cultures" in reference to the unique collective *Volk*, or organic people of a particular place united in language, institutions, arts and literature. A Volk possessed its own, unique culture, and all were equal before God. German historiography picked up this idea of the Volk as a dynamic whole and made it a central object of study.[12] This focus unleashed a wave of scholarly activity in historicism, a movement that essentially created the modern discipline of history in Germany. Historicism affirmed the possibility of real understanding of the past and that all phenomena of past life "had to be grasped in terms of unique entities (such as persons, cultures, or nations)."[13] Cultures should be interpreted in their own terms and not judged by other cultures or outside, abstract ideals—as the French had attempted to impose on German people under Napoleon. The unfolding of cultures was totally unique and possessed no universal aim.

Anthropologists rejected Tylor's idea of studying the universal development of culture according to the law of stages as a false universalism, and favored the German approach of studying unique cultures on their own terms. This happened in early-20th century American anthropology through the German transplant Franz Boas, who had been influenced by historicism in his studies back home. The universal "culture" of Tylor became plural as Boas spoke of *cultures*. One had to approach the development of culture historically and sociologically. In other words, both diachronic and synchronic perspectives needed to inform the science of culture Boas proposed. He contributed three major ideas to modern anthropology. The first was historical particularism, which meant that cultures developed along their own unique paths depending on the historical influences that affected them, not according to predetermined progressive movement, as Tylor had argued. Second, Boas and his students showed that cultures must be encountered directly by anthropologists through fieldwork. Third, cultures should be understood on their own terms without judgment by external standards (cultural relativism).[14]

These principles have served the socio-historic study of culture well ever since. Through the books of Boas' students Alfred Kroeber, Clark Wissler and R.H. Lowie, American anthropology influenced Christopher Dawson during the 1920s, and, in turn, Catholic Studies programs later in the 20th century. For example, in their study of particular Christian cultures, Catholic Studies students realize that no historic Christian culture is absolute or independent of influences from non-Christian cultures (historical particularism); they encounter actual Christian cultures ("fieldwork") through Rome programs, mission trips, tours, student activities on campus, and, above all, through the liturgy and traditional forms of Christian prayer (see Jared Staudt's essay on poetic knowledge); and they come to realize that there have been many Christian cultures in the ages of the Church, all equal before God in some sense, and that today's secular culture is not absolute but relative in that there are and have been other ways of living and thinking (cultural relativism). This realization of the relativity and historicity of their world takes considerable study and imagination for students to come to, Dawson remarks, yet it can free them to appreciate other ways of Christian life in past and present.[15]

But if one emphasizes the particular and the unique, as Boas did, how can one evaluate facts according to a larger meaning? If cultural relativism is a necessary methodological principle in the study of cultures, how can one account for the fact that, for people within cultures, truth, goodness and beauty really matter in an ultimate sense? Some anthropologists wonder whether, for instance, it is logically possible to subscribe to both the idea of the relativity of culture and to that of universal human rights.[16] These are pressing questions if the concept of culture is to be serviceable in Catholic Studies.

For social scientists and Catholic Studies practitioners, one way around the problem of relativism lies in Tylor's other legacy to anthropology: his confidence in scientific (empirical) methods and reasoning discovering the laws of nature that govern human life. After all, the "history of mankind is part and parcel of the history of nature," and human life is governed by laws as definite as those that rule the motion of waves and the growth of plants and animals, Tylor wrote. He specifically compared the development of a culture with that of a plant or animal species, an observation that Christopher Dawson made too when he pointed out that the development of culture does indeed have a considerable analogy to the development of a species in Darwinian terms. A new species arises in response to its environment and not according to Tylor's universal law of evolution, just as a human culture results from the intimate communion between a people and the region in which and by which they live, as well as from influences of other peoples.[17] Geography, geology, climatology, mineralogy, agriculture, economics and urban design all have a place in the study of actual cultures that have existed and do exist. The laws of nature studied in these fields introduce an authentically universal perspective on culture, for at the root of any culture lies its relations to its environment. These relations are not "culturally relative."

Nevertheless, the problem of cultural relativism returns as one reaches the limits of an empirical understanding of the human person. Ethnographic fieldwork has demonstrated the tremendous variation in marriage and family arrangements around the world, for example, but to the burning questions in our contemporary culture of "What is marriage? What *should* marriage be?" this empirical research cannot yield answers. Our questions have non-empirical dimensions to them. The postmodern movement has noted the limits of empiricism too, alerting contemporary anthropologists of their own cultural background as an influence on their assumptions and fieldwork. One must now use the words "objective" and "scientific" with caution.[18] The human factor is always at work such that however much culture is molded by environmental conditions, it is never the mere passive result of material forces. Human action, creativity and reason introduce the real possibility of cultural interaction and progressive development.[19]

This is where the humanistic tradition of culture-study enters the stage, and a quotation from Socrates is helpful in responding to the problem of relativism: "When Socrates was asked to which [country] he belongs, he would say, 'To the world,' for he thought that he was an inhabitant and citizen of the whole world."[20] Socrates did not merely belong to one city or one culture. He could, in some way, transcend them. Through reason he could partake of a universal human conversation and could communicate to others in distant times and places. In a limited way he could enjoy genuine contact with *being* that all human beings, of whatever culture, have access to. While cultural relativity is a true insight into human life, relativism can confuse *how* knowledge is acquired with the validity of that knowledge.[21] Because Socrates arose in Greek culture, does this mean his ideas are only true for that culture? No. There *can* be a basis of judgment about human reality discoverable through the moral imagination and the *intellectus* of reason.[22] There can be an "ought," a prescriptive understanding of how we should live, and an urgency about preserving and handing on the permanent things of a culture. In this way the work of Socrates himself has been handed down to today by Romans, Christians, Muslims and many others.

CULTURE: THE HUMANISTIC ACCOUNT

While I distinguish in this essay between the socio-historic and humanistic traditions of culture-study, they often overlap—as in the Society for Humanistic Anthropology, founded in 1974, which recognizes that "professional inquiry takes place in a context of human value" and is concerned with the "personal, ethical, and political choices facing humans." This is a recognition that empirical study cannot be completely cut off from universal values. In addition, its journal publishes a variety of genres, including fiction, an acknowledgment that the creativity and interpretation of anthropologists themselves enter into their research. Anthropologist Clifford Geertz famously showed this by his "dramatistic approach" to cultural artifacts as texts. Thus, humanistic anthropology blends both traditions to some degree.[23]

With this overlap in mind, and in contrast to the socio-historic view of culture as a complex, whole way of life of a particular people, the humanistic tradition has much to say about culture as the sphere of true values that humanize people. Matthew Arnold's 1869 book *Culture and Anarchy* was a milestone in this tradition. He castigated religious people of his day for their privatization of religion and neglect of the wider culture. Arnold treated culture itself as a kind of replacement for religion. He argued that those with culture should redeem English society by conveying it to all people through education. He defined culture as the pursuit of intellectual and moral perfection for the good of individuals and society. Culture is the holistic, inner perfection of our humanity as distinguished from animality. Arnold placed culture in opposition to the "mechanical" world of the new industrial age, the sphere of the workaday utilitarian values that by themselves reduce a person's humanity. His conception of culture sought to humanize people, to "make the best that has been thought and known in the world current everywhere; to make all men live in an atmosphere of sweetness and light... ."[24] Arnold's view of culture as "the best that has been thought and known" soon took on a more specific meaning in the early 20th century in reference to the works of intellectual and artistic activity. Culture came to refer to music, literature, painting, sculpture, theater and film, and it retains this derivative meaning today for many people, as a description of the "cultured person."[25]

In the mid 20th century, the philosopher Josef Pieper took up Arnold's urgency in defending humanistic culture from the mechanical and utilitarian values of the modern world. Pieper defines culture as those human spiritual and intellectual gifts and qualities not immediately useful to wants and needs. In *Leisure the Basis of Culture* (1952), he argues that culture depends on leisure for its existence and leisure in turn depends on *cultus*, divine worship. This is because in divine worship a definite space of time is withdrawn from working hours. So, Christianity forbids servile work on Sundays. It does so not as a negation of work but as an affirmation of all that transcends the world of work and directs it toward higher ends, such as works of mercy or building Gothic cathedrals. Alexis de Tocqueville illuminates this insight of Pieper's by remarking that in ages of faith the final end of life is in the next world, serving as an immovable object or organizing principle for social activity. People suppress passing desires in pursuit of higher objects, and when these same people engage in affairs of this world, the same habits mark their conduct. But as the light of faith dims, the range of higher objects shrinks. Pieper argues that Sunday worship of God raises our sights and reserves time and space from the world of work, opening up fertile ground for human activity as varied as philosophical thought, music and visiting the sick. He defines leisure not as relaxation or entertainment, but as the contemplative affirmation of creation and the Creator. Resting in this peaceful affirmation of being preserves freedom and that "undiminished humanity which views the world as a whole." This is why Pieper argues that leisure, rightly understood, really is the basis of culture understood in this second, humanistic sense.[26]

At this point, the historian and the anthropologist might object that Pieper has trespassed on their empirical study of culture with a much too spiritual and intellectual approach to culture that has little to do with real life. Yet perhaps what Pieper has to say offers profound insight into real life. Perhaps Pieper's words will strike a chord with the student who has experienced emotional isolation because of a distant, workaholic father, who is too caught up in the values of contemporary culture to "waste" time in leisure with him or her, passing on a cultural inheritance that could make life worth living. Maybe Pieper can help the scholar trying to understand the religious prohibitions of another people and the human sense of the sacred. Pieper is coming at culture from another direction than the historian and the anthropologist: He is a participant living within a cultural tradition communicating universal principles of supreme value for our humanity. This is his claim.

In fact, Pieper has tapped into the humanistic tradition of understanding culture in largely intellectual, spiritual and creative terms—from the "inside," so to speak, and as something worth defending because it humanizes us. This is culture as the peaceful and lush public park one steps into off the busy street in order to reflect and pray, wandering among the elm trees and purple thyme, enjoying time away from *doing* to simply *be* with nature, literature or God. One can "waste" time in contemplative reflections on truth that so often bear fruit in creative activity through which one feels more human. This, too, is culture.

Intellectual life can only thrive within a humanistic culture rooted in leisure. Contemplative realization of the goodness of an end gives direction and meaning to empirical research. In fact, humanistic culture is necessary to support those values that make the socio-historic study of culture possible. Only people of humanistic culture would even *want* to spend years in pursuit of disinterested study of the cultures of *other* people because such an effort is ultimately based on the desire to "know thyself." It is also grounded in the contemplative realization of the goodness of knowing something for its own sake. Historians and anthropologists ought to take a keen interest in such a humanistic view of culture for the sake of their own disciplines, if nothing else.

Another objection historians and anthropologists might have to this humanistic view of culture is the dangerous implication of judgmental universalism that it contains. Matthew Arnold wrote of making the best known *everywhere* and to make *all* men live in an atmosphere of "sweetness and light." This is just another example of 19th century British imperialist ambitions, they might say. The study of culture does not lead to universal truths but only to understanding of particular cultures.

Surely humanistic culture has been used as a weapon against others, and the chastened humanist is grateful for this warning. Also, the universalism of the humanistic account of culture can be overemphasized. This is the danger of idealism. The legitimate materialism of the socio-historic view of culture is a counterweight to this weakness of the humanistic account.

This objection against universalism raises an important issue in the study of culture. Is culture particular or universal? Should it be studied empirically or contemplatively? Boas would favor the former, respectively, and Pieper the latter. Yet, as Raymond Williams notes in his book *Keywords: A Vocabulary of Culture and Society*, the still active and complex history of the word "culture" belies any attempt to nail down one "true" meaning of the word. In fact, it is the range and overlap of the humanistic and the socio-historic meanings that is significant. He writes:

> The complex of senses indicates a complex argument about the relations between general human development and a particular way of life, and between both and the works and practices of art and intelligence. Within this complex argument there are fundamentally opposed as well as effectively overlapping positions; there are also, understandably, many unresolved questions and confused answers. But these arguments and questions cannot be resolved by reducing the complexity of actual usage.[27]

Williams means here that the relation between universal values and particular cultures is so complex that multiple traditions of thinking about culture have developed. We need both the socio-historic and the humanistic perspectives because culture is not only something outside us that is empirically observable but also *in us* and worth defending. The universal element in the scientific study of culture cannot be reduced to the laws of nature or an abstract principle of progress. Nor can the view that culture is relative and local fully express it.

Perhaps "universal" and "particular" present a false dichotomy. They can both serve as a path to the truth of things, one through the unchanging universal and one through the constantly shifting particulars of time. One can approach truth through the universally true mathematical equation, for example, *and* through the particulars of a poem, such as William Blake's "Auguries of Innocence," in which one can "see a World in a Grain of Sand."[28] There is what Dawson calls the "intuition of pure being" that lies at the heart of every culture.[29] The human mind in any time and place can correspond to reality. The truths of reality can pass down from generation to generation by tradition, enshrined in the institutions, customs, morals and habits of the particular culture. Culture really can be a "bearer of human and divine truths."[30] These truths can be transferred from culture to culture through contact by trade, education or war. Just because knowledge is gained in particular times and places does not mean it is only applicable in those historically limited instances. Its spread from one culture to another does not necessarily imply cultural imperialism. The current popularity of Western classical music in China testifies to the humanistic view of culture that certain traditions can be refined and enriched through their encounter with other cultures.[31]

Conclusion: Implications for Catholic Studies

Catholic Studies is not a special kind of theology, a catechetical program, a cultural studies program or a Great Books program. It is an integrated, liberal arts-based education rooted in the study of Christian culture, a cultural object that has become obscured by the separation of specialized disciplines in a modern, secular academia. Just as the Oxford undergraduate *Literae Humaniores* is an interdisciplinary degree focused on the classical cultures of Greece and Rome, Catholic Studies is an interdisciplinary study of Christian culture. It is decisively different than contemporary fields such as *Literae Humaniores* or cultural studies because it rests on a science of culture that embraces both the socio-historic and humanistic traditions in its study of Catholicism as artifact and as revelation together in an integrated whole. Its material object is stable—Christian culture—but its formal object shifts depending on the expertise of the professor and the questions asked. The complex nature of the object demands this, as we have seen through the etymology of the word "culture" and the two traditions of culture-study. Some will approach Christian culture from the point of view of theology or philosophy, some from the point of view of history and others from that of literature. The key, however, to a successful Catholic Studies course is to focus on one while keeping the others in mind so as not to reduce culture to theology, to philosophy, to history or to literature. These fields have their own legitimate autonomy, and Catholic Studies professors advance the knowledge and teaching of Christian culture from within their particular disciplines. They must avoid blurring boundaries and sacrificing methodological rigor by recognizing the limits of disciplines in light of the whole view of culture sketched here.

How can this be done on a practical level? As an historian, I strive to keep both traditions of culture-study in front of my students in the course "Catholicism and America." This is a junior-level history class cross-listed in Catholic Studies offered every other year at the University of Mary. It surveys the interaction of American culture and Catholic culture from colonial times to the present. These two traditions meet in institutions such as families, parishes, schools and voluntary associations as the places where people try to work out in their daily lives what it means to be both American and Catholic. Students read primary sources, including letters and speeches and selections from important commentators on America such as Alexis de Tocqueville and Orestes Brownson. They also read key secondary texts in the field such as those by James O'Toole and John McGreevy.[32] They seek to answer empirical questions: "How did Catholics adopt Protestant/American patterns of church governance? Why did many Irish Catholics respond differently to the Prohibition movement than many German Catholics?" Questions like these lead to empirical research and empirical answers, as historical questions in the social science tradition should.

But what makes this class something other than just a history class is that in addition to empirical questions, students also examine historically situated principled questions like: "How are American Catholic views on social justice today influenced by the wider American culture? What are some of the difficulties and opportunities within American culture for the reception of the Gospel?" These are not simply empirical but principled questions that rely on taking Catholic theology, philosophy and the American cultural environment seriously, with an eye to the present. These are questions that spring from a concern for how we should live now as Catholics and cultural protagonists. Students read, for example, two chapters from Francis Cardinal George's *The Difference God Makes,* which examine socio-historic and humanistic views of American culture in the light of Christian faith.[33] The combination of descriptive, empirical questions with prescriptive, principled ones is a central characteristic of this Catholic Studies course in history, recalling an older tradition of humanistic history before the discipline came to be regarded as an empirical social science in the early 20th century, for better and for worse.

The science of culture that combines socio-historic and humanistic culture-study traditions with both empirical and principled questions helps many of the students in my course Catholicism and America, even non-Catholic ones, connect personally with the material. It gives them insight into living responsibly in America today as Christians. This bond to the material at a deep level is a key factor, I have found, in student enthusiasm over this course and Catholic Studies in general. They learn to think about their culture with the tools of the Catholic intellectual tradition.[34] They begin to see ways to relate faith and ideas to the rest of life. They start linking classes to each other on the basis of underlying philosophical and theological principles, overcoming some of the fragmentation of knowledge according to methods and subjects. Students can work toward a synthesis of knowledge around real questions and problems that require interdisciplinary and integrated thinking rather than simply accumulating disconnected facts. This is made possible by the science of culture that combines the socio-historic and humanistic culture-study traditions, and that, along with theology and philosophy, forms the academic backbone of Catholic Studies.

NOTES

[1] John C. Cavadini, "Catholic Studies? A Cautionary Note," in *The Idea of the Catholic University,* ed. Kenneth D. Whitehead (Chicago: University of Scranton Press, 2009): 95, 96, 97.

[2] Christopher Dawson, *The Crisis of Western Education* (1961; Washington, DC: The Catholic University of America Press, 2010), 115.

[3] Ibid., 105-06, 116.

[4] *Gaudium et Spes,* ch. II "The Proper Development of Culture," §53, and *Ex Corde Ecclesiae,* footnote 16.

[5] *Oxford English Dictionary Online,* http://www.oed.com/ (accessed October 21, 2006),

senses 2, 3, and 4; Raymond Williams, *Culture & Society: 1780-1950* (1958; New York: Columbia University Press, 1983), 335; Romano Guardini, *Letters from Lake Como: Explorations in Technology and the Human Race* (1924-1925; Grand Rapids: William B. Eerdmans, 1994), 12, 17; Napoleon A. Chagnon, *Yanomamo*, 5th ed. (1968; USA: Wadsworth, 1997), 55.

[6] Peter Melville Logan, "On Culture: Edward B. Tylor's *Primitive Culture*, 1871," *BRANCH: Britain, Representation and Nineteenth-Century History*, http://www.branchcollective.org/?ps_articles=peter-logan-on-culture-edward-b-tylors-primitive-culture-1871; Peter Melville Logan, "On Culture: Matthew Arnold's *Culture and Anarchy*, 1869," *BRANCH: Britain, Representation and Nineteenth-Century History*, http://www.branchcollective.org/?ps_articles=peter-logan-on-culture-matthew-arnolds-culture-and-anarchy-1869; George W. Stocking, "Matthew Arnold, E.B. Tylor, and the Uses of Invention," *American Anthropologist* New Series, 65, no. 4 (Aug. 1963): 783-799.

[7] Romano Guardini, *Letters from Lake Como: Explorations in Technology and the Human Race*, 43; Josef Pieper, *Leisure the Basis of Culture* (San Francisco: Ignatius, 2009), 26, 28.

[8] Edward Tylor, *Primitive Culture*, 2 vols. (1871; New York: Harper & Row, 1958), vol. 1, 1.

[9] John Monaghan and Peter Just, *Social & Cultural Anthropology: A Very Short Introduction* (Oxford: Oxford University Press, 2000), 34, 48; Stanley R. Barrett, Sean Stokholm, and Jeanette Burke, "The Idea of Power and the Power of Ideas: A Review Essay," *American Anthropologist* 103, no. 2 (2001): 468, 477; Peter Burke, *What Is Cultural History?* (Cambridge: Polity, 2008), 25.

[10] Garrick Bailey and James Peoples, *Essentials of Cultural Anthropology*, 3rd ed. (Belmont, CA: Wadsworth Cengage Learning, 2014), 21-22.

[11] Barrett, Stokholm, and Burke, "The Idea of Power and the Power of Ideas: A Review Essay." Eric Wolf is quoted on p. 469 of this article, and the authors reference Wolf's *Envisioning Power: Ideologies of Dominance and Crisis* (Berkeley: University of California Press, 1999), 288.

[12] Ernst Breisach, *Historiograhy: Ancient, Medieval, and Modern*, 3rd ed. (Chicago: University of Chicago Press, 2007), 222-23.

[13] Ibid., 325.

[14] Bailey and Peoples, *Essentials of Cultural Anthropology*, 86; Franz Boas, "The Methods of Ethnology," *American Anthropologist* 22, no. 4 (October-December, 1920): 316, 317.

[15] Dawson, *The Crisis of Western Education*, 112.

[16] Monaghan and Just, *Social & Cultural Anthropology: A Very Short Introduction*, 52. For the reference to Kroeber, Wissler and Lowie, see the bibliography to Christopher Dawson, *Progress and Religion: An Historical Enquiry* (1929; Washington, DC: The Catholic University of America Press, 2001).

[17] Tylor, *Primitive Culture*, vols. 1, 2; Dawson, *Progress and Religion: An Historical Enquiry*, 51-53.

[18] Bailey and Peoples, *Essentials of Cultural Anthropology*, 94-95, 99.

[19] Dawson, *Progress and Religion: An Historical Enquiry*, 53, 55, 64.

[20] Quoted in Eric Brown's "Socrates the Cosmopolitan," *Stanford Agora: An Online Journal of Legal Perspectives* vol. 1:1 (2000), 74, http://agora.stanford.edu/agora/

libArticles/brown/brown.pdf (accessed August 7, 2014). Brown cites Cicero's *Tusculum Disputations*, 108.

21 David Hackett Fischer, *Historians' Fallacies* (New York: HarperPerennial, 1970), 181.

22 Russell Kirk, *Eliot and His Age: T.S. Eliot's Moral Imagination in the Twentieth Century* (New York: Random House, 1971), 47. Here Kirk describes the moral imagination as having connections to John Henry Newman's "illative sense" in chap. 9 of *The Grammar of Assent*. Kirk writes that the evidences of the moral imagination "may be fragmentary and irregular, but they are numerous; and, entering the mind over a long period of time, they may bring conviction. The moral imagination, embracing tradition, looks to theology and history and humane letters, especially, for evidences of human nature and of the permanent things."

23 Society for Humanistic Anthropology, "Welcome!," accessed December 29, 2014, http://www.aaanet.org/sections/sha/welcome/; Burke, *What Is Cultural History?*, 37-39.

24 Matthew Arnold, *Culture and Anarchy* (Cambridge: Cambridge University Press, 1935), 45, 47, 49-50, 69, quotation on 70.

25 Raymond Williams, *Keywords: A Vocabulary of Culture and Society* (London: Fontana/ Croom Helm, 1976), 80.

26 Alexis de Tocqueville, *Democracy in America*, 2 vols. (New York: Vintage Books, 1972), vol. 2, 149; Pieper, *Leisure the Basis of Culture*, 53.

27 Williams, *Keywords: A Vocabulary of Culture and Society*, 80-81.

28 William Blake, "Auguries of Innocence," Poetry Lovers Page, http://www. poetryloverspage.com/poets/blake/ to_see_world.html (accessed August 18, 2014).

29 Dawson, *Progress and Religion: An Historical Enquiry*, 76.

30 Dermot Quinn, "Christopher Dawson and Historical Imagination," *The Chesterton Review* XXVI, no. 4 (2000): 484.

31 Joseph Kahn and Daniel J. Wakin, "Western Classical Music, Made and Loved in China," *The New York Times*, April 2, 2007, http://www.nytimes.com/2007/04/02/ world/asia/02iht-china.html?pagewanted=all&_r=0 (accessed August 9, 2014).

32 Mark Massa and Catherine Osborne, eds., *American Catholic History: A Documentary Reader* (New York: New York University Press, 2008); Alexis de Tocqueville, *Democracy in America*, trans. by Henry Reeve (Ware: Wordsworth Classics, 1998); Orestes Brownson, *The American Republic: Its Constitution, Tendencies and Destiny* (Wilmington, DE: ISI Books, 2003); James O'Toole, *The Faithful: A History of Catholics in America* (Cambridge, MA: Belknap Press of Harvard University Press, 2008); John McGreevy, *Catholicism and American Freedom: A History* (New York: W.W. Norton, 2003).

33 Francis Cardinal George, *The Difference God Makes: A Catholic Vision of Faith, Communion, and Culture* (New York: Crossroad, 2009), chaps. 2 and 3.

34 Church in the 21st Century Center (Boston College), "The Catholic Intellectual Tradition: A Conversation at Boston College," July 2010, http://www.bc.edu/content/ dam/files/top/church21/pdf/cit.pdf (accessed August 8, 2014).

IO

A Roman View of American Catholicism: Thinking Hemispherically

PAUL G. MONSON

Shortly after Pope Benedict XVI's resignation, reporters asked Timothy Cardinal Dolan of New York whether he might emerge from the impending conclave as the first American pope. The jocular archbishop replied that any hopes for an "American" papacy intimated the smoking of a controlled substance rather than a firm grasp of reality.[1] The question, however, may not have been so absurd. An "American" cardinal did in fact step onto the Loggia, albeit as the Church's first *Latin* American pope. This observation is more than a cheeky triviality. Rather, it is magisterial, at least in the sense of Pope St. John Paul II's Post-Synodal Apostolic Exhortation, *Ecclesia in America*. In this largely forgotten papal document, the late pontiff audaciously speaks of "America" as a single, hemispheric "continent." He refuses to distinguish between two separate "Americas," but rather insists on thinking of "America" as a "single entity, by reason of...[its] shared Christian identity."[2] This hemispheric perspective, so counterintuitive and even caustic to many in the United States, frames the exhortation's map for the "new evangelization" in the New World at the dawn of a new millennium.

Nevertheless, this document is worth retrieving for more than its provocative definition of "America." For the astute historian, *Ecclesia in*

America is something of an ironic indictment, or put more poignantly, a gentle papal slap on the cheeks of Yankee Catholics. John Paul II signed the document on January 22, 1999, exactly 100 years *to the day* of Pope Leo XIII's blistering condemnation of "Americanism" in his encyclical *Testem benevolentiae*. This intentional, inescapable gesture continues to elude most scholarship on U.S. Catholicism, as it not only challenges the definition of "American Catholicism" but also interrupts a stubborn narrative of American exceptionalism among U.S. Catholics.[3]

The narrative goes something like this: A progressive contingent of 19th-century bishops, led by the indefatigable John Ireland of St. Paul, attempted, with great foresight, to accommodate Catholicism to American pluralism and modern values, only to be thwarted by Leo and his Teutonic minions. After decades of darkness and despair, the vindication of these "Americanists" arrived with Vatican II, especially through the contribution of John Courtney Murray in *Dignitatis humanae* and the Church's engagement of modernity in *Gaudium et spes*. Both conciliar documents testify to how the American experience informed the development of Catholic doctrine in the great "American Century." Here, however, this triumphalist narrative splits into two camps. Some idolize the Americanists as the first "liberal Catholics," challenging the Church to adapt to the spirit of the age rather than retreating to the "ghettos" of pre-conciliar Catholicism. Others celebrate the Americanists as sowing the seeds for later papal endorsements of American democratic capitalism in the face of godless socialism. The former bemoan *Veritatis splendor,* the latter demur to *Caritas in veritate.* These joint narratives of a so-called "Americanist tradition" continue to overshadow the character and thought of Catholicism in the United States, such that many Roman Catholics in this country view their faith from the perspective of Washington's beltway, New York's stock exchange or Hollywood's screen, but rarely from the perspective of Rome's apostolicity.

Addressing this enduring problem, this paper retrieves the insights of *Ecclesia in America* into what constitutes "American Catholicism," a project that is timely in light of both Francis' papacy and U.S. bishops' plight for immigration reform. I argue that a Catholic Studies Rome program, properly conceived, presents an indispensible key to shattering a myopic sense of "American exceptionalism" among Catholics in the United States. In support of this argument, this essay first asks: "Why Rome?" Answering this question, I adopt the three paths that John Paul outlines for his "American" audience in *Ecclesia in America*: the paths of conversion, communion and solidarity. I demonstrate how Rome, by virtue of its apostolic heritage, proffers the student an unparalleled, tangible grasp of each papal path. In Rome, the student witnesses three essential elements of Catholicism in a new light: the conversion of history, the communion of saints and the solidarity of pilgrims. Overall, this paper shows how rooting a student's understanding of Catholic conversion, communion and solidarity in Rome can fulfill the spirit of *Ecclesia in America* and inculcate a more hemispheric view of "American Catholicism."

WHY ROME?

Before proceeding down our three paths, let us begin with an obvious question: "Why *Rome*?" Why send students to another hemisphere to gain a hemispheric vision of Catholicism in the Americas? Is this idea not absurd? Would not Mexico City or Sao Paulo or Pope Francis' own Buenos Aires be more congenial to a "hemispheric" objective? Moreover, does not an appeal to Rome only perpetuate the Church's penchant for "Eurocentrism," oblivious to Christianity's rise in the "Global South"? The skeptical ecclesiologist might go one step further: Is this appeal to Rome little more than the return of ultramontanism from its cold conciliar grave? The skeptical parent, plagued by a student's debt, might enjoin a further question: How does study abroad benefit the study of Catholicism, which can be experienced at home through campus ministries, Newman centers or local parishes? If a student wants to *study* in Rome, there are plenty of academic venues, like John Cabot, or professional programs in art, politics or international business.

Indeed, the question of Rome cannot be answered apart from the question of what constitutes Catholic Studies. Despite a proliferation of competing models in U.S. higher education, Catholic Studies ultimately comes down to a reconciliation of the dichotomy between campus ministry and rigorous academics, between spiritual conversion and intellectual conversion, between faith and reason. The study of faith's impact on culture, divorced from the life of faith itself, becomes woefully impoverished. One must *experience* true catholicity to make sense of Catholicism, just as one must practice law to understand law, work abroad to understand international business or examine an original masterpiece in person to understand artistic technique and genius. Books only go so far. For John Henry Newman, the difference is between a noetic and a real apprehension of an object, between theory and things.[4] The study of Catholicism can begin with the theoretical; it can begin with cultural studies or great books. Yet to apprehend Catholicism fully, at least in Newman's epistemology, requires the experience of Catholicism itself. And Rome is the best primer, the best framework, the best lens for experiencing Catholicism, as Rome presents the student eye with three things not found in any other city in the West: the apostolic conversion of history; the transcultural and transtemporal nature of ecclesial communion; and the call for Christian solidarity with fellow pilgrims. Each experience corresponds to one of John Paul's poignant paths in *Ecclesia in America*, paths that escape most Yankee Catholics.

FIRST PATH: APOSTOLIC CONVERSION OF HISTORY

Let us begin by examining the first path for the student in Rome: the apostolic conversion of history. I, like every impatient adolescent, was incessantly informed that "Rome was not built in day," a vacuous adage for modern ears. And then, as a young adult, I arrived in Rome and realized something my parents did not intend. A visit to Rome unveils how this adage more aptly applies to Rome's Christian heritage than her ancient imperial ruins. In Rome the Christian transformation of history stares one in the face, in a way unparalleled by any city in North or South America. In Rome the stones and artwork are witnesses of conversion, such that one might call Rome a "sacrament" of conversion for the simple reason that it is not an ossified museum collection but rather a living city. This living sacrament communicates two essentials about conversion in Catholicism: Conversion operates within a diverse tradition, and it consists of an unresolved drama rather than a triumphal narrative.

Let us take the first lesson: conversion as operating in a diverse tradition. Rome's visual testimony of conversion offers more than a superficial juxtaposition of ancient temples and modern technology, a struggle between Roman monuments and Roman motorini. Rather, the judicious eye, the student's eye, learns to discern the convergence and melding of ages within the Church. The city testifies not only to faith transforming culture but also to culture nourishing faith. Pagan customs inform early Christian symbolism in the catacombs; Jewish ritual and the Roman basilica merge in liturgical architecture; exquisite Byzantine mosaics grace Baroque altars over ancient temples. Rome presents a cacophony of beauty that does what beauty, in the Platonic sense, is supposed to do: "shock" our complacency and reawaken us from our slumber.[5] The intersection of beauty and conversion comes to life in Rome's oldest basilicas, from Santa Maria in Trastevere to Santa Maria Maggiore to San Clemente, where the bewildered Yankee Catholic encounters a potpourri of styles and ages in architecture, art and liturgical arrangement. Catholic Studies embraces this organic assemblage as a moment of learning, such that the student comes to realize that pre- and post-conciliar fashions in American churches, be they neo-gothic chapels or Cold War cubes, are not paradigmatic for the Church's tradition. Rome's ecclesial art and architecture are witness not only to authentic Catholic diversity but also to continuity and unity within the tradition. The typical American tourist often misses this complementarity, dismissing any style that does not conform to personal tastes. It is precisely this meeting of faith and culture in Rome's churches that presents an unparalleled opportunity for the American student to grasp the complexity and diversity of the tradition, which, in the words of Newman, "changes...in order to remain the same."[6] Each age's appropriation of the faith manifests new expressions of Catholic conversion in history. No city in the Western hemisphere offers both the catacomb and the Caravaggio.

In a similar manner, the cacophony of Rome's aesthetic presents the student with insights into the nature of Christian conversion. The history of Christian conversion is not a folk tale but rather a gripping drama. Rome took centuries to build not because of the Roman siesta but rather because of the Roman rejection of the Gospel for a life of violence, greed, lust or treachery. Rome bears the mark of the papacy's development and records both its sin and salvation. The splendor of the Vatican is both masterpiece and scandal, as much a *maxima culpa* as a *felix culpa*. The back and forth of the Church's reform through the ages epitomizes Newman's insight into the nature of ecclesial development: There is good development and there is bad development, progress and regress. Development is not reducible to random evolution but rather the growth and refinement of an idea, and in Rome that idea is the apostolic nature of the conversion. Each age returns to the tombs of Peter and Paul, and each age bears marks of development and corruption. There are Borgias and there are Bergoglios, and the interplay of both in Rome's history, both ancient and modern, reminds the Catholic that he or she does not have the luxury of triumphalism. Rome's ongoing conversion to the apostles' proclamation of Christ reveals Catholicism's symphony of grace and sin, divine providence and human free will, faith and reason. The story of Christianity's baptism of culture is still being written, if for no other reason than that the baptized often rebel. Rome's famous Pantheon captures this reality, where both an icon of the Virgin and a sarcophagus of Vittorio Emanuele compete for attention, and Rome's gargantuan monument for the latter demonstrates how the worshiping of idols is anything but dead. The conversion of culture is slow and stubborn, more a labyrinth than a straight road. Rarely is conversion as simple as falling off a horse; usually it is the gradual transformation of culture that challenges and matures a nascent faith. Another poignant image of this process is the story of Christopher Dawson looking over the domes and ruins of Rome on Easter Day as he sat on the steps of the *Ara Coeli*, a church built over Caesar Augustus's altar to a prophesied "Son of God."[7] Dawson did not adopt the Catholic faith the next day, but his decision that day to pursue a history of culture eventually led him to the other side of the Tiber.

Yet even if the path of conversion is difficult to chart, it leads somewhere. In the words of *Ecclesia in America*, conversion "fosters new life." Conversion "leads to fraternal communion, because it enables us to understand that Christ is the head of the Church, his Mystical Body; it urges solidarity, because it makes us aware that whatever we do for others, especially for the poorest, we do for Christ himself."[8] These are the other two paths John Paul outlines for American Catholics. Thus we proceed to Rome's second experience awaiting the student: the communion of saints.

SECOND PATH: THE NATURE OF ECCLESIAL COMMUNION

If Rome's history manifests the path of conversion, then her collection of the faithful at St. Peter's exemplifies the path of communion. The square in front of St. Peter's, host to countless papal audiences, masses and canonizations, presents the American student with a tangible grasp of two "things" —in the Newmanian sense—that are at the heart of Catholic communion: the Church as transcultural and transtemporal. The first witnesses to Catholicism's ecclesiology of a visible church, the second to its ecclesiology of a communion of saints, past and present.

Let us begin with the first element of Catholic communion: its transcultural character. Catholicism, by its very definition, is not a church of a specific nation or culture. And by the same token, Catholicism is not a melting pot, precisely what Leo accused 19th-century "Americanism" of doing. The most successful missionaries in history have consistently been those who have taken the gospel to transform a culture without destroying its language, heritage and customs. Ironically, those very cultures that resisted the Americanists—the Germans, Italians and Poles—now, after decades of affluence, are often the ones confounded by the obstinacy of other immigrants—Latin Americans, Asians and Africans—to conform to Anglo-American worship. Despite American Catholicism's ethnic diversity, most U.S. Catholics remain aloof to the presence of other non-English-speaking Catholics in their area, thus overlooking the transcultural nature of their own religion. This tragedy, of course, stems from the American tradition of the ethnic parish: The English-speaking majority do their thing; the Spanish-speaking theirs, the Vietnamese, Korean and Hmong present curiosities, and no one is quite sure what to do with the Maronite, Melkite and Ukrainian Catholics.[9] This arrangement has the great advantage of preserving the cultural diversity of Catholicism in the United States, yet it also tends to hide this same diversity. Rarely on these shores does the shared communion of these cultures manifest itself in common worship, and this is where Rome can open the U.S. Catholic mind to John Paul's point that "plurality and diversification ...are not obstacles to unity but...give the character of communion."[10]

Let us return to St. Peter's Square. Anyone who has attended a papal liturgy in the square faces an unexpected reality. Thousands come to see the pope, but the pope is little more than a distant white dot projected on Jumbotrons. Aside from the occasional drive through the crowd, the pope's presence is frankly underwhelming. A student in Rome, however, comes to understand a greater beauty at such an event. He or she comes to recognize the different language groups in the square, the variety of flags and even dress and, most importantly, that Catholicism is much more than a collection of pale European faces. This collection enters into deeper, supernatural communion during a papal mass, during which worship transcends language boundaries and the sharing of the same Eucharist manifests visibly an invisible kinship. Granted, there exist special gatherings, such as World Youth Day, that can also open one's eyes to this reality. However, in Rome this encounter is a weekly, sometimes even daily occurrence, and its frequency invites the student to contemplate and digest this reality over time rather than merely to observe it in passing.

Likewise, liturgies in the square further inculcate a sense of the Church that transcends not only culture but also time. The statues of saints crowning the square's twin porticoes signal the church's memory of its own and their witness of sanctity. These statues are more than decoration. They are reminders that the papal liturgies of the square participate in a communion that extends beyond the confines of time and space and includes all of the Church's saints, canonized and non-canonized. Just as history is always before one's eyes in Rome, so too is the witness of the dead. Every church is crammed with tombs of the famous, the infamous and the obscure. And then there are the reliquaries that inundate any remaining space, often occupying a prominent place on or within an exquisite altar or below an artistic masterpiece. What might scandalize the tourist can help a student reflect on the transtemporal nature of ecclesial communion, in a way that stained glass and colorful statues cannot. The Eucharistic invocation for saints and souls gains new light. Nowhere does this reality strike the student more than the Clementine Chapel containing the Fisherman's bones. Curiosity gives way to contemplation, and the student begins to realize that the cultural force that built Rome was ultimately not the power of popes but the devotion of pilgrims. Countless pilgrims, who over the centuries have descended upon the Eternal City to pray before the relics of Peter and Paul, become more than a peculiarity; they become brothers and sisters in Christ. They are recognized as fellow sinners in search of sanctity similarly imploring the apostles' intercession in the same square before St. Peter's. This realization, fostered through a sense of pilgrimage, brings us to John Paul's third path of solidarity. In the word of *Ecclesia in America*, "Sharing in the Eucharist must lead to a more fervent exercise of charity."[11]

Third Path: Solidarity through Pilgrimage

Rome's third path flows from the first two. Rome presents the conversion of history; the transformation of history invites a deeper sense of ecclesial communion; and most of all, a greater sense of Catholic communion challenges the student to develop a real, authentic understanding of Christian solidarity through an experience of the fellow pilgrim in Rome. Rome pushes the student to see the face of Christ in a neighboring pilgrim, and from this realization matures an understanding of the Church's mission as prayerful service toward one's neighbor in the world.

Rome begins its first lesson in solidarity with a harsh reality: The swarm of pilgrims that descends upon Rome constitutes a fickle and homely bunch. An up-close experience of Rome's pilgrims quickly deromanticizes any notion of pious pilgrims reverently approaching the tombs of Peter and Paul. Rather, pilgrims push their way to the front and jabber along on the way. They blur the lines between the praying faithful and the camera-crazed tourist. They sweat and smell, they occasionally swear and they have short attention spans. It is one thing to walk a cathedral's labyrinth, or indulge in *Canterbury Tales*, or watch Martin Sheen trek the *Camino* on-screen; it is quite another to experience the fellow pilgrim in person, with poor manners and questionable hygiene.

Nevertheless, *Ecclesia in America* consistently refers to the "pilgrim Church in America," in paragraphs 1, 11, 37 and 75, highlighting conversion, communion and solidarity as paths rather than states of being. Catholic Studies capitalizes on this encounter with the fickleness and, one might say, depravity of fellow pilgrims to show how the paths of conversion and communion seek the face of Christ in the most unexpected of places: one's physical neighbor. The idea of one's "neighbor" can become ephemeral and noncommittal at the theoretical level. In Rome, however, one's "neighbor" is often a fellow pilgrim in crowded St. Peter's Square, invading personal space and trying one's patience. This experience of "neighbor" in a fellow pilgrim reveals an opportunity to recognize a bond that transcends the flaws of facades: a mutual journey or search for the love of Christ. This love may vary in degrees of maturity and authenticity, yet this common bond reveals a common struggle with fellow sinners. Catholic Studies pushes the student to recognize this bond with fellow pilgrims, which is one often missed in the familiarity of a parish or Newman center.

It is easier to love a neighbor who shares the same physical neighborhood than it is to love a foreign neighbor who shares nothing in common culturally or linguistically. However, the experience of Rome places pilgrims on common ground. One cannot assume a cultural superiority over the other; both are strangers in the same home, seeking the same Father through the same Son in the same Spirit. From this recognition of the face of Christ in the fellow pilgrim in St. Peter's Square is born a recognition of the face of Christ in the world beyond the square. This epiphany is the threshold of a student's path to solidarity, what John Paul calls "the service of our neighbors in all their needs, material and spiritual, since the face of Christ shines forth in every human being."[12]

Nevertheless, Rome's potential to instill a sense of solidarity extends beyond enlightenment. A vibrant Catholic Studies program further introduces students to those who live the Christian call to serve others, a service that is both material and spiritual. The city invites the student to experience the reality of St. Lawrence's description of the poor as the true treasures of the Church. The city is full of examples of solidarity with the poor and marginalized: the Community of Sant'Egidio serving migrants; the Missionaries of Charity serving the city's elderly homeless; the Little Sisters of the Lamb dignifying the poor through the mendicant tradition. In the United States, Catholics still find themselves polarized between the liturgy and justice, a choice between highlighting prayer or promoting service. Rome's new religious communities, however, awaken students to the travesty of this dichotomy. These communities witness to Christ's call to service while maintaining a vibrant prayer life through chant, Eucharistic adoration or even all-night vigils. It should come as no surprise that *Ecclesia in America* ends with a call for the justice of the disenfranchised, especially the migrant, while simultaneously proclaiming the need for a new evangelization on the American "continent." Indeed, John Paul ends the exhortation with a prayer, one further imploring the intercession of none other than Our Lady of Guadalupe as "Mother of America." In fact, it was the synod behind the exhortation that promoted the universal celebration of her feast day, December 12, both as a reminder of the humble origins of Christian evangelization in the New World, especially among the poor, and as a gesture of unity between North and South as one America.[13]

CONCLUSION

In highlighting the various avenues that Rome presents for student paths toward conversion, communion and solidarity, I have demonstrated how Rome can be a key to retrieving the vision of John Paul's *Ecclesia in America* and moving beyond an insular sense of cultural exceptionalism among U.S. Catholics. The convergence of apostolic witness, historical transformation, intercultural liturgies, sacred relics, diverse pilgrims and religious communities provides unparalleled experiences that together form a framework for broadening a student's understanding of Catholicism beyond familiar boundaries.

How might a truly "hemispheric" vision of American Catholicism flow from a student's encounter of Rome? Although a more thorough answer lies beyond this current study, a few possible trajectories are worth noting. For instance, a student might come to recognize how the Latin American roots of U.S. Catholic history, both in the Southeast and the Southwest, are as important, if not more so, than the founding of a Catholic colony in Maryland. In this sense, a student would develop a greater appreciation for how Spanish and French missionaries sowed the seeds of Catholicism in the present-day United States. Given Pope Francis' recent (and I believe, "hemispheric") announcement, a ready example of this new perspective would place Junípero Serra alongside John Carroll in the history of American Catholicism. A student might also take greater interest in the liturgies of other ethnicities at home, recognizing with new eyes how Catholic communion transcends cultures and ages. Here a truly "Roman" view of Catholicism would recall the presence of eparchs and Eastern Catholics at papal events and appreciate how the Church's liturgical tradition is much deeper than Trent or Vatican II. Likewise, a sense of solidarity rather than suspicion would take root, embracing these "other" Catholic immigrants in America as full members of the same family—an explicit objective of John Paul II's vision in *Ecclesia in America*.[14] Furthermore, a student might approach the question of immigration policy in the United States from the perspective of Catholic communion and solidarity rather than from the antics of cable news and politicians. Such a shift would more fully grasp American bishops' concerns for immigrant families and their welfare and see how a more constructive conversation on immigration listens to the voices and needs of fellow Catholics on the *other* side of the border. All of these trajectories would manifest John Paul's "hemispheric" idea of America as one continent with a shared faith.

Even if a student returns from Rome without this new vision, he or she has at least encountered something that one cannot avoid in Rome: the beauty of Catholicism. Pope Francis has made a strong case for how the New Evangelization should begin with an appeal to beauty if it is to make inroads in our highly visual culture.[15] Rome facilitates such an introduction to the beauty of the Catholic faith, yet the city's introduction to this mystery lies beyond the works of Michelangelo and Bernini. Rather, Rome introduces one to the beauty of Catholicism made flesh: its people, its pilgrims, its sinners, its saints. The Eternal City is the great primer of the eternal Church, the Body of Christ.

NOTES

[1] Antonio Antenucci, "Pope Hope Is Dope," *New York Post*, February 18, 2013.

[2] Pope John Paul II, *Ecclesia in America*, §5.

[3] A notable exception is William Portier, "Americanism and Inculturation, 1899–1999," *Communio* 27 (Spring 2000): 139-60. See also Michael Baxter's response, "The Unsettling of Americanism," ibid.,161-70, especially his designation of "Americanism" as a "Newmanian idea" (165). References to *Ecclesia in America* are practically nonexistent in recent works on U.S. Catholicism. The only one I could find was in Patrick Carey's *Catholics in America: A History*, updated ed. (New York: Sheed and Ward, 2004), 142.

[4] John Henry Newman, *An Essay in Aid of a Grammar of Assent*, introduction by Nicholas Lash (Notre Dame, IN: University of Notre Dame Press, 1979), 49-86.

[5] See Benedict XVI, "Address to the Participants in the Meeting with Artists," November 21, 2009, Libreria Editrice Vaticana, 2009, http://w2.vatican.va/content/benedict-xvi/en/speeches/2009/november/documents/hf_ben-xvi_spe_20091121_artisti.html.

[6] Newman, *An Essay on the Development of Christian Doctrine*, 6th ed. (Notre Dame, IN: University of Notre Dame Press, 1989), 40.

[7] Christina Scott, *A Historian and His World: A Life of Christopher Dawson* (New Brunswick: Transaction, 1992), 49-50.

[8] Pope John Paul II, *Ecclesia in America*, §26.

[9] For an enlightening new take on the experience of language and cultural convergence in U.S. Catholic parishes, see Brett Hoover, *The Shared Parish: Latinos, Anglos, and the Future of U.S. Catholicism* (New York: New York University Press, 2014).

[10] Pope John Paul II, *Ecclesia in America*, §36.

[11] Ibid., 35.

[12] Ibid., 52.

[13] Ibid., 11. Peter Casarella describes the exhortation as "thoroughly Guadalupan" in "Solidarity as the Fruit of Communion: *Ecclesia in America*, 'Post-Liberation Theology,' and the Earth," *Communio* 27 (Spring 2000): 123.

[14] John Paul II, *Ecclesia in America*, §17.

[15] See *Evangelii Gaudium*, §167.

Afterword

Maintaining the Light: Don J. Briel, Catholic Studies and the Future of Catholic Intellectual Life in America

Wilson (Bill) D. Miscamble, C.S.C

When Don Briel was an undergraduate at Notre Dame in the late 1960s, he was influenced by a number of notable teachers who surely helped lay some of the seeds that have borne fruit in the notable Catholic Studies Program he developed at the University of St. Thomas.[1] One thinks of the legendary teacher of Catholic literature, Frank O'Malley, and the demanding theologian and priest in the Congregation of Holy Cross, James Tunstead Burtchaell. Such scholars as O'Malley and Burtchaell instilled within Briel a deep love for the Catholic intellectual tradition and a familiarity with such great Catholic thinkers as John Henry Newman and Christopher Dawson.

During the planning phase and the initial years of the Catholic Studies endeavor at the University of St. Thomas in the early 1990s, Briel's former teacher James T. Burtchaell was at work on a massive study that was published by Eerdmans under the title *The Dying of the Light: The Disengagement of Colleges and Universities from their Christian Churches.*[2] The book emerged in 1998, although Burtchaell had offered glimpses of its contours as early as 1991 in essays published in *First Things.*[3] One reviewer labeled the book "a jeremiad, a lamentation for what has been lost."[4] Certainly Burtchaell's conclusion gave a justification for these descriptions. He asked whether "the story within the [17 distinct] stories" that he told actually "meant the end of Christian colleges and universities." He regretted that there had been such "little learned rage against the dying of the light" as these colleges surrendered their Christian identities.[5] He was in no doubt that the light was going out.

Yet he ended with a tantalizing challenge, after first explaining that it was not the purpose of his book to give "instruction on how to avoid the failures of the past (and present)." He wrote: "The failures of the past, so clearly patterned, so foolishly ignored and so lethally repeated, emerge pretty clearly from these stories. Anyone who requires further imagination to recognize and remedy them is not up to the task of trying again, and better."[6]

Even as Burtchaell was writing these searing words, Don Briel was "about the work" (as Frank O'Malley might have said) of recognizing the problems of "the present" at the University of St. Thomas and of working to remedy them.[7] He wanted to restore and to maintain "the light." He had the imagination, and also the courage and leadership abilities, to shape Catholic Studies as a way of addressing the specific and long-simmering crisis in Catholic higher education that Burtchaell and others identified in the 1990s.[8] Inspired by Pope John Paul II and his apostolic constitution *Ex Corde Ecclesiae,* Briel wanted to provide both students and faculty with a program that gave them "an opportunity to experience the rich diversity of the Catholic intellectual tradition—politics, psychology, history, science, literature, theology, philosophy, culture and more—and understand it in an integrated way." The integration was key. Briel put it well himself in suggesting that his program's students would "discover the Catholic faith as the 'integrating principle that helps make sense of everything,' instead of seeing it as a disconnected, 'private value.' "[9] He hoped to develop a new generation of Christian humanists who could engage the challenges of our time.

Briel and his collaborators developed Catholic Studies at St. Thomas as an alternative path to the aping of secular peers that was pursued in many Catholic schools at the time. This sad and unreflective imitation of secular peers is now much further advanced in some Catholic higher education institutions than others. Indeed, some are already in the situation that Reinhold Hütter recently described as the "Polytechnic Utiliversity." He observed and decried that in our day, "university education delivers goods that are seen as commodities, as purchasable means to satisfy individual desires and solve collective problems." Furthermore, he noted that "all academic disciplines in the late modern research university have become servile arts, and the university an accidental agglomeration of advanced research competencies gathered in one facility for the sake of managerial and logistical convenience."[10]

There is of course much more that could be said of the contemporary higher education landscape, but let us accept that this critical analysis captures much of the general context in the United States. What then has been the extent of the impact of Catholic Studies in response to it? Is Catholic Studies an approach that might help meet some of the challenges that Catholic higher education faces at this time? Has it aided in fostering and enhancing Catholic intellectual life? Has it enriched the Catholic intellectual tradition? Has the Catholic Studies model served as an exemplar and inspiration to encourage a revival in the form and content of Catholic higher education more broadly?

The model of Catholic Studies pursued at the University of St. Thomas draws on *Ex Corde Ecclesiae* in seeing a close relationship between Catholic institutions of higher learning and the institutional Church. Furthermore, it draws inspiration from Pope John Paul II's *Fides et Ratio* in holding to "the unity of knowledge and to the ultimate complementarity of faith and reason."[11] This model of Catholic Studies is obviously more developed and rich in content than those efforts at institutions that have established a single "Chair in Catholic Studies."[12] Don Briel assuredly worked to demonstrate in practice the viability of the vision for a Catholic university outlined by Cardinal Newman over a century ago and, more recently, analyzed with customary brilliance by Alasdair MacIntyre in his *God, Philosophy, Universities*.[13] The program at St. Thomas held possibilities of calling other places forward to offer an education for the whole person and to engage in the pursuit of truth. Sympathetic observers, including the author, hoped that the success of the St. Thomas program might serve either to encourage or even to "shame" other Catholic colleges and universities into offering well-integrated programs for their own students.

Such hopes regrettably have not been fully realized. They certainly have not borne marked fruit on the older established campuses like Fordham, Boston College, Notre Dame, Georgetown and St. Louis. Reviewing the last two decades at Notre Dame, a case study of sorts, it is clear that there were some positive developments. Some genuine renewal in the Theology Department under John Cavadini's leadership and the creative and good work of the Center for Ethics and Culture under David Solomon's guidance are obvious illustrations. Some similar positive developments also occurred on other Catholic campuses. Yet none of the major Catholic universities sought to offer to their students the integrated Catholic education and formation that Don Briel supplied to his Catholic Studies students at the University of St. Thomas. The larger universities were headed in a different and really quite opposite direction.

An explanation for their contrary development is provided by the Notre Dame philosopher Alfred Freddoso. He outlined a number of historical trends to explain the situation at Notre Dame, but these trends have a much broader applicability. They are still operative and they explain why it can be so hard for students to get a rich Catholic education. Among the factors that Freddoso noted are "the university's steadily intensifying and often frustrated aspiration to be regarded as a major player in the American educational scene." Such "aspirations" lead institutions to imitate their preferred and secular peers in significant areas of academic life. In light of this, Freddoso noted "the concomitant segregation of faith from reason," along with "the deterioration of the core curriculum into a series of disjointed 'course distribution requirements' guided by no comprehensive conception of what an educated Catholic should know." Continuing on and getting further to the heart of the matter, Freddoso also noted "the easy transition from a faculty dominated by 'progressive' Catholics to a faculty more and more dominated by people ignorant of the intellectual ramifications of the Catholic faith." He also pointed to "a succession of high-level administrators lacking in a philosophical vision of Catholic higher education and intent on diffusing throughout the university a pragmatic mentality at once both bureaucratic and corporate."[14]

This circumstance prevails, it must be understood, even as many exemplary ventures occur on Notre Dame's campus and beyond it. Notre Dame sponsors the Alliance for Catholic Education and the Echo Program and endless "service learning opportunities." It advises Catholic Charities USA and Catholic Relief Services on their programs. It supports the Tantur Ecumenical Institute in the Holy Land. The sacramental life on campus remains rich. A significant number of faculty pursue work that is in some way related to Catholic intellectual life. But honest observers will note the reality of those factors identified by Freddoso. They understand that the idea of an integrated Catholic education is considered as a relic of a bygone age at schools like Notre Dame. It (and other major Catholic institutions) has become much more like "public schools" located in "Catholic neighborhoods."[15] The situation on the older and larger campuses reflected little influence from the integrated Catholic Studies model. Certainly it did not inform their curricular decisions in any notable way.

The situation was much different in some other parts of the landscape of Catholic intellectual life and higher education. There a different narrative prevailed than the one Burtchaell had foreshadowed in his book. In fact, from the 1970s onward there have been a significant number of creative efforts made to keep the distinctive "light" of Catholic higher education burning. Don Briel's efforts at St. Thomas should be seen as an important part of this larger—if rather diffuse—effort. In this broader effort, a number of notable developments must be included. An illustrative, but certainly not exhaustive, list would include:

1. The foundation of a new group of small Catholic liberal arts colleges like Thomas Aquinas (1971) and Christendom College (1977). These schools are still small but quite academically rigorous. Also formed more recently is Ave Maria University in Ave Maria, Florida, which aspires to be a more comprehensive university while still offering an integrated Catholic education.

2. The real renewal of other Catholic colleges, which had seemed likely to secularize or to simply shut down. The most notable examples are Franciscan University in Steubenville, Ohio; Benedictine University in Atchison, Kansas; the University of Dallas in Texas; and more recently, the University of Mary in Bismarck, North Dakota. They are places with a lively religious and intellectual life and spirit.

3. The revitalization in American seminaries over the past two decades. Such revitalization is well evidenced at Mundelein Seminary, which is being refashioned as a center for reflection on Catholic theology and as a force for the New Evangelization.

4. The lively Catholic Chaplaincies and Newman Centers at major state universities such as the University of Illinois in Urbana-Champaign, Texas A&M University and the University of Nebraska at Lincoln. These are places with a vibrant Catholic liturgical and social life that also provide various programs to deepen students' knowledge about their Catholic faith.

5. The establishment of "Catholic Studies" chairs at a range of institutions—public and private. Such single chairs can make important contributions. A fine example of this is the case of Russell Hittinger, who occupies the William L. Warren Professorship of Catholic Studies at the University of Tulsa.

6. The development of new institutes associated with the New Evangelization, of which the Augustine Institute in Denver would be a notable example.

7. The establishment of centers for Catholic thought and reflection near some of the great secular schools to engage sympathetic scholars for their faculties and to offer a range of programs for their students. Notable here would be the Lumen Christi Institute at the University of Chicago.

8. The contributions of various think tanks and public intellectuals housed within them, such as the Ethics and Public Policy Center in Washington, D.C., and the Witherspoon Institute at Princeton, where such thinkers as George Weigel and Robert George respectively pursue their crucial labors.

Clearly there is much going on in contemporary Catholic intellectual life. While no clear cause and effect lines can be drawn here, the Catholic Studies movement begun at St. Thomas not only contributed to but also benefited from the general impetus that produced these various endeavors. The inspiration of St. Pope John Paul II played a crucial role in inspiring these initiatives both intellectually and spiritually, but individuals like Don Briel drew strength and encouragement from this witness to hope and have played their own parts in the renewal of Catholic intellectual life. Briel fashioned a notable program but was also a key player in connecting people so that collaborative ventures might be undertaken. In this sense, Catholic Studies has been important beyond its own campus confines. In ways that can't always be well-documented and measured, the Catholic Studies approach helped give new energy and spirit to Catholic intellectual endeavors. It notably did this at a crucial time when those who should have been leading the way in this effort shirked their responsibilities. The question, however, remains: Where to now?

The former president of Notre Dame, Fr. Theodore Hesburgh, was fond of saying that the Catholic University (and he really meant Notre Dame) was "the place where the Church did its thinking." This was always something of a conceit, of course, but it is helpful to ask: Where will future Catholic thought occur? Christopher Dawson proved, from his life as an independent scholar, that no institutional affiliation is needed in order to contribute to the study of Catholic culture and life. Yet institutions truly matter. Looked at in a broad span, one can appreciate that during the first millennium of Christianity, the monasteries, the cathedral and the convent schools were extremely important in advancing learning and in the pursuit of "both wisdom and holiness."[16] In the second millennium—or certainly from the 13th century forward—the universities were the key locales for Catholic thinking. Will they continue to be so?

Certainly Catholic universities and colleges remain places where some individuals can do some thinking beneficial to the Church. The aforementioned Alasdair MacIntyre surely illustrates the point. Another example would be the work of the Notre Dame sociologist of religion Christian Smith. He recently authored a study entitled *Young Catholic America: Emerging Adults In, Out Of, and Gone from the Church*.[17] It is a bracing read and is inspired by religious convictions and insights. Incidentally, it also reveals what a challenging task lies ahead for Catholic educators to pass along the faith to students and to deepen their understanding and love for it. Despite the stellar examples of such scholars as MacIntyre and Smith, however, Catholic colleges and universities now are hardly the only locations where serious Catholic thought occurs. Some of the best thinking and writing about crucial social and policy questions occurs beyond their boundaries. An important example for contemporary discussion by Catholic intellectuals is the excellent study by Sherif Girgis, Ryan T. Anderson and Robert P. George, *What Is Marriage? Man and Woman: A Defense.*[18]

Going forward, Catholic Studies programs have important contributions to make in this larger intellectual effort, which will be pursued on Catholic campuses and beyond them. Serious Catholic Studies programs are designed so as to encourage interdisciplinary collaboration and also to bring a Catholic perspective to bear on entire areas of research and teaching, as Michael Naughton and others have demonstrated in their work on business and Catholic social teaching.[19] Notably, from a longer-term perspective, these programs should be crucial incubators to generate the Catholic intellectuals of the future who will sustain Catholic culture and thought.

To do this, Catholic Studies programs will have to maintain their commitment to providing both a broad and integrated approach in educating their students. This approach will always have a crucial place for liturgy and prayer and for art and drama. It will truly give to its students an appreciation for Catholic culture in its beauty and richness. This approach, of course, must hold out against the merely utilitarian approach that characterizes so much of contemporary education. It must help keep alive the real promise of a Catholic education.

This will not be easy, especially in a national context of direct assaults on the religious liberty of Catholic institutions such as hospitals, universities and social agencies. Furthermore, higher education in general is going through a challenging period of change. Who knows how it might develop in the world of Massive Open Online Courses (MOOCS) and other Web-based learning innovations. Clearly the humanities are in some retreat and the utilitarian approach is dominant. Even in those Catholic colleges and universities that offer Catholic Studies programs there can be jealousy and resentment if these programs are "too successful" or, dare we say, even "too Catholic."

While the challenges are there, so also is a rich promise. Catholic Studies Programs must keep alive the treasured education that helps students and faculty to grasp the complementary nature of faith and reason and to receive a deep understanding and love for the truth and for the

One who is "the way, the truth and the life" (John 14:6). They must be crucial locales that allow students to obtain a clear appreciation of the Catholic moral and social vision and to reflect on how it might be used to engage the world. They have the special duty to keep the flame of integrated Catholic learning burning brightly. Don Briel has shown well how to realize this promise over these past two decades. The best honor that can be given to him is to sustain and extend his labors in Catholic higher education. Each of us must do what we can—wherever we are located—to maintain "the true light." May the Holy Spirit guide and inspire us.

NOTES

1 Don J. Briel, "Catholic Studies at the University of St. Thomas," *Catholic Education* 12, no. 3 (2009): 384-98.

2 James Tunstead Burtchaell, *The Dying of the Light: The Disengagement of Colleges and Universities from Their Christian Churches* (Grand Rapids: Wm. B. Eerdmans Publishing Company, 1998).

3 James Tunstead Burtchaell, "The Decline and Fall of the Christian College," *First Things* 12 (April 1991): 16-29; and "The Decline and Fall of the Christian College (II)," *First Things* 13 (May 1991): 30-38.

4 Richard T. Hughes, "The Dying of the Light (Book Review)," *Catholic Historical Review* 85, no. 4 (October 1999): 666.

5 Burtchaell, *The Dying of the Light*, 851.

6 Ibid.

7 For more information on Don Briel's teacher, Frank O'Malley, see John W. Meaney, *O'Malley of Notre Dame* (Notre Dame, IN: University of Notre Dame Press, 1991).

8 For a later discussion of the "crisis," see Melanie M. Morey and John J. Piderit, S.J., *Catholic Higher Education: A Culture of Crisis* (New York: Oxford University Press, 2006).

9 Peter Jesserer Smith, " 'Catholic Studies' Program Excels as Founder Bids Farewell," *National Catholic Register*, August 24, 2014, 11.

10 Reinhold Hutter, "Polytechnic Utiliversity," *First Things* 237 (November 2013): 47.

11 Don Briel, as quoted in Smith, "'Catholic Studies' Program Excels as Founder Bids Farewell," 11. Also see John Paul II, *Fides et Ratio, Encyclical Letter on the Relationship between Faith and Reason* (Washington, DC: U.S. Catholic Conference, 1990).

12 The Chauncey Stillman Chair in Catholic Studies at Harvard, which Christopher Dawson once held, might be seen as a forerunner of such appointments.

13 Alasdair MacIntyre, *God, Philosophy, Universities: A Selective History of the Catholic Philosophical Tradition* (Lanham, MD: Rowman & Littlefield, 2009).

14 This list comes from Alfred J. Freddoso's "Introduction" to Charles E. Rice, *What Happened to Notre Dame* (South Bend, IN: St. Augustine's Press, 2009), xi-xii.

[15] Ibid., xii.

[16] Here I rely on the wonderful essay of Matthew Lamb "The Millennial Challenges Facing Catholic Intellectual Life," *Nova et Vetera* 11, no. 4 (2013), 969-91. For the specific quotation, see 982.

[17] Christian Smith et al., *Young Catholic America: Emerging Adults In, Out of, and Gone from the Church* (New York: Oxford University Press, 2014).

[18] Sherif Girgis, Ryan T. Anderson, and Robert P. George, *What Is Marriage? Man and Woman: A Defense* (New York: Encounter Books, 2012). Note that the authors would distinguish that this work is not an explicitly Catholic book, but rather is grounded in natural law theory accessible to all.

[19] See Michael Naughton and Helen Alford, *Managing as if Faith Mattered: Christian Social Principles in the Modern Organization* (Notre Dame, IN: University of Notre Dame Press, 2001).

Consolidated Bibliography

Abbott, Claude Coller, ed. *Further Letters of Gerard Manley Hopkins Including His Correspondence with Coventry Patmore.* London: Oxford University Press, 1956.

Alighieri, Dante. *Convivio.* Translated by William Walrond Jackson. Oxford: Oxford University Press, 1909.

———. *Purgatory.* Translated by Dorothy Sayers. New York: Penguin, 1955.

Antenucci, Antonio. "Pope Hope Is Dope." *New York Post,* February 18, 2013.

Aristotle. *The Metaphysics.* Translated by W.D. Ross. Oxford: Clarendon Press, 1924.

———. *Poetics.* Translated by S.H. Butcher. London: Macmillan, 1907.

Arnold, Matthew. *Culture and Anarchy.* Cambridge: Cambridge University Press, 1935.

Augustine. *Confessions.* Translated by Henry Chadwick. Oxford: Oxford University Press, 2009.

———. *On Genesis: Two Books on Genesis Against the Manichees; And, On the Literal Interpretation of Genesis, an Unfinished Book.* Fathers of the Church, Vol. 84. Washington, D.C.: Catholic University Press, 2001.

———. *Expositions on the Psalms.* Vol. VIII. Nicene and Post-Nicene Fathers, Series I. Edited by Philip Schaff. Translated by J.E. Tweed. Buffalo, NY: Christian Literature Publishing Co., 1888.

———. *Select Works and Letters.* Vol. IV. Nicene and Post-Nicene Fathers, Series II. Edited by Philip Schaff and Henry Wace. Grand Rapids, MI: Eerdmans, 1980.

Bailey, Garrick, and James Peoples. *Essentials of Cultural Anthropology.* 3rd ed. Belmont, CA: Wadsworth Cengage Learning, 2014.

Balthasar, Hans Urs von. *Bernanos: An Ecclesial Existence.* Translated by E.

Leiva-Merikakis. San Francisco: Ignatius Press, 1998.

Barrett, Stanley R., Sean Stokholm, and Jeanette Burke. "The Idea of Power and the Power of Ideas: A Review Essay." *American Anthropologist* 103, no. 2 (2001): 468-480.

Barron, Robert. *Catholicism: A Journey to the Heart of the Faith*. New York: Image, 2011.

Baxter, Michael. "The Unsettling of Americanism." *Communio* 27 (2000): 161-70.

Benedict XVI (Joseph Ratzinger). "Address to the Bishops of the United States of America. (Regions X-XIII) on Their '*Ad Limina*' Visit." May 5, 2012. Libreria Editrice Vaticana. http://w2.vatican.va/content/benedict-xvi/en/ speeches/ 2012/may/documents/hf_ben-xvi_spe_20120505_us-bishops. html.

———. "Address to the Participants in the Convention of the Diocese of Rome." June 11, 2007. Libreria Editrice Vaticana, 2007. http://w2.vatican.va/ content/benedict-xvi/en/speeches/2007/june/documents/hf_ben-xvi_ spe_20070611_convegno-roma.html.

———. "Address to the Participants in the First European Meeting of University Lecturers." June 23, 2007. Libreria Editrice Vaticana. http://w2.vatican. va/content/benedict-xvi/en/speeches/2007/june/documents/hf_ben-xvi_spe_20070623_european-univ.html.

———. "Address to the Participants in the Meeting with Artists." November 21, 2009. Libreria Editrice Vaticana, 2009. http://w2.vatican.va/content/ benedict-xvi/en/speeches/2009/november/documents/hf_ben-xvi_ spe_20091121_artisti.html.

———. "Address to the Participants in the Meeting with Catholic Educators." April 17, 2008. Libreria Editrice Vaticana. http://w2.vatican.va/ content/benedict-xvi/en/speeches/2008/april/documents/hf_ben-xvi_ spe_20080417_cath-univ-washington.html.

———. "Address to the Participants in the Meeting on the 50th Anniversary of the Encyclical *Mater et Magistra*." May 16, 2011. Libreria Editrice Vaticana. http://w2.vatican.va/content/benedict-xvi/en/speeches/2011/may/ documents/hf_ben-xvi_spe_20110516_justpeace.pdf.

———. *Caritas in Veritate*. Vatican: Libreria Editrice Vaticana, 2009.

———. *Deus Caritas Est, Encyclical Letter on Christian Love*. Libreria Editrice Vaticana, 2005. http://w2.vatican.va/content/benedict-xvi/en/encyclicals/ documents/hf_ben-xvi_enc_20051225_deus-caritas-est.html.

———. *God and the World: A Conversation with Peter Seewald*. San Francisco: Ignatius, 2003.

———. "Homilies of His Holiness Bartholomew I Ecumenical Patriarch of

Constantinople and His Holiness Pope Benedict XVI: Homily of the Holy Father." Libreria Editrice Vaticana, 2008. http://w2.vatican.va/content/benedict-xvi/en/homilies/2008/documents/hf_ben-xvi_hom_20080629_pallio.html.

———. *On the Way to Christ Jesus.* San Francisco: Ignatius Press, 2005.

———. "Relativism: The Central Problem for Faith Today." *Origins* 26, no. 20 (1996): 309-316.

———. *Spe Salvi, Encyclical Letter on Christian Hope.* Libreria Editrice Vaticana, 2007. http://w2.vatican.va/content/benedict-xvi/en/encyclicals/documents/hf_ben-xvi_enc_20071130_spe-salvi.html.

———. *Values in a Time of Upheaval.* San Francisco: Ignatius Press, 2006.

———. *Without Roots: The West, Relativism, Christianity, Islam.* Translated by Michael F. Moore. New York: Basic Books, 2006.

Bennis, Warren, and James O'Toole. "How Business Schools Lost Their Way." *Harvard Business Review* 83, no. 5 (2005): 96-104.

Blum, Christopher O. *Rejoicing in the Truth: Wisdom and the Educator's Craft.* Front Royal, VA: Christendom Press, 2015.

Boas, Franz. "The Methods of Ethnology." *American Anthropologist* 22, no. 4 (1920): 311-21.

Bonhoeffer, Dietrich. *The Cost of Discipleship.* Translated by R.H. Fuller. New York: Macmillan Publishers, 1960.

Breisach, Ernst. *Historiography: Ancient, Medieval, and Modern.* 3rd ed. Chicago: University of Chicago Press, 2007.

Briel, Don J. "Catholic Studies at the University of St. Thomas." *Catholic Education* 12, no. 3 (2009): 384-98.

———. "The Idea of a University: A Contemporary Reappraisal." Unpublished lecture, last modified August 29, 2014. http://www.donbriel.org/articles/.

———. "Liberal Learning and Professional Education in Newman's *The Idea of a University*." Unpublished lecture. University of St. Thomas, St. Paul, MN. 1997.

———. "Mission and Identity: The Role of Faculty." *Journal of Catholic Higher Education* 31 (2012): 169-79.

Brooks, David. "The Organization Kid." *Atlantic,* April 1, 2001.

Brown, Eric. "Socrates the Cosmopolitan." *Stanford Agora: An Online Journal of Legal Perspectives* 1, no. 1 (2000): 74-87.

Brown, Peter. *The World of Late Antiquity.* New York: Harcourt, 1971.

Brownson, Orestes. *The American Republic: Its Constitution, Tendencies and*

Destiny. Wilmington, DE: ISI Books, 2003.

Buckley, Michael. "The Catholic University and Its Inherent Promise." *America* 168, no. 19 (1993): 14-16.

Burke, Peter. *What Is Cultural History?* Cambridge: Polity, 2008.

Burtchaell, James T. "Catholic Institutions of Higher Learning: Dutiful yet Free in Church and State." *Current Issues in Catholic Higher Education* 9 (1988): 19-21.

———. "The Decline and Fall of the Christian College (I)." *First Things* 12 (April 1991): 16-29.

———. "The Decline and Fall of the Christian College (II)." *First Things* 13 (May 1991): 30-38.

———. *The Dying of the Light: The Disengagement of Colleges and Universities from Their Christian Churches*. Grand Rapids: Wm. B. Eerdmans Publishing Company, 1998.

Caldecott, Stratford. *Beauty for Truth's Sake: On the Reenchantment of Education*. Grand Rapids, MI: Brazos Press, 2009.

———. *Beauty in the Word: Rethinking the Foundations of Education*. Tacoma, WA: Angelico Press, 2012.

———. "Kairos: Towards a Culture of Life." *Communio* 21 (1994): 128-59.

Callahan, Daniel, ed. *The Role of Theology in the University*. Milwaukee: The Bruce Publishing Company, 1967.

Carey, Patrick. *Catholics in America: A History*. Rev. ed. New York: Sheed and Ward, 2004.

Casarella, Peter. "Solidarity as the Fruit of Communion: Ecclesia in America, 'Post-Liberation Theology,' and the Earth." *Communio* 27 (2000): 98-123.

Cavadini, John. "Catholic Studies? A Cautionary Note." In *The Idea of the Catholic University*, edited by Kenneth D. Whitehead, 95-97. Chicago: University of Scranton Press, 2009.

———. "An Open Letter to the Notre Dame Community Regarding Catholic Identity." *The Observer*, April 19, 2006.

Chagnon, Napoleon A. *Yanomamo.* 5th ed. Wadsworth, 1997.

Chesterton, G.K. *Orthodoxy*. South Orange, NJ: Chesterton Institute Press, 2008.

The Catholic Intellectual Tradition: A Conversation at Boston College. Boston College. July 2010. http://www.bc.edu/content/dam/files/top/church21/pdf/cit.pdf.

Congregation for Catholic Education. "The Religious Dimension of Education in a Catholic School: Guidelines for Reflections and Renewal." Rome, April 7, 1988. http://www.vatican.va/roman_curia/congregations/ccatheduc/documents/rc_con_ccatheduc_doc_19880407_catholic-school_en.html.

Cortright, S.A., and Michael Naughton, eds. *Rethinking the Purpose of Business.* Notre Dame, IN: University of Notre Dame Press, 2002.

Cortright, Steve. "Sacramental Identification." Lecture presented at the 7th International Symposium on Catholic Social Thought and Management Education, University of Notre Dame, Notre Dame, Indiana, June 11-13, 2008. http://www.stthomas.edu/media/catholicstudies/center/johnary-aninstitute/conferences/2008-notredame/Cortright-final-pape.pdf.

Damascene, John. "Exposition of the Orthodox Faith." In *Nicene and Post-Nicene Fathers*, Vol. 4, edited by Philip Schaff and Henry Wace. Grand Rapids: Eerdmans Publishing, 1963.

———. *Three Treatises on the Divine Images.* Translated by Andrew Louth. New York: St. Vladimir's Seminary Press, 2003.

Dawson, Christopher. *The Age of the Gods: A Study in the Origins of Culture in Prehistoric Europe and in the Ancient East.* Washington D.C.: Catholic University of America Press, 2012.

———. *The Crisis of Western Education.* Washington D.C.: Catholic University of America Press, 2010.

———. *Enquiries into Religion and Culture.* Washington D.C.: 2009.

———. *The Gods of Revolution.* Washington D.C.: Catholic University of America Press, 2015.

———. *The Judgment of the Nations.* Washington D.C.: Catholic University of America Press, 2011.

———. *The Making of Europe: An Introduction to the History of European Unity.* Washington D.C.: Catholic University of America Press, 2003.

———. *Medieval Essays.* Washington D.C.: Catholic University of America Press, 2002.

———. *The Movement of World Revolution.* Washington D.C.: Catholic University of America Press, 2013.

———. *Progress and Religion: An Historical Inquiry.* Washington D.C.: Catholic University of America Press, 2001.

———. *Religion and Culture.* Washington D.C.: Catholic University of America Press, 2013.

———. *Understanding Europe.* Washington D.C.: Catholic University of America Press, 2009.

De Blaauw, Sible. *Cultus et decor: Liturgia e architettura nella Roma tardoantica e medievale.* 2 vols. Città del Vaticano : Biblioteca Apostolica Vaticana, 1994.

Delbecq, Andre. "A Leadership Perspective on Catholic Business Education." Unpublished lecture presented at the 7th International Symposium on Catholic Social Thought and Management Education. University of Notre Dame, Notre Dame, Indiana, June 11-13, 2008.

Dessain, Charles Stephen, and Thomas Gornall, eds. *The Letters and Diaries of John Henry Newman.* London: Nelson, 1961-72; Oxford: Clarendon Press, 1973.

Drew, Katherine Fischer. *The Lombard Laws.* Translated by Katherine Fischer Drew. Philadelphia: University of Pennsylvania Press, 1973.

Dulles, Avery. "Seven Essentials of Evangelization." *Origins* 25, no. 23 (1995): 397-400.

Eco, Umberto. "History and Historiography of Semiotics." In *Semiotics: A Handbook on the Sign-Theoretic Foundations of Nature and Culture,* edited by Roland Posner. New York: Walter de Gruyter, 1996.

Eliot, T.S. "Metaphysical Poets." London: Faber and Faber Limited, 1932.

Epstein, Edwin M. "Catholic Social Teaching and Education in Business and Economics: A Non-Catholic's Perspective." *Educational Perspectives* 14, no. 1 (1996): 20-27.

Finney, Paul C. *The Invisible God: The Earliest Christians on Art.* New York: Oxford University Press, 1994.

Fischer, David Hackett. *Historians' Fallacies.* New York: Harper Perennial, 1970.

Fisher, James T., and Margaret M. McGuinness, eds. *The Catholic Studies Reader.* New York: Fordham University Press, 2011.

Flannery, Austin, ed. *Vatican Council II: The Conciliar and Post Conciliar Documents.* Volume 1. Collegeville, MN: Liturgical Press, 1996.

———. *Vatican Council II: Constitutions, Decrees, Declarations.* Rev. ed. Collegeville, MN: Liturgical Press, 1996.

Francis I. "Easter Vigil Homily." April 19, 2014. Libreria Editrice Vaticana. http://w2.vatican.va/content/francesco/en/homilies/2014/documents/papa-francesco_20140419_omelia-veglia-pasquale.html.

———. *Evangelii Gaudium, Apostolic Exhortation on the Proclamation of the Gospel in Today's World.* Libreria Editrice Vaticana, 2013. http://w2.vatican.va/content/francesco/en/apost_exhortations/documents/papa-francesco_esortazione-ap_20131124_evangelii-gaudium.html.

———. "Meeting with the Bishops of Brazil: Address on the Occasion of the XXVIII World Youth Day." July 28, 2013. Libreria Editrice Vaticana. http://w2.vatican.va/content/francesco/en/speeches/2013/july/documents/papa-francesco_20130727_gmg-episcopato-brasile.html.

———. "Video Message to the Faithful of Buenos Aires on the Occasion of the Feast of Saint Cajetan." August 7, 2013. Libreria Editrice Vaticana. http://w2.vatican.va/content/francesco/en/messages/pont-messages/2013/documents/papa-francesco_20130807_videomessaggio-san-cayetano.html.

George, Francis Cardinal. *The Difference God Makes: A Catholic Vision of Faith, Communion, and Culture*. New York: Crossroad, 2009.

Gilby, Thomas, O.P. *Poetic Experience: An Introduction to Thomist Aesthetic*. New York: Sheed & Ward, 1934.

Girgis, Sherif, Ryan T. Anderson, and Robert P. George. *What Is Marriage? Man and Woman: A Defense*. New York, NY: Encounter Books, 2012.

Gleason, Philip. *Contending with Modernity: Catholic Higher Education in the Twentieth Century*. New York: Oxford University Press, 1995.

Goodpaster, Ken. *Conscience and Corporate Culture*. Malden, MA: Wiley-Blackwell, 2006.

Greenleaf, Robert K. *The Institution as Servant*. Cambridge, MA: Center for Applied Studies, 1972.

Guardini, Romano. *Letters from Lake Como: Explorations in Technology and the Human Race*. Grand Rapids: William B. Eerdmans, 1994.

Gutierrez, Gustavo. *A Theology of Liberation*. New York: Maryknoll, 1973.

Hahn, Cynthia. "What Do Reliquaries Do for Relics?" *Numen* 57, no. 1 (2010): 284-316.

Hamel, Gary. "Moon Shots for Management." *Harvard Business Review* 87, no. 2 (2009): 91-98.

Havard, Alexandre. *Created for Greatness: The Power of Magnanimity*. 2nd ed. New Rochelle, NY: Scepter, 2014.

———. *Virtuous Leadership: An Agenda for Personal Excellence*. 2nd ed. New Rochelle, NY: Scepter, 2007.

Heclo, Hugh. *On Thinking Institutionally*. Boulder, CO: Paradigm Publishers, 2008.

Heft, S.M., James L. and Fred P. Pestello. "Hiring Practices in Catholic Colleges and Universities." *Current Issues in Catholic Higher Education* 20, no. 1 (1999): 89-97.

Hegel, George W.F. *The Philosophy of Right*. Translated by T.M. Knox. Oxford: Oxford University Press, 1967.

Hesburgh, Theodore M., ed. *The Challenge and Promise of a Catholic University*. Notre Dame, IN: University of Notre Dame Press, 1994.

Hobbes, Thomas. *The Leviathan*. New York: Penguin, 1982.

Hoffer, Eric. *The True Believer: Thoughts on the Nature of Mass Movements*. New York: Harper and Row, 1951.

Hoover, Brett. *The Shared Parish: Latinos, Anglos, and the Future of U.S. Catholicism*. New York: New York University Press, 2014.

Hopkins, Gerard Manley. *Poems and Prose*. New York: Penguin, 1963.

Hughes, Richard T. "The Dying of the Light (Book Review)." *Catholic Historical Review* 85, no. 4 (1999): 666-69.

Hunter, James Davison. *To Change the World: The Irony, Tragedy, & Possibility of Christianity in the Late Modern World*. New York: Oxford University Press, 2010.

Hütter, Reinhold. "Polytechnic Utiliversity." *First Things* 237 (2013): 47-52.

International Theological Commission. *Theology Today: Perspectives, Principles, and Criteria*. 2011.

John Paul II. "Address to the Catholic University of the Sacred Heart." April 13, 2000. Libreria Editrice Vaticana. http://w2.vatican.va/content/john-paul-ii/en/speeches/2000/apr-jun/documents/hf_jp-ii_spe_20000413_univ-catt-sacro-cuore.html.

———. *Ecclesia in America, Post-Synodal Apostolic Exhortation on the Encounter with the Living Jesus Christ: the Way to Conversion, Communion and Solidarity*. Libreria Editrice Vaticana, 1999. http://w2.vatican.va/content/john-paul-ii/en/apost_exhortations/documents/hf_jp-ii_exh_22011999_ecclesia-in-america.html.

———. *Ex Corde Ecclesiae, Apostolic Constitution on Catholic Universities*. Washington, D.C.: U.S. Catholic Conference, 1998.

———. *Fides et Ratio, Encyclical Letter on the Relationship between Faith and Reason*. Libreria Editrice Vaticana, 1998. http://w2.vatican.va/content/john-paul-ii/en/ encyclicals/documents/hf_jp-ii_enc_14091998_fides-et-ratio.html.

———. "Homily of His Holiness John Paul II, Oriole Park at Camden Yards, Baltimore." October 8, 1995. http://w2.vatican.va/content/john-paul-ii/en/homilies/1995/documents/hf_jp-ii_hom_19951008_baltimore.html.

———. "Homily of His Holiness John Paul II, Victory Square, Warsaw." June 2, 1979. Libreria Editrice Vaticana, 1979. http://w2.vatican.va/content/john-paul-ii/en/homilies/1979/documents/hf_jp-ii_hom_19790602_polonia-varsavia.html.

———. "Mass for Students of the Pontifical Major Seminary of Rome: Homily of John Paul II." October 13, 1979. https://w2.vatican.va/content/john-paul-ii/fr/homilies/1979/documents/hf_jp-ii_hom_19791013_roman-seminary.html.

———. *Redemptoris Missio, On the Permanent Validity of the Church's Missionary Mandate*. Libreria Editrice Vaticana, 1990. http://w2.vatican.va/content/john-paul-ii/en/encyclicals/documents/hf_jp-ii_enc_07121990_redemptoris-missio.html.

Kahn, Joseph, and Daniel J. Wakin. "Western Classical Music, Made and Loved in China." *The New York Times*, April 2, 2007.

King, Jason, and Shannon Schrein, eds. *God Has Begun a Great Work in Us: Embodied Love in Consecrated Life and Ecclesial Movements*. Maryknoll, NY: Orbis, 2015.

Kirk, Russell. *Eliot and His Age: T.S. Eliot's Moral Imagination in the Twentieth Century*. New York: Random House, 1971.

Keyne, Geoffrey, ed. *Poetry and Prose of William Blake*. London: Random House, 1927.

Kosslyn, Stephen M., et al. *Report of the Task Force on General Education*. Harvard University. 2007. http://isites.harvard.edu/fs/docs/icb.topic830823.files/Report%20of%20the%20Taskforce%20on%20General%20Education.pdf.

Krautheimer, Richard. *Early Christian and Byzantine Architecture*. New York: Penguin Books, 1970.

Lamb, Matthew. "The Millennial Challenges Facing Catholic Intellectual Life." *Nova et Vetera* 11, no. 4 (2013): 969-91.

———. "Will There Be Catholic Theology in the United States?" *America* 162, no. 20 (1990):523-34.

Laurent, Marcel. *L'Art chrétien des origines à Justinien*. Brussels: Société Royale d'Archéologie de Bruxelles, 1956.

Leclercq, Jean. *The Love of Learning and the Desire for God: A Study of Monastic Culture*. New York: Fordham University Press, 1982.

Lev, Elizabeth. "Reading Theological Context: A Marian Interpretation of Michelangelo's Roman Pieta." In *Revisioning: Critical Methods of Seeing Christianity in the History of Art*, edited by James Romaine and Linda Stratford, 207-223. Eugene, OR: Cascade Books, 2013.

Lev, Elizabeth, and Jose Granados. *A Body for Glory: Theology of the Body in the Papal Collections*. Vatican City: Edizioni Musei Vaticani, 2014.

Lewis, C.S. *Christian Reflections*. London: Fount/Harper Collins, 1981.

Lewis, Harry R. *Excellence without a Soul: How a Great University Forgot Education*. New York: Public Affairs, 2006.

Logan, Peter Melville. "On Culture: Edward B. Tylor's *Primitive Culture*, 1871." *Branch: Britain, Representation and Nineteenth-Century History*. http://www.branchcollective.org/?ps_articles=peter-logan-on-culture-edward-b-tylors-primitive-culture-1871.

———. "On Culture: Matthew Arnold's *Culture and Anarchy*, 1869." *Branch: Britain, Representation and Nineteenth-Century History*. http://www.branchcollective.org/?ps_articles=peter-logan-on-culture-matthew-arnolds-culture-and-anarchy-1869.

MacIntyre, Alasdair. "Catholic Universities: Dangers, Hopes, Choices." In *Higher Learning and Catholic Traditions*, edited by Robert E. Sullivan, 1-21. Notre Dame, IN: University of Notre Dame Press, 2001.

———. *God, Philosophy, Universities: A Selective History of the Catholic Philosophical Tradition*. Lanham, MD: Rowman & Littlefield, 2009.

———. *The Tasks of Philosophy: Selected Essays*. Cambridge: Cambridge University Press, 2006.

Maritain, Jacques. *Art and Scholasticism*. Translated by Joseph W. Evans. New York: Charles Scribner's Sons, 1962.

———. *Creative Intuition in Art and Poetry*. New York: Pantheon Books, 1953.

———. *The Education of Man*. Edited by Donald and Idella Gallagher. Garden City, NY: Doubleday & Company, Inc., 1962.

Massa, Mark, and Catherine Osborne, eds. *American Catholic History: A Documentary Reader*. New York: New York University Press, 2008.

McGreevy, John. *Catholicism and American Freedom: A History*. New York: W.W. Norton, 2003.

McInerny, Daniel. "Poetic Knowledge and Cultural Renewal." *Logos* 15, no. 4 (2012): 17-35.

McNabb, Vincent, O.P. *An Old Apostle Speaks*. Edited by G. Vann. Oxford: Blackfriars, 1946.

Meaney, John W. *O'Malley of Notre Dame*. Notre Dame, IN: University of Notre Dame Press, 1991.

Mengler, Thomas. "Why Should a Catholic Law School Be Catholic?" *Journal of Catholic Social Thought* 7, no. 2 (2010): 211-29.

Miller, J. Michael, C.S.B. *The Holy See's Teaching on Catholic Schools*. Manchester, NH: Sophia Institute Press, 2006.

Mommsen, Theodore E. "Petrarch's Conception of the 'Dark Ages.' " *Speculum* 17, no. 2 (1942): 226-42.

Monaghan, John, and Peter Just. *Social & Cultural Anthropology: A Very Short Introduction*. Oxford: Oxford University Press, 2000.

Morey, Melanie M., and John J. Piderit, S.J. *Catholic Higher Education: A Culture in Crisis*. New York: Oxford University Press, 2006.

Miscamble, Wilson D., C.S.C., ed. *Go Forth and Do Good: Memorable Notre Dame Commencement Addresses*. Notre Dame, IN: University of Notre Dame Press, 2003.

Naughton, Michael J., and Helen Alford, O.P. *Managing as if Faith Mattered: Christian Social Principles in the Modern Organization*. Notre Dame, IN: University of Notre Dame Press, 2001.

———. *Vocation of the Business Leader: A Reflection*. 4th ed. Vatican City: Pontifical Council for Justice and Peace, 2012.

Naughton, Michael and Thomas Bausch. "The Integrity of an Undergraduate Catholic School of Management: Four Integrating Characteristics." *California Management Review* 38 No. 4 (1996): 118-40.

Nerlich, Brigitte, and Zazie Todd, Vimala Herman, and David D. Clarke, eds. *Polysemy: Flexible Patterns of Meaning in Mind and Language*. Berlin: Walter de Gruyter, 1996.

Newman, John Henry. *Apologia Pro Vita Sua*. Edited by Ian Ker. London: Penguin Books, 1994.

———. *Discussions and Arguments on Various Subjects*. London: Longmans, 1907.

———. *An Essay in Aid of a Grammar of Assent*. Oxford: The Clarendon Press, 1985.

———. *Essays Critical and Historical*. Vol. 1. New York: Longmans, Green and Co., 1907.

———. *An Essay on the Development of Christian Doctrine*. Notre Dame, IN: University of Notre Dame Press, 1989.

———. *Historical Sketches*. Vol. 2. London: Longmans, Green and Co., 1906.

———. *Historical Sketches*. Vol. 3. London: Longmans, 1903.

———. *The Idea of a University*. Edited by Ian Ker. Oxford: The Clarendon Press, 1976.

———. "The Infidelity of the Future." In *Faith and Prejudice and Other Unpublished Sermons of Cardinal Newman*, 52-62. New York: Sheed and Ward, 1956.

———. "Intellect: the Instrument of Religious Training." In *Sermons Preached on Various Occasions*. London: Longmans, Green and Co., 1921.

———. *Oxford University Sermons*. London: Longmans, 1909.

———. *Parochial and Plain Sermons*. Vol. 4. London: Longmans, 1909.

———. *Sermons Preached on Various Occasions*. London: Longmans, 1908.

———. *The Via Media of the Anglican Church*. London: Longmans, Green and Co., 1897.

Nietzsche, Friedrich. *Beyond Good and Evil: Prelude to a Philosophy of the Future*. Translated by Walter Kauffman. New York: Vintage, 1989.

O'Connor, Flannery. *Collected Works*. Edited by Sally Fitzgerald. New York: Library of America, 1988.

O'Connor, Flannery. *Mystery and Manners*. Edited by Robert Fitzgerald. New York: Farrar, Straus, and Giroux, 1969.

O'Dea, Thomas. *American Catholic Dilemma*. Chicago: University of Chicago Press, 1958.

O'Toole, James. *The Faithful: A History of Catholics in America*. Cambridge, MA: Belknap Press of Harvard University Press, 2008.

Origen. *Contra Celsum*. Translated by Henry Chadwick. Cambridge: Cambridge University Press, 1980.

Paleotti, Gabriele. *Discourse on Sacred and Profane Images*. Translated by William McCuaig. Los Angeles: Getty Publications, 2012.

Paul VI. *Evangelii Nuntiandi, Apostolic Exhortation*. Libreria Editrice Vaticana, 1975. http://w2.vatican.va/content/paul-vi/en/apost_exhortations/documents/hf_p-vi_exh_19751208_evangelii-nuntiandi.html.

Pieper, Josef. *Happiness and Contemplation*. Translated Introduced by Ralph McInerny. South Bend: St. Augustine's Press, 1998.

———. *Leisure, the Basis of Culture* and *The Philosophical Act*. Translated by Alexander Dru. Introduced by James V. Schall, S.J. San Francisco: Ignatius Press, 2009.

———. *Only the Lover Sings*. San Francisco: Ignatius Press, 1990.

———. *In Tune with the World: A Theory of Festivity*. Translated by Richard and Clara Winston. South Bend: St. Augustine's Press, 1999.

Pierucci, Ernest. "Restoring the Broken Image: The Centrality of the Subjective Dimension of Labor and Liberal Education in Catholic Business Education." Unpublished lecture presented at the 7th International Symposium on Catholic Social Thought and Management Education. University of Notre Dame. Notre Dame, Indiana. June 11-13, 2008.

Pontifical Council for Culture. *The Via Pulchritudinis: Privileged Pathway for Evangilisation and Dialogue*. March 27, 2006. http://www.vatican.va/roman_curia/pontifical_councils/cultr/documents/rc_pc_cultr_doc_20060327_plenary-assembly_final-document_en.html.

Porter, Lyman W., and Lawrence E. McKibbin. *Management Education and Development: Drift or Thrust into the 21st Century?* New York: McGraw-Hill Book Company, 1988.

Porth, Stephen J., John J. McCall, and Joseph A. DiAngelo. "Business Education at Catholic Universities: Current Status and Future Directions." *Journal of Catholic Higher Education* 28, no. 1 (2009): 3-22.

Portier, William. "Americanism and Inculturation, 1899–1999." *Communio* 27 (2000): 139-60.

Pseudo-Macarius. *The Fifty Spiritual Homilies.* Edited by G.A. Maloney. Mahwah, NJ: Paulist Press, 1992.

Quinn, Dermot. "Christopher Dawson and Historical Imagination." *The Chesterton Review* 26, no. 4 (2000): 471-89.

Rice, Charles E. *What Happened to Notre Dame?* South Bend, IN: St. Augustine's Press, 2009.

Russello, Gerald J., ed. *Christianity and European Culture: Selections from the Work of Christopher Dawson.* Washington, D.C.: Catholic University of America Press, 1998.

Schindler, David, ed. *Hans Urs von Balthasar: His Life and Work.* San Francisco: Ignatius Press, 1991.

Schindler, David. "The Anthropological Vision of *Caritas in veritate* in Light of Economic and Cultural Life in the United States." *Communio* 37, no. 4 (2010): 558-79.

Scola, Angelo. *Test Everything, Hold Fast to What Is Good: An Interview with Hans Urs von Balthasar.* Translated by M. Shrady. San Francisco: Ignatius Press, 1989.

Scott, Christina. *A Historian and His World: A Life of Christopher Dawson.* New Brunswick: Transaction, 1992.

Selznick, Philip. *Leadership in Administration: A Sociological Interpretation.* New York: Harper & Row, 1957.

Senior, John. *The Restoration of Christian Culture.* Norfolk, VA: IHS Press, 2008.

Seton, Elizabeth Bayley. *Collected Writings: Vol. 1, Correspondence and Journals 1793-1808.* Edited by Regina Bechtle, S.C. and Judith Metz, S.C. New York: New City Press, 2000.

Shaw, Russell. *American Church: The Remarkable Rise, Meteoric Fall, and Uncertain Future of Catholicism in America.* San Francisco: Ignatius, 2013.

Smith, Christian, Kyle Longest, Jonathan Hill, and Kari Christoffersen. *Young Catholic America: Emerging Adults In, Out of, and Gone from the Church.* New York: Oxford University Press, 2014.

Smith, Peter Jesserer. "'Catholic Studies' Program Excels as Founder Bids Farewell." *National Catholic Register,* August 24, 2014.

Stocking, George W. "Matthew Arnold, E.B. Tylor, and the Uses of Invention." *American Anthropologist New Series* 65, no. 4 (1963): 783-99.

Stratford, Caldecott. *Beauty for Truth's Sake: On the Reenchantment of Education.* Grand Rapids, MI: Brazos Press, 2009.

Sullins, Paul. "The Difference Catholic Makes: Catholic Faculty and Catholic Identity." *Journal for the Scientific Study of Religion* 43, no. 1 (2004): 83–101.

Suzawa, Yukako. *The Genesis of Early Christian Art: Syncretic Juxtaposition in the Roman World.* Oxford: Oxford University Press, 2008.

Sybel, Ludwig V. *Christliche Antike: Einführung in die altchristliche Kunst.* Marburg: N.G. Elwertsche Verlagsbuchhandlung, 1909.

Taylor, James. *Poetic Knowledge: The Recovery of Education.* New York: State University of New York Press, 1998.

Thomas Aquinas. *Summa Theologiae.* Translated by Fathers of the English Dominican Province. London: Burns, Oates & Washburne, 1920.

Tocqueville, Alexis de. *Democracy in America.* 2 Vols. New York: Vintage Books, 1972.

Trinkaus, Charles. *In Our Image and Likeness: Humanity and Divinity in Italian Humanist Thought.* Vol 1. Notre Dame, IN: University of Notre Dame Press, 2009.

Tylor, Edward. *Primitive Culture.* New York: Harper & Row, 1958.

Ward-Perkins, Bryan. *The Fall of Rome and the End of Civilization.* Oxford: Oxford University Press, 2005.

Waugh, Evelyn. *Brideshead Revisited.* New York: Back Bay Books, 2012.

Wickham, Chris. *Inheritance of Rome: Illuminating the Dark Ages.* New York: Viking, 2009.

Williams, Raymond. *Culture & Society: 1780-1950.* New York: Columbia University Press, 1983.

———. *Keywords: A Vocabulary of Culture and Society.* London: Fontana/Croom Helm, 1976.

Wiman, Christian. *My Bright Abyss: Meditations of a Modern Believer.* New York: Farrar, Straus and Giroux, 2013.

Wood, Mark. "Poverty, Chastity and Disillusion." *The Malta Independent*, March 30, 1997.

Zeff, S.A. "Does Accounting Belong in the University Curriculum?" *Issues in Accounting Education* 4, no. 1 (1989): 203-10.

Zizola, Giancarlo. *The Utopia of Pope John XXIII.* Maryknoll, NY: Orbis Books, 1978.

Zwick, Mark, and Louise Zwick. *The Catholic Worker Movement: Intellectual and Spiritual Origins.* NY: Paulist Press, 2005.

Contributors

Don J. Briel is holder of the Blessed John Henry Newman Chair of Liberal Arts at the University of Mary.

Matthew T. Gerlach is Dean of the Institute for Lay Ministry at Sacred Heart Major Seminary, Detroit. Formerly he served as founding director of the Catholic Studies Program at the University of Mary.

F. Russell Hittinger is holder of the William K. Warren Professor of Catholic Studies and a Research Professor of Law at the University of Tulsa, working at the intersection of philosophy, law and theology.

Joshua M. Hren is Assistant Professor of English at Belmont Abbey College, Managing Editor of *Dappled Things*, and Editor-in-Chief of Wiseblood Books, engaging the intersections of religion, literature and political philosophy.

Elizabeth Lev lives in Rome as an author, tour guide, and professor of art history, teaching for the Pontifical University of St. Thomas (Angelicum) and for Catholic Studies at the Bernardi Campus, University of St. Thomas, Rome.

Wilson D. Miscamble, C.S.C. is Professor of History at the University of Notre Dame and a priest in the Congregation of Holy Cross and writes on Catholic identity in higher education and Catholics in the public square.

Paul G. Monson is Assistant Professor of Church History at Sacred Heart Seminary and School of Theology, Hales Corners, Wisconsin. His research is focused on developments of American Catholic thought and culture.

Paul Murray, O.P. is an Irish Dominican priest, scholar, and poet presently serving as President of the Spirituality Faculty at the Angelicum and teaching literature of the mystical tradition to Catholic Studies students in Rome.

Michael J. Naughton is Director of the Center for Catholic Studies and holder of the Koch Endowed Chair in Catholic Studies at the University of St. Thomas (Minnesota).

Jonathan J. Reyes is the Executive Director of the Department of Justice, Peace, and Human Development (USCCB), previously serving in leadership at the Augustine Institute of Denver, FOCUS, and Christendom College.

R. Jared Staudt teaches Theology and Catholic Studies at the University of Mary and the Augustine Institute and serves in the Office of Evangelization and Family Life Ministries in the Archdiocese of Denver.

Joseph T. Stuart is Associate Professor of History and teaches Catholic Studies at the University of Mary, having earned his Ph.D. in modern history from the University of Edinburgh, publishing widely on Christopher Dawson.

George Weigel is Distinguished Senior Fellow at Washington's Ethics and Public Policy Center, where he holds the William E. Simon Chair in Catholic Studies.